Global P

THE (Delicate) ART

Reviews from the USA, Ireland, UK, Nigeria, Colombia, Singapore, Brazil, Cyprus, Switzerland, and Denmark

---

"Bureaucracy has never been discussed in such an entertaining and educational way before. Learn how to clean out the organizational 'scar tissue' that is slowing you down."

—Adrian Cockcroft (USA), VP Cloud Architecture Strategy, Amazon Web Services

"What do ancient Egypt, Louis XIV, Napoleon, Thomas Hobbes, *Moby Dick*, and the very-often-referred-to Max Weber have to do with digital transformation? A great deal, because bureaucracy is a permanent guest in history and a necessary evil. So whether you have fallen in love with bureaucracy or hate it, you should read this book. Bad bureaucracy can dehumanize, promote blind spots and stifle innovation. But good bureaucracy can introduce fairness and provide efficiency through scalability and predictability, e.g., in regulatory compliance. Once again, Mark manages to combine exciting storytelling with tangible analogies from history and daily life."

—Chris Russ (Switzerland), Program Director and Senior Lecturer, ZHAW School of Management and Law

"My brain continues to turn around quantum bureaucracy. How to get the right amount of it at the right time and in the right place, but no more and not there unless you look. Maybe Schrodinger's Bureaucracy is something I need to work on and think about.... Great read, and I'm so thankful to Mark for writing this book to reform bureaucracy. With his insight into razor-bearing sumo monkeys, we can progress toward a more modern way of managing. Like Jonah, I felt trapped with no way to determine my own direction. Mark provides great tools for guiding the whale."

—Josh Seckel (USA), Specialist Leader, Deloitte Digital

"Mark has done it again: with his usual wit and verve, he has cut past normal lazy blather about 'bloated bureaucracies' to get to the truth about their place in the world. In doing so, he outlines not only why bureaucracies are necessary, but how they are best fought through a deep understanding of their internal logic and weak points. [*The (Delicate) Art of Bureaucracy*] serves as a handbook on how to fight the good fight not just for IT, but for the world too."

—**Ian Miell (UK)**, Cloud Native Consultant, Container Solutions

"A must read for leaders trying to break the vicious circle of 'it can't be done' in complex organizations. Based on history, sociology, and his own experiences, Mark Schwartz explains the different perspectives on bureaucracy and how to bust it with practical steps. The perfect handbook for transformation under constrained circumstances."

—**Renato Garcia Pedigoni (Brazil)**, CDO, Grupo Boticário

"My organization launched an internal program called 'Kill Bureaucracy' (Kill B). Reading this book made me realize the obvious: One does not simply kill bureaucracy. Following the guidelines and practical examples in this great book, one will understand that he has to simply transform from 'Homo bureaucraticus' to a monkey, a sumo wrestler, or a razor!"

—**George Chr. Georgiou (Cyprus)**, Enterprise Architect, Bank of Cyprus

"*The (Delicate) Art of Bureaucracy* is so creative, clever, and enlightening, it will help me remove digital transformation headwinds for years to come. It's a must read for government and business leaders as they embark on digital transformation. It will make you a better digital leader by giving you the knowledge to use bureaucracy as a digital accelerator, and it belongs on your office desk today."

—**Chris Radich (USA)**, VP Digital Strategy, Salesforce

"A shrewd and entertaining account of how bureaucracy becomes entrenched in social organizations and of its encumbering effects on the process of change. But its greatest value is in the sharing of strategies and tactics for knowledge workers trammeled by bureaucracy to—like Sumo wrestlers—turn the weight of the red tape to their advantage and become innovator-makers."

—**Renata Brogan (UK)**, Solutions Architect,
Women in Tech, Women in IT

"It takes great curiosity to deeply understand organizational bureaucracy, great courage to challenge it, and pure genius to know how to bend it to your will. In this book, Mark delivers a razor-sharp analysis on all of the above and then shares with us a comprehensive roadmap to a better future, where bureaucracy finally becomes the organizational enabler it was always intended to be."

—**John Walsh (Ireland)**, Business Relationship Manager, PepsiCo

"Mark Schwartz has written a classic on bureaucracy that will always be relevant. A very readable, insightful, playful, useful, and enjoyable book that will help readers who are bureaucrats of any flavor—and any of us who think we don't need bureaucracy but do—as long as it is a lean and learning bureaucracy. Mark provides the techniques of the Monkey, the Razor, and the Sumo Wrestler to effect the required change. As always, a bonus in Mark's books are enjoyable mini-lessons in literature, philosophy, mythology, and pasta!"

—**Tom Michelli (USA)**,
Former Acting Department of Defense Principal Deputy CIO,
CIO US Coast Guard, and CIO US Immigration and Customs Enforcement

"Need ideas to accelerate change and disrupt bureaucracy? This book brings analogies that will relate to your world. Mark uses three levers as themes, each with usable playbooks, that will give you the confidence and early wins to maintain momentum as you break through the barriers most organizations face."

—**Chris Richardson (USA)**, Deputy CIO, IT Development, Mobility,
Smart Cities, Arizona State University

"Mark Schwartz turns the tables on bureaucracy, offering a practical guide to stripping out a labyrinth of rules and replacing them with simplicity, ease, and automation. His version of a benevolent bureaucracy paves the path for digital transformation and facilitates creativity and innovation."

—**Kimberly Johnson (USA)**, COO, Fannie Mae

"I identified with every chapter. Although we tend to think that bureaucracy is a disease and there are no magic recipes to change our way of thinking, we can always think of leaving it on the light side of the force."

—**Laura Caceres (Colombia)**,
Operations Director, DevOps LATAM

"This fascinating book will make you rethink bureaucracy and give you actionable tools to manage in increasingly complex environments. Mark's ability to weave philosophy, history, and humor throughout his reflections on real-life experiences puts important concepts in a completely new and important context. His playbook for addressing bureaucracy is compelling and clear—I look forward to adopting many of his recommendations. Hooray for the intersection of Liberal Arts and Computer Science!"

—**Rich Seltz (USA)**, CIO, CDO, Cabot Microelectronics

"Informative, interesting, and thought provoking piece that raises the veil on bureaucracy. It elucidates bureaucracy's history, evolution, practices, approaches, perceptions, and learnings. This book comes with a great deal of objectivity that propels the mind to seek innovative ways to create an enabling bureaucracy!"

—**Ikoabasi Akpan (Nigeria)**, Sales Manager, Air France-KLM

"A remarkable and eye-opening journey on bureaucracy written with spark and wit. It will give you a completely different perspective on bureaucracy—particularly entering the next normal. A must-read for all who want to realign and shift bureaucracy towards learning instead of using it as a *Schimpfwort* (a great word)!"

—**Eveline Oehrlich (Germany)**,
Chief Research Director, DevOps Institute

"As someone who has been a cog in large, faceless corporations, I found bureaucracy stifling enough to abandon the heavy-handed rules and processes of large enterprise for the startup world. But even startups can become victims of senseless and unbending rituals. I discovered that bureaucracy has no preferred host. You may not come to love bureaucracy, but you will appreciate the wisdom in Mark's sage advice. In his battles with the Leviathan that is the USCIS, he brings levity and plenty of Moby Dick references as he deftly avoids the traps set by the devilish MD-102 by channeling the ways of the Monkey, the Razor, and the Sumo Wrestler and becoming a force for positive change."

—**Mark Birch (Singapore)**, Founder, Enterprise Sales Forum;
Founder DEV.BIZ.OPS

"Bureaucracy has long been a major impediment to transformation. With his usual style of complementing his progressive thinking with a variety of literary references and wit, Mark provides an engaging, insightful, and balanced view on a topic that could easily make one's eyes bleed! In this book you will find a practical guide to busting bureaucracy and turning it into a force for good, all while staying true to the modern techniques of Agile and DevOps—with the help of a Monkey, a Razor, and a Sumo Wrestler."

—**Keith Madsen (Ireland)**, SVP,
Cloud and Advanced Technology, Bank of America

"Mark is to bureaucracy as Sun-Tzu is to the art of war. Read this book to capitalize on the good intended from bureaucracy and have the scissors you always hoped for to reshape it to be enabling, learning, and lean. Leverage the weight of bureaucracy to your advantage like a champion organizational Sumo wrestler."

—**Jamie Scott Berniker (USA)**, Executive Director,
Corporate Development, Global Bank

"Mark has done it again, giving us IT professionals insights into how we, with our software and our creative software development processes, can change heavy, unproductive bureaucratic corporations into adaptable, human-friendly, value-driven bureaucratic corporations that we all love to work for. Red tape is here to stay; it's a matter of being smart about it. This book for sure will be one I am going to refer to when meeting my colleagues and peers."

—**Allan Nyland Christensen (Denmark)**,
Senior Transformation Manager, LEGO

(Delicate)

THE ART OF BUREAUCRACY

BUREAUCRACY

Digital Transformation with the Monkey,
the Razor, and the Sumo Wrestler

MARK SCHWARTZ

author of *A Seat at the Table*

IT Revolution
Independent Publisher Since 2013
Portland, Oregon

25 NW 23rd Pl, Suite 6314
Portland, OR 97210

First Edition
Printed in the United States of America
25 24 23 22 21 20   1 2 3 4 5 6 7 8 9 10

Cover and book design by Devon Smith

Library of Congress Catalog-in-Publication Data

Names: Schwartz, Mark, author.
Title: The (delicate) art of bureaucracy : digital transformation with the
monkey, the razor, and the sumo wrestler / by Mark Schwartz.
Description: First edition. | Portland, OR : IT Revolution Press, LLC,
[2020] | Includes bibliographical references.
Identifiers: LCCN 2020021721 (print) | LCCN 2020021722 (ebook) |
ISBN 9781950508150 (Trade Paperback) | ISBN 9781950508174 (eBook) |
ISBN 9781950508181 (Kindle)
Subjects: LCSH: Bureaucracy. | Organizational learning.
Classification: LCC HD38.4 .S48 2020 (print) | LCC HD38.4 (ebook) |
DDC 658.4—dc23
LC record available at https://lccn.loc.gov/2020021721
LC ebook record available at https://lccn.loc.gov/2020021722

For information about special discounts for bulk purchases or for information on
booking authors for an event, please visit our website at www.ITRevolution.com.

THE (DELICATE) ART OF BUREAUCRACY

To the bureaucratic trolls, tasked with the endless, thankless work of keeping us chaos monkeys in line.

CONTENTS

PLAYBOOK SUMMARY

THE BLACK BELT BUREAUCRAT

A NOTE FROM THE PUBLISHER

As you can imagine, we are exhausted here at Exothermic Press, having finally wrangled Mark Schwartz's new book into the space between two covers. If you know Mr. Schwartz's writing, you will not be surprised to hear that this book's ideas kept expanding along all nine known dimensions of the universe (I speak of those posited by string theory), so this task required hearty geometric exertions. We had to cut the chapter on "Bureaucracy and Ballet" and an unfinished one on "Quantum Bureaucracy," but perhaps they'll turn up in a later book.

You will notice something new in this book *comparari prioribus*: I have done my best to annotate some of Schwartz's more far-flung leaps of imagination to make sure they are accessible to those of us without philosophy degrees or who just want to get right to the meat of Schwartz's ideas on how to endure the torments of bureaucracy and thrive despite them. Without wishing to spoil the ending, I can tell you that the alliance of the Monkey, the Razor, and the Sumo Wrestler proves a potent one.

The annotations seemed necessary because, as I pointed out in my conversations with Mr. Schwartz, few readers have as much as noticed his favorite devices in earlier books; to wit, the "fortune cookie" self-referential (he calls it recursive) footnote on page xviii of *The Art of Business Value*, or the dozen or so references to obscure types of pasta he employed in *A Seat at the Table* to avoid the IT cliché of "spaghetti code." He responded as he usually does: with a giggle.

There are several things you should know before you enter the world of *The (Delicate) Art of Bureaucracy: Digital Transformation with the Monkey, the Razor, and the Sumo Wrestler*. The first is that you might be challenged to figure out what Mr. Schwartz really thinks of bureaucracy. We were when first we read the manuscript. At times, he seems almost to be arguing that bureaucracy is a good thing, which for a DevOps and Agile proponent seemed, frankly, mystifying. In other instances he speaks of its crushing soullessness, the burdens it placed in his way as he tried to reform government IT, and the alienation and hopelessness it engenders. So, I asked him. Here's his response, verbatim:

> You can't fight bureaucracy if you see it as an existential condition, a nightmare, an agent of dread and loathing. It's strange how viscerally people react to the mention of bureaucracy. The word is almost shorthand for evil, the way "Satan" might have been in the past. And no one thinks of themselves as a bureaucrat—it's always the person in the next cubicle over. Now bureaucracy *is*, of course, evil, hey, but let's laugh rather than tremble before it.

In other words, I still don't know whether Mr. Schwartz stands pro or con, or what he wishes us to think.

Another thing to keep in mind as you make your way through *The (Delicate) Art of Bureaucracy* is that in Mr. Schwartz's books, motifs tend to surface in odd ways. You will find that *Moby Dick* plays an important part in this volume. In Herman Melville's book, Captain Ahab monomaniacally pursues, with murderous intent, a tremendous albino sperm whale that once chewed off his leg. Every omen informs Ahab and his superstitious crew that they will not succeed. Moby Dick is the leviathan of the Bible, a tremendous, angry force of nature, far more powerful than his tiny human opponents who float helplessly in small, unstable boats in a churning, limitless ocean. Fighting Moby Dick is fighting nature, but Ahab tries anyway. His fight is an expression of his freedom.

Similarly, Mr. Schwartz says, bureaucracy is a powerful monster, a force of nature, much larger than us, and largely undefeatable. Cut off a tentacle and another grows in its place. Or as Kafka says, it merely restabilizes and becomes ever more malevolent. Just how powerful is the leviathan of bureaucracy? Mr. Schwartz's description of the bureaucratic *Physeter macrocephalus* MD-102 with its eighty-seven required documents and twenty-one oversight roles echoes Melville's description of a sperm whale:

> Between eighty-five and ninety feet in length, and something less than forty feet in its fullest circumference, such a whale will weigh at least ninety tons; so that, reckoning thirteen men to a ton, he would considerably outweigh the combined population of a whole village of one thousand one hundred inhabitants.[1]

A NOTE FROM THE AUTHOR

To produce a mighty book, you must choose a mighty theme. No great and enduring volume can ever be written on the flea, though many there be who have tried it.

—Herman Melville, *Moby Dick*

As for the metaphysical thoughts, my dear sir, allow me to say that any brain is capable of producing them, it's just that we cannot always find the words.

—José Saramago, *All the Names*

Someone must have been telling lies about Mark S., because one day, without having done anything wrong, he woke in his bed to find himself suddenly transformed into a giant insect—a bureaucrat.* Crawling through government office buildings, his exoskeleton examined by puzzled security folks; burrowing through great piles of bureaucratic waste; propping himself upright in meeting-room chairs never designed for creatures with more than two legs; learning to tell his I-90s from his I-485s and his SF-86s from his TPS reports;† peeling off the paperwork that stuck to him like flypaper, he flapped his antennae helplessly—for the first few years at least—but with an insect's sniffing curiosity.

Over time, he realized that everyone else around him, private sector and public, while railing against bureaucracy—who doesn't?—was also beginning to grow antennae and take on the shape of bureaucrats without noticing it. Upon

---

* Mr. Schwartz is conflating the opening sentence of Kafka's *The Trial* with that of *The Metamorphosis*. -ed.

† TPS Reports are a recurring bureaucratic joke in the movie *Office Space*. -ed.

leaving the federal bureaucracy he found the insect apocalypse well underway: banks, insurance companies, educational institutions, and even those tech companies that are admired for their agility and speed had long since settled into that energetic languor that makes a bureaucracy busy on paper and sticky and gooey on execution.

Yes, I, Mark S., had become the CIO of US Citizenship and Immigration Services, a part of the Department of Homeland Security. By definition, a bureaucrat. By inclination, an iconoclastic, playful, get-things-done ex-software-developer who imagined he could sit down at a keyboard and change the world. By chronology, an incoming government employee at precisely the moment when it had finally become interested in agile ways of working and wanted to stop manufacturing huge, monolithic IT projects that went over budget, fell behind schedule, and were featured on the front page of the *Washington Post*. But the government couldn't help itself. *Agile* was a word, and the bureaucracy could not rest until it had redefined it and formalized it and surrounded it with rules and constraints—in other words, until it had drained Agile of its agility.

My colleagues and I spent some years trying to convince policymakers to accept the dictionary definition of agility. We looked for ways to nudge the bureaucracy in the direction of what we were all calling digital transformation. After we'd banged our little insect heads against the wall for several years, the wall slowly began to move. Where before we'd only been able to release IT capabilities once every eighteen months or so, we found we were delivering new software as often as three times a day. Our multibillion-dollar, five-plus-year projects shrank to a size where we could actually execute them. We became a case study in the IT buzzwords of today—DevOps, microservices, cloud, containers, kombucha. And we did it as bureaucrats.

Somehow, along the way, I thought I'd begun to understand bureaucracy. Don't get me wrong, I hate sluggish officialdom as much as the next *Homo sapiens*. But it turned out that the evil trolls of bureaucracy—the ones who lived in a cave somewhere and only popped out now and then to shout "No!" and hand the public more forms to fill out—well, they were human too, trying to do the right thing. And much of what we see as wasteful government bureaucracy, it turned out, had been put there deliberately to accomplish social or political goals that you and I supported. There was a frightening beauty to the way the bureaucracy worked once you cleared away the red tape and got a good look at it.

These days I meet with executives from about 120 companies a year and speak with enterprise leaders at conferences, at dinner roundtables, and while waiting to use the restroom at industry events. And, amazingly, my stories of bureaucracy light them right up. They tell me about how their companies' bureaucracies are pinning them under mountains of red tape*—ironically, in many cases bureaucracies they've set up themselves. Sometimes they say they need "cultural change"—but what they mean is they need to break free of their companies' rigid rules and rigid authorities, the controls that control innovation and change by making sure they don't happen.

It's strange to be writing a book on bureaucracy. Who'd want to read such a thing? I'm inspired by a couple of books I've read over the last year. One was *Death*, by Shelly Kagan, a great philosopher and professor at Yale. For Khepri's[†] sake, who'd want to read a book on death? Well, I heartily recommend it. Kagan will make you think and rethink and puzzle and wonder why you've never read one before. The other book was *Gut: The Inside Story of Our Body's Most Underrated Organ* by Giulia Enders. Who'd want to read such a thing? But she just seems so excited about digestion that the book is hard to put down. I'm hoping that my fascination for bureaucracy will similarly shine through, and that I'll be able to make bureaucracy as interesting as she makes human excrement. Or Kagan makes death.

I figured I'd drop a few stories throughout the book from my experience in the big bureaucracy. I left a few good ones out too. Like the time I was in a contentious government meeting and one of the participants suddenly leapt up and excused himself, saying, "I have to go move a supercomputer!" I wasn't sure if that was a sly way to say that he badly needed a bathroom break, a reference to some new government bloat, or just a "dog ate my homework" excuse for shutting down my ideas on bureaucracy-busting.[‡]

Anyway, I have reason to think that we all have a secret fascination with bureaucracy. Take the universal appeal of Kafka's writing. We know that Joseph K. is not going to be acquitted and we know that the Land Surveyor will never make it to the Castle. Yet we read of their adventures with some kind of compulsion to see how bureaucracy inevitably triumphs. We replay to ourselves the mechanism of Catch-22 and want to scream at the officials of the Ministry

---

* A reference to the Monkey King, who reappears in Chapter 12. -ed.

† An Egyptian god who winds up playing a large role in this book. See Introduction. -ed.

‡ See Giulia Enders, *Gut*, above. -au.

of Circumlocutions as they circumlocute.* We laugh as the good soldier Svejk makes his way through a military bureaucracy filled with buffoons and mortal danger.†

Bureaucracy moves us, mystifies us, and represents something deep about the human condition. It has something to do with the tension between freedom and constraint, order and chaos, accountability and authority, and how humans organize socially to accomplish common objectives. In writing this book, I wanted to peel away the blubber and find its heart.

Bureaucracy is also a critical player in enterprises' digital transformations, which, nominally, is my subject. I've written a series of books on leadership in the digital world: *The Art of Business Value*, *A Seat at the Table*, and *War and Peace and IT*. In them I've tried to help leaders of large enterprises "unstick" their organizations so that they can become digital. My books have described how new ways of delivering technology are also changing how leaders lead, and how digitally inspired techniques can be used to succeed in today's digital economy. But when my readers try to apply those ideas, they often find themselves stymied by the roles and rules and formalities they've set up to bring order and control to their enterprises.

So a book on bureaucracy seems as essential today as a book on human waste, and one that you can read while you're eating. I might ask you to think a little bit differently about bureaucracy. I will definitely ask you to join me and become a Chaos Monkey, a Knight of Occam, and a Lean Sumo Wrestler. Together we can wield bureaucracy as a superpower and bust through it at the same time.

Press 1 to bust a bureaucracy, 2 to forge a new bureaucracy, or hold the line if you wish to speak to a reader care associate. Ding dongle, the functionary's dead. Long live the functionary!

Mark S.
Boston, 2020

---

* That's from Charles Dickens's *Little Dorrit*. -ed.

† A bureaucratic romp through the Czech military by Jaroslav Hašek, often compared to Heller's *Catch-22*. -ed.

I own thy speechless, placeless power;
but to the last gasp of my earthquake life
will dispute its unconditional, unintegral mastery in me.
In the midst of the personified impersonal,
a personality stands here.

—Herman Melville, *Moby Dick*

INTRODUCTION: WE'RE BUREAUCRATS ALL

To catch hold of fleeting appearance he must shackle it with rules, tear into its fair body with concepts, and preserve its living spirit in a meagre frame of words.

—Friedrich Schiller, *On the Aesthetic Education of Man*

He tasks me; he heaps me; I see in him outrageous strength, with an inscrutable malice sinewing it. That inscrutable thing is chiefly what I hate; and be the white whale agent, or be the white whale principal, I will wreak that hate upon him.

—Herman Melville, *Moby Dick*

Bureaucracy Is Us

Homo bureaucraticus: humankind is truly the bureaucratic animal. Psychologists have watched children spend more time arguing over the rules of a game than actually playing it.[1] Children learn rule-making, of course, from their parents, those power-crazy authorities who invent and enforce arbitrary decrees about bedtimes and TV watching. We all begin structuring the world bureaucratically long before we learn to develop interactive voice response systems ("Your call is important to us. Please listen distractedly as our options have never changed."), join congressional subcommittees, or set acceptable use policies for IT systems. Someday, archaeologists will sniff out today's humans by following our trail of bureaucracy through the zeros and ones of our big data streams.

Perhaps it's no wonder, stamped as we are in the image of celestial beings, or vice versa. The Jade Emperor, after all, has always presided over a "celestial hierarchy" of Chinese gods that looks suspiciously like a Chinese political bureaucracy. When the Monkey King* of legend is not invited to the Jade Empress's party, he wants to know who was. "It's all according to rule, you know . . . the Venerable Immortals of the Ten Continents and Three Islands, the Mystic Divinity of the North Pole . . . the Star Lords of the Five Constellations, the Three Pure Ones, the Four Emperors and the Heavenly Immortal of the Great Nomad from the Eight High Caves . . . [sorry, not done yet] . . . the Immortal of the Nine Mounds, the Gods of the Seas and Mountains . . ." Oh yes, and also the terrestrial deities.[2]

Christian angelology, formalized in the Early Middle Ages, was already quite familiar with the principle of division of labor. It organized the angels into nine "choirs": Seraphim, Cherubim, Thrones, Dominions, Virtues, Powers, Principalities, Archangels, and Angels.[3] Virtues are responsible (accountable?) for miracles, Thrones for presenting the prayers of humans, and Cherubim for guarding the tree of life.

Judaism has its rabbinic law, the 613 commandments of the Torah, the pseudo-legal document it calls the covenant, and the many pages of Exodus describing exactly how to build an Ark of the Covenant and who may use it. All in the service of implementing rules and regulations laid down by the supreme parental authority—rules we *must* live by (laws of nature) and rules we *should* live by (laws of morality).

The gods of the ancient Aegean, though not big on following rules themselves, nevertheless had functional specialties, like employees in a factory: Eros for arrows, Momus for mockery, Alastor for family feuds, Chaos for Information Technology, and Morpheus, presumably, for bureaucracy.[†] If you wanted wind, you had to get a sign-off from Aeolus; if you wanted a hangover, from Dionysus.

Aeolus—Homer-certified wind deity tasked with air moving, reporting directly to Zeus, the chief executive deity—was surely hired into his position for his wind skills, although he generally delegated to one of his four Anemoi, depending on the wind's required compass direction. It takes just a small imaginative leap to think of Aeolus as rather busy and needing to prioritize his

---

* See Chapter 12, "The Way of the Monkey." -ed.

† I'm lying. But the ones I didn't make up are here: https://greekgodsandgoddesses.net /gods/. And by the way, it's Atlas who carries the world on his back, not a succession of turtles. -au.

workload, doesn't it? Sure, if you have a wind need you can go ahead and pray, but if you really want service, it's best to file a ticket and get onto his queue.

I mean no disrespect to religions or dead Greeks, because when I label something a bureaucracy, I make no value judgment. We've come to view bureaucracy as an evil—maybe even as evil itself since the philosopher Hannah Arendt used the memorable phrase "the banality of evil" to describe the highly bureaucratized Nazi genocide.

But in this book I suggest we step back and consider bureaucracy for what it really is: a way to impose a structure on the world so that we can link general principles to actions. I don't want to mire you now in the precise definition of *bureaucracy** —we'll get to that in a few chapters—but for now, let's just say that a *bureaucracy is a form of social organization with formal, rigid rules and formal, rigid hierarchies of authority*. That's not too far from the definition sociologists use.

Digital Transformation

In today's digital economy—one of rapid change, uncertainty, and complexity—bureaucracy is an impediment. It's the sticky stuff that prevents companies from dancing nimbly to the music of change. It's the no-saying choir of a shrouded and inscrutable sub-sub-sub-department, the vampire forms in triplicate that drain employees of motivation, the rules that lock in yesterday's worst practices, and the impersonal languages of corporatese, legalese, political doublespeak, and—I'm not sure why—the speech of airplane flight attendants ("This is your last and final boarding call for flight 666 with service to Inferno International.").

As enterprises accept information technologies into the hearts of their corporate personalities, they find today's tools for rapid change slowed by rules that seem arbitrary, their high-tech Teslas stuck on muddy, potholed rural roads. They need fast 0–60 capability and nimble cornering, but instead they get meetings, sign-offs, and email nastygrams from the guardians of expense-reporting policies. Bureaucracy is a mature company's symptom of aging, a deteriorating condition that will inevitably lead it to aimless wandering,

---

*Don't you hate books that start out by quoting Wikipedia or dictionary definitions of their terms? -au.

fits and starts, fear of new technologies, intervention by concerned shareholders, and finally assisted demise at the hands of a Dr. Icahn.*

In IT today we want *fast flow*. We want to deliver. And what gets in our way? Mysterious corporate rules that can't be questioned. Signatures we need from people we've never heard of. Pleading requests we have to make for tools we need. Time we spend occupying a seat in meetings. Policies that suddenly land on our desks and demand our attention just when we're on the verge of delivering business value for the company that auto-deposits our paychecks.

At the same time, IT leaders must confront their own bureaucratic instincts. We speak of IT *governance*—the word just drips with bureaucratic goo, doesn't it?—and IT *standards*. We work and breathe within the constricted space allowed us by compliance acronyms—GDPR, SOX, HIPAA, PCI-DSS. Our security engineers, overwhelmed by constant taunting from nation-states and professional hackers, slam rules on the enterprise to protect it. IT organizations balance centralization with decentralization; standards with evolving architectures; rulebooks, runbooks, and standard operating procedures with ad hoc attempts to be useful. They promote agility but only within a framework of backlogs, stand-ups and burn-downs, and sprint reviews—artifacts and ceremonies redolent of red tape.

Like the Venerable Immortals of the Ten Continents and Three Islands, we find ourselves a part of a hierarchy we didn't invent or choose, yet we cope with it by electing to manufacture yet more bureaucracy. It comes naturally to us *Homo bureaucraticuses*—we have our Midas touch that turns even smiley faces into standardized icons and protocols regulating when they should and shouldn't be used.

Modernity Is Bureaucracy

Bureaucracy has long been seen as a cornerstone of advanced industrial societies, and even as constitutive of modernity itself.[4] It sounds strange, but bureaucracy has been called the "primary institutional characteristic of highly complex and differentiated societies, epitomizing 'the modern era.'"[5]

For the pioneering sociologist Max Weber, whom we'll be encountering throughout this book, bureaucracy was just the application of reason to orga-

---

* Famed corporate raider. -ed.

nizational design, a way of setting up rules and accountabilities to promote efficiency.[6] To John Stuart Mill, the nineteenth century British philosopher, it was a form of administration that "accumulates experience, acquires well-tried and well-considered maxims, and makes provision for appropriate practical knowledge in those who have the actual conduct of affairs."[7] In our modern age, where we've seen science and engineering triumph, where we like to base decisions on hard data, bureaucracy is the application of those types of rational thought patterns to structuring and running a social organization.

Modern bureaucracy developed during the nineteenth century, as science rose and the privileged aristocracy declined, and as business enterprises became larger and clashed in global markets. It so dominated organizations that management historians could say that "almost all the benefits we take for granted in today's society—modern medicine, modern science, modern industry—rest on a bureaucratic foundation.[8] To see the connection between bureaucracy and modernity, it helps to think about what it replaced: in the public sphere, the arbitrariness, capriciousness, and nepotism of monarchies or the chaos of revolutionary governments; in the business world, a lack of formal discipline and management strategies that sounded a lot like "let's make friends with the king and hope he gives us a charter to exploit a new colony."

There's no more dramatic illustration of bureaucracy's deep impact on modern society than its use by terrorist networks.

> From the mid-1990s through late 2001, al-Qa'ida made every effort to become a fully bureaucratized organization, complete with employment contracts specifying vacation policies, explicitly documented roles and responsibilities for different jobs including detailed descriptions of the experiences required for senior leadership roles, security memos written by a specialized security committee, and standardized questionnaires for those arriving at training camps.[9]

The three-page application to join al-Qa'ida asks applicants to list their hobbies and pastimes, and asks "What objectives would you like to accomplish on your jihad path?"[10] Terrorist operatives complain about the burdensome rules they face, particularly the requirements that they get targets approved centrally before striking them.[11] There are even stories of would-be suicide bombers being asked to fill out forms in triplicate before being allowed to take exams to assess their suitability.[12]

History of Bureaucracy (Part One): Pharaoh to Sade

Despite its deep connection to modernity, bureaucracy is hardly new. In ancient Egypt the pharaohs set up a sizable hierarchy to deal with irrigation, mining, and pyramid building, with scribes as their chief bureaucrats.[13] Supervisors were assigned a span of control of precisely ten subordinates, and a grand vizier (Joseph in the Bible being the most famous[14]) presided over the hierarchy. By planning carefully, dividing work among departments, and employing professional full-time administrators, the ancient Egyptians became experts at forecasting the rise of the Nile and coping with its consequences.[15]

China too developed a bureaucracy as early as 1000 BCE, introduced the division of labor as early as CE 1, and, influenced by Confucian principles, began using merit exams to fill positions sometime during the Han Dynasty (206 BCE–CE 220).[16]

Diocletian bureaucratized the Roman Empire; the heavy taxes he then needed to support the administration became one of the reasons for the empire's fall.[17] The Middle Ages saw Roman bureaucracy replaced by the feudal system, which (according to the economist and historian Ludwig Von Mises) was an attempt at governing *without* a centralized bureaucracy—an effort that failed miserably. "The modern state," he says, "is built upon the ruins of feudalism. It substituted bureaucratic management of public affairs for the supremacy of a multitude of petty princes and counts."[18]

At the same time, the church was evolving its own formal structure. By the third century CE it had organized into a hierarchy of bishops, presbyters, deacons, subdeacons, and acolytes, later adding a pope at the Council of Nicaea.[19]

Happily for our English language we were able to borrow the useful term *byzantine* to honor the intricacies of its namesake empire's administration. And it was the Holy Roman Emperor Charles V of Spain who, in modernizing the administration of his empire—yes, modernizing—gave us another useful term when he bound important documents with *red tape* instead of plain white string.[20]

The intellectual history of bureaucracy goes way back as well. Plato's *Republic* is an argument for government by an elite bureaucracy of philosophers.[21] Aristotle's description in *Politics* of the attributes of a good organization is surprisingly similar to the bureaucracy we know today: (1) specialization of labor, (2) departmentation, (3) centralization, decentralization, and delegation, (4) synergy, and (5) leadership.[22]

As long as there have been bureaucracies there have been people complaining about them. Well, almost as long, since the ranks of Egyptian and Roman bureaucracies were largely filled with slaves. When Diocletian expanded the Roman bureaucracy, Lactantius (c. 250–325 CE), a Christian apologist and advisor to Emperor Constantine, raged about the burden it imposed on the people:

> There were also many stewards of different degrees, and deputies of presidents. Very few civil causes came before them: but there were condemnations daily, and forfeitures frequently inflicted; taxes on numberless commoditie. . . . While Diocletian, that author of ill, and deviser of misery, was ruining all things, he could not withhold his insults, not even against God.[23]

The term *bureaucracy* itself—"rule by offices" or "rule by desks"—was meant to be sarcastic when the French gave it to us in the mid-eighteenth century.[24] No one willingly describes themselves as a bureaucrat; the sociologist Robert Merton uses the colorful German word *Schimpfwort*—that is, an invective or epithet[25]—to describe the term.

Speaking of bureaucracy and words the French gave us, there's also the useful word *sadism*. In an article in *Lapham's Quarterly*, the critic Lucy Ives tells us that the Marquis de Sade's works, particularly *The 120 Days of Sodom* (written in 1785), are best read as narratives about bureaucracy, tales of cold, formal, and even boring implementations of rules around outrageous sexual practices. Four friends bring together a group of people and occupy an abandoned chateau to practice acts of "dispassionate intensity." Their debauched activities are constrained by a set of laws they agree to before they enter the chateau. Roles are carefully delineated: "The four friends form an executive committee, which is overseen by the four procuresses, four duennas, and four storytellers, who operate like a toothless board of directors."[26] Bureaucracy and sadism: products of Enlightenment France.

Ludwig Von Mises has the last word on the exquisite pain of bureaucracy:

> There cannot be any doubt that this bureaucratic system is essentially antiliberal, undemocratic, and un-American, that it is contrary to the spirit and to the letter of the Constitution, and that it is a replica of the totalitarian methods of Stalin and Hitler.[27]

Well, then.

The Keynote Story

I'll use the following story, one that I've also related in my previous books, to illustrate the subtleties of bureaucracy.

I was working with a team of software developers as a product owner, charged with representing the business's needs to the technologists. We were building a software system to help employees process applications submitted by our customers. As is typical in Agile software delivery, we divided the work into two-week iterations and held a retrospective after each to explore ways to improve our process. In one of those retrospectives the team asked me to prepare a certain requirements document—a "state transition" diagram showing all of the states a customer application could pass through as it was processed. That was a bit unusual for us; we typically preferred to flesh out requirements iteratively and face-to-face during each two-week period. But since this was a complex area of the system, they'd need to coordinate their work carefully, and having more formal documentation would make sure that all the pieces fit together well.

It seemed reasonable, but I wanted to avoid the risk of having different copies of this document floating around while we were still refining the requirements. So we agreed that I would sketch the state transition flow and pin it to the corkboard in the team room. That way we'd all be looking at the same diagram and we could easily change it when we needed to.

Two weeks later we were back for another retrospective. The diagram had been a great success, the team members agreed. But one of them complained that when she'd looked for it on the corkboard it wasn't there. It turned out that another team member had taken it and used it at his desk for a few days, forgetting to return it.

The process improvement parts of our brains locked onto the problem. One team member suggested we pin a sign-out sheet to the corkboard next to the diagram. Whenever someone took the sketch off the board they could write their name on the sign-out sheet, the date and time they took it, and which desk they were sitting at, in case someone else needed to find it. I saw where this was going and made a counter-suggestion. "How about," I asked, "if whoever takes the diagram remembers to return it quickly?"

Do you see where I'm going with this? The team's solution was good—it would solve the problem. It was also bureaucratic. Yes, it would mitigate the risk that someone wouldn't have access to the diagram when they needed it. At the same time, it would impose a cost (the effort of signing out the document) on everyone, regardless of whether they were the kind of person who would remember to return the document promptly. Later, after the incident was forgotten, team members would view the sign-out process as pointless bureaucracy. It was a solution, all right—effective, but not lean. Remembering to return the document would be leaner, as would simply writing one's initials on the sign-out sheet and nothing else.

Process improvement had led unthinkingly to bureaucracy. This is common. The cycle of formalizing, optimizing, documenting, and then applying a process uniformly is the essence of the bureaucratic art. It institutionalizes "the surest way we've found to do this particular task." Software developers are particularly adept at formalizing and optimizing processes—after all, that is what programming a computer is all about.

When something goes wrong, employees meet in a "postmortem" or "root cause analysis." Someone asks, "How will we make sure this doesn't happen again?" Brainstorming ensues. They usually decide to set up a process that adds more controls. Of course they do—their boss would be horrified if they decided not to take any corrective action. Errors require correction, and correction, when designed to *avoid* an occurrence, almost always adds constraints. But, I say, in many cases doing nothing is precisely the right solution, because the cost of new controls may be higher than the risk-adjusted cost of the error happening again.

It is the layers and layers of these rules and accountabilities, created to "improve" business processes, that make the Frankenstein's monster we think of as bureaucracy.

A Different View

Bureaucracy, in another sense, is simply form—it's the structure of our corporate environment, the architectural elements *within* which we are free to innovate and gratify our customers.[28] In our everyday lives, we consider ourselves free. But we're not free from the law of gravity. We're not free to violate moral laws (we *can*, but we may be punished). We can't tickle a sperm whale to death or eat strozzapreti while winning the Boston Marathon. We exercise our freedom within boundaries that have been set without our involvement or consent. "On one level, all this is obvious," says David Graeber, the author of *The Utopia of Rules*. "We are just talking about the emergence of form. Freedom has to be in tension with something, or it's just randomness."[29]

When I write a book, I start by preparing an outline. Then I begin to fill in sections. I invariably wind up changing the outline later, but in the meantime the outline gives form to the book. Although it constrains the content I will create, "create" is still the right word—the outline also provides a structure that allows me to play with silly whale analogies and obscure types of pasta. As long as I "comply" with it, the pieces of the book will assemble themselves into a coherent whole, or in this case perhaps a combatant whale.

Form is constraining, yes, but it also keeps us safe and lets us make decisions based on a knowledge of probable outcomes. Contrast that with the ancient world, where humans were just playthings of the gods. One day you go to the woods for a little walk to clear your head, accidentally stumble onto the goddess Diana taking a bath, get turned into a stag, and wind up being torn apart by dogs. This is not what you expect when you go for a walk.*

Bureaucracy is the inverse of science: while the latter seeks to find rules for *understanding* the world, the former creates rules for how we are to *operate* in the world. Both bring order to chaos. Because bureaucracy is concerned with how we *should* act, it is a form of ethics.

Bureaucracy memorializes best practices. As long as the concept of "better" exists, bureaucracy must exist, which is why it's a distinctive competence of *Homo bureaucraticus*. It's about structure and creativity, governance, transparency, fairness, morality, standards and exceptions, coolness under pressure, institutionalization of shared knowledge, religion, superstition, planning and foresight, retrospection and evidence, and stability in flux. It is subtle and delicate.

Bureaucracy, a wonderful thing, a gift of the gods to humanity! A string that leads you through a labyrinth;[†][‡][§] the cumulative knowledge of a long tradition of sages. In this book you'll learn to command it as Zeus commands lightning. We wax bureaucratic when the muses allow.

---

* The story of Actaeon in Ovid's Metamorphoses. -ed.

† The Athenian hero Theseus finds his way in and out of the Minotaur's labyrinth with the help of thread provided to him by Ariadne. Mr. Schwartz no doubt means to suggest the difficulty of moving through a bureaucracy's labyrinthian rules. -ed.

‡ You know, I keep feeling like I'm being followed by an auditor—sorry, editor—who insists on dropping footnotes into my text. -au.

§ Cute. -ed.

Executive Summary, TL;DR

My argument in this book will go something like this:

1. We have a bizarre aversion to bureaucracy, a visceral reaction that prevents us from coping effectively with it. Bureaucracy isn't just frustrating to us, it's frustration itself, to such an extent that we call anything that frustrates us bureaucracy. We, and Kafka, have nightmares about it. I suggest that we stop this right now.
2. In fact, we're natural bureaucrats. We make bureaucracy to be able to act socially in the world despite its complexity. We generalize to simplify the world, and then make rules for action based on those generalizations. In particular, we bureaucratize as a way to turn our problem-solving successes into problem-solved routines.
3. Bureaucracy is a way to structure organizational interactions. That's all. Not a nightmare, not a prank by minions of Satan. Sometimes it's even useful (when dealing with compliance and audits, for example).
4. Nevertheless, the bureaucracies we encounter every day are, in fact, frustrating, Satanic, soul-destroying, and Kafkaesque. That's because they aren't *lean*, *learning*, and *enabling*, the three characteristics of good, not evil, bureaucracy.
5. We can overcome bureaucracy by blasting holes in it, by shrinking it, and by forcing it to turn upon itself and become *lean*, *learning*, and *enabling*. We have all the devices of mythology and science available to us. We do so by employing the arts of the Monkey, the Razor, and the Sumo Wrestler. I'll show you how.

Read This Book

This book is for leaders who want their companies to succeed in the digital age. It's an exploration of the gooey stuff that holds us back and a tactical manual for yanking our boots out of it. I'll show that it's not bureaucracy *per se* that drives us crazy, but rather certain qualities that bureaucracy tends to take on, and which can be reversed.

It's good news that we can manipulate bureaucracy in this way, because we need it. If nothing else, those acronyms we must comply with—our FISMAs and

KYCs, LOLs, and R2D2s*—demand bureaucracy, since they require structural controls and formal accountabilities. Bureaucracy also provides a framework for our activities where it makes sense to have one; it's the guardrails and constraints within which we practice our digital arts.

This is a book about information technology, because technology makes vivid the tension in our corporate lives today between speed and freedom on the digits of one hand, and sludge and constraint on the digits of the other. It also happens to be my field. But though I'll use examples from the technology world, I'm really talking about how any group of people works together. I'll do my best to explain the technology examples so everyone can follow them.

Because my emphasis will be on information technology and digital transformation, I'll be devoting a lot of attention to a particular kind of bureaucracy: the kind that oversees, or governs, projects and investments. This is bureaucracy that affects mostly white-collar workers, and it's enforced not only by officials in high-power positions, but also by administrators who have the power to say no and demand paperwork, and frequently use that power. I refer to them, tongue-in-cheek, as "bureaucratic trolls in caves." In doing so, I don't intend anything personal against them; in my imagination, trolls are those cute plastic dolls with big smiles on their faces. I too have moments of troll-like behavior, and I'll suggest throughout this book that you probably do as well.

I'll also draw a lot of my examples from the government. Not because it's only government that faces bureaucratic challenges in its digital transformations, but because government is extreme, so its examples tend to be clearer and more dramatic. It also happens to be where I spent some time and, with the help of some motivated, brilliant bureaucrats, pulled off a surprising digital transformation. There are important differences between government and corporate bureaucracies (see James Q. Wilson's book *Bureaucracy*), but the similarities are also striking.

Warnings on Terminology

Traditionally one speaks of *managers* as the bureaucrats, who apply their bureaucracy coercively to *workers*. Career, or civil service, government functionaries (as opposed to politicians) are also called bureaucrats. But as bureaucracy has changed, the terminology has become problematic. The bureaucrats in a

---

* Probably needless to say, but the last is not a compliance acronym, but rather a *Star Wars* reference. -ed.

large enterprise are often not managers but line employees who enforce policies—the trolls in caves that periodically appear and stop productive work until forms are filled out. And line employees who work with customers also act as bureaucrats when they enforce rules and demand paperwork.

Also, an apology: I'm going to use the term *digital transformation*, which we all know is a trendy buzzword that's quickly being emptied of all meaning. I'll do so because I don't have a better word for this important trend in enterprises today: the movement from slow-moving, don't-change-too-often management to fast-moving, change-is-normal management. Technology is important in this transformation because it not only makes it possible but also makes it necessary—competitors have access to the same enabling technology, and customers and employees have come to demand it. I use the term while holding my nose.

Structure of the Book

In Part I of this book I'll tease out the true meaning of bureaucracy from its emotional baggage. I'll examine how it works, why we hate it, and what we may even be able to borrow from it.

In Part II I'll draw on contemporary organizational theory to propose a new model for bureaucracy, one that retains its fundamental nature—controls and structure—but is lean, learning, and enabling rather than bloated, stale, and coercive. I know this sounds crazy or pointless, but as you'll see in Part III it's both possible and purposeful.

With that new model in mind, in Part III I'll provide a playbook. I'll show how we can break through bureaucratic obstructions using the skills of the Monkey, the Razor, and the Sumo Wrestler. And then—get ready for it—I'll show you how to become a master bureaucrat yourself, so you can wield bureaucracy for the good of society and your organization.

You Know Who You Are

This is a guide for IT practitioners and corporate leaders who (I'd never refer to them as bureaucrats) wish to impose structure and controls (I'd never call them bureaucracy) . . . um, without driving others crazy. Actually, I *will* call them by those names.

If you're leading an IT transformation, you're frustrated by bureaucracy. Without realizing it, you're probably also manufacturing it. This book is for you. Do you impose standards? Security controls? Does your exception process involve lots of forms and approval signatures? Do you insist that everyone who wants to talk to you fill out a service ticket first? See my point? You, puny human, *Homo bureaucraticus*, are (ouch) a bureaucrat.

If you're an enterprise leader, a CEO, say, or a CFO, COO, board director, legal counsel, or some other chief something, you're frustrated that your company—IT in particular—doesn't move fast enough; your folks seem enthusiastic but quickly bog down in execution; your enterprise is not innovative enough. The problem just might be the bureaucracy you're secretly manufacturing while no one is looking. We're on to you. This book is for you.

If you're a technologist, trying to enjoy your work and deliver value to your company, your frustrations are endless, and bureaucracy is chief among them. You need a playbook for dealing with it so you can do your job. Read on.

If you're an alien from a planet that is bureaucracy-free and you never negotiated the rules of your games as a child, have never been frustrated by your cable company's customer service, and have never filled out a form with little boxes that are too small, don't bother with this book. I can recommend plenty of *good* authors to read, like Franz Kafka and Herman Melville.

Benediction: A Ball of Dung

Let's call on the ancient Egyptian deity most closely associated with transformation. His name is Khepri, and he's the god who moves the sun along so that each day can start fresh—an apt metaphor for transformation. His symbol is the dung beetle, which is also the Egyptian hieroglyphic for *transformation*. Apparently the Egyptians equated his way of nudging the sun from one day to the next with the way a beetle pushes along his little ball of dung.

Khepri is also a qualified bureaucrat: the *Egyptian Book of the Dead*, envisioning the entrance to the afterlife as a bureaucracy where the newly dead must answer a series of questions precisely and formulaically, suggests burying a dung beetle image with a body to whisper into its ear the required answers.

As if this wasn't enough to make Khepri our patron deity for bureaucratic transformation, Franz Kafka, the writer most associated with the terrors of bureaucracy, had the protagonist of "The Metamorphosis" metamorphose (transform) into—you guessed it—a dung beetle.*

---

* You might have thought he was transformed into a cockroach. The cockroach/dung beetle controversy is a longstanding debate in academia, but the Dungists appear to

Oh, Khepri! We ask you to bless our efforts at bureaucratic transformation! Please assist us in rolling this ball of odorous bureaucracy toward the abyss, that we may successfully enter the realm of the digital afterlife! Amen!

---

be winning; in the story, the maid does specifically call Gregor a dung beetle, whereas cockroaches are never mentioned. -au.

PART I

DIGITAL TRANSFORMATION AND BUREAUCRACY

OVERTURE:
TRY IT YOURSELF

He gains consciousness from sensuous slumber, sees that he is a man, looks around and finds himself to be living in a state. Force of need cast him there before he was capable of freely choosing this condition.
—Friedrich Schiller, *On the Aesthetic Education of Man*

Everything is simpler than we can imagine, at the same time more complex and intertwined than can be comprehended.

—Goethe

A Revelatory Puzzle

Imagine that you're going to create a large organization from scratch to produce a product or accomplish a mission. Or perhaps you've been asked to take over management of a big group of people who are standing around waiting for you to tell them what to do. Organizations grow and evolve, but let's just shortcut all of that and say that you suddenly have, oh, 100,000 people or so sitting in your corporate cafeteria and twiddling their thumbs impatiently. Incidentally, this is in some ways the situation DHS found itself in when it was founded in 2003 after the 9/11 attacks—it was created by bringing together people from twenty-two existing agencies to somehow keep the country safe.[1]*

Now how will you set up your organization? More precisely, how will you coordinate those 100,000 people to work toward a common goal—your goal?

---

*Fun fact: speaking of bureaucracy, over 108 congressional subcommittees oversee DHSR.[2] Surprised that it's hard to get anything done? -au.

You'll probably need someone to be in charge, right? We'll call that person the CEO. And unless you want to have 100,000 people reporting to the CEO, you'll probably need some sort of a hierarchy to keep the thing organized. Perhaps you'll have one part of the company focus on sales, another part on marketing, and another on producing the product. That's particularly sensible because people tend to be skilled or at least educated in one thing or the other, and with that kind of structure you can use their skills efficiently.

For each part of the hierarchy, you'll probably need to tell them what their job description is—what they're responsible for. Perhaps their goals will involve some quantifiable metrics. You also know that since they'll all be spending money, there's a danger that they'll spend too much. In fact—it's virtually guaranteed that they will, other things being equal, because spending more will always allow them to do more of whatever you're holding them responsible for. So perhaps you'll assign each group a maximum they can spend and set up some processes to keep track of the cash they toss around so you can do your tax returns at the end of the year.

You can't just *create* these hierarchies—you also need ways for people in them to interact to get the job done. And because the organization is large, you can't count on informal communications. So, you work with them to set up some formal interaction patterns. For example, Marketing will generate and capture leads, and then pass them on to Sales. Salespeople might learn from their customers what product attributes are valuable, so you'll make sure they have a way to communicate that information to the product design team.

The financial market regulators and the government want to make sure you're transparent and have controls in place, for example, to protect investors. So, you make someone a CFO and charge them with reporting on what everyone else is doing and with establishing controls that will satisfy auditors.

Let's see what you've done. You've set up a hierarchy based on a division of labor, a separation of responsibilities. You've instituted a merit system where the good marketers are placed into Marketing, the good operators into Operations, and the Royal Fools* into disciplinary proceedings. You've structured their interactions to best achieve the company's goals and established formal ceremonies to facilitate those interactions. And you've thrown in some rules-based, auditor-friendly controls as guardrails to satisfy authorities.

Congratulations. You've created a bureaucracy.

Don't feel bad about yourself, *Homo bureaucraticus*. You're not the first.

---

* See next chapter for more on Royal Fools. -ed.

WHAT ARE WE TALKING ABOUT?

I mistrust all systematizers and I avoid them. The will to a system is a lack of integrity.

—Nietzsche, *Twilight of the Idols*

And what thing soever besides cometh within the chaos of this monster's mouth, be it beast, boat, or stone, down it goes all incontinently that foul great swallow of his, and perisheth in the bottomless gulf of his paunch.

—Plutarch, *Moralia*

Authorities and Royal Fools

Let's take any social organization, by which I mean a group of people working together toward common goals. It could be, perhaps, a government, or a business corporation, or a nonprofit. By what authority do leaders lead in this organization, and how can they set up their organization to make sure it accomplishes their goals?

There are three ways. The first is through *tradition*—leaders become leaders because . . . well, tradition says they should be. For example, kings and queens are generally kings and queens and not acrobats and newscasters because they're born into the right families. Pharaohs commanded their people to build pyramids because pharaohs commanded people to build pyramids—there were no skate parks back then. The role of *monarch* is defined pretty loosely*—search

---

* Of course, there has been a tendency toward constitutional monarchies in the modern era and even during medieval times in Britain. -au.

online for "king" and you'll find jobs in King County and at Burger King, but no job description for "ruler."

A cool thing about monarchs is that they're necessarily right about everything—because they say so. To the political philosopher Thomas Hobbes, writing in *Leviathan*,* that's exactly the point. People are born naturally into a "brutish" state—if they don't cede power to a sovereign and accept the sovereign's judgement as binding, they'll spend their time killing each other rather than making cat videos. Melville, compiling references to whales for his introduction to *Moby Dick*, gleefully quotes the opening line of Hobbes's *Leviathan*: "By art is created that great *Leviathan*, called a Commonwealth or State—(in Latin, Civitas) which is but an artificial man."[1] I do the same here, just as gleefully.†

In traditional organizations, officials act in traditional roles. The *Cup-Bearer* bears cups. A *Royal Fool* acts foolishly. A *Gentleman of the Bedchamber* oversees a king's "physicians and entertainments." A *Bearded One*, in Byzantine times, was responsible for not being a eunuch, while a *Nipsistiarios* was beardless and held the water basin. And, yes, the *Groom of the King's Stool* did precisely what it sounds like.‡ Let's just say that a traditional hierarchy is not always organized logically for the most efficient management of the realm.

A second type of authority is that of the charismatic leader, such as, say, Hitler, Napoleon, Joan of Arc, Mother Teresa, the Pied Piper, or—I have to assume—the first lemming in a suicide parade. Here it's the leader's personal magnetism that inspires their followers and powers their administration. A problem for organizations of this type is continuity—charismatic leaders tend to hold power only briefly. Consider the lemming.

These two types of authority—*traditional* and *charismatic*—can be referred to as *leadership by notables* or *patrimonial leadership*. Notables exercise leadership in their own names—their interests are the state's or business's interests. They may profit personally from their administration, and they

---

* Note Schwartz's indirect reference to Moby Dick and whales here. Leviathan is the huge monster of the sea cited in the Bible, and the term is often used to refer to whales. -ed.

† That is, happily drawing the connection between whales and state bureaucracies. -ed.

‡ No lie. For details you can refer to Giulia Enders's *Gut: The Inside Story on Our Body's Most Underrated Organ*. -au.

may grant the authority to profit to the officials who act in their names—for example by allowing tax collectors or grooms of the stool to collect a little extra for themselves.

Is it possible that a notable is sometimes also acting in the best interests of the business or state? To ask that question, I think, is to misunderstand the idea of leadership by notables. In the famous words of Louis XIV (which he probably never uttered), "*L'etat, c'est moi*" ("the state—that's me!").[2] The kingdom was the ruler's, personally; there was no separation between the role and the person who filled it—at least until the rise of constitutional monarchies, when the power of monarchs became restricted to waving at the public and perpetrating sex scandals.

The third possible source of authority is *rational-legal* authority, where roles are defined according to some agreed-upon logic and then occupied by individuals who thereby gain the power and accountabilities assigned to the role. *Occupying* the role is the crucial concept—the person is no longer acting as an individual but in an official capacity. They are not authorized to seek personal profit, nor to bring their prejudices, personal vendettas, or family relationships into their jobs. Roles and the relationships between them are specified in rules that have been chosen to promote the success of the organization.

Such authority is *rational* in the sense that reason is used to design the best set of roles and practices for achieving the desired outcomes. It is *legal* in the sense that rules determine behavior rather than whim, caprice, or personal interests. Rational-legal authority allows for continuity because different people may fill the roles over time. Each role is occupied by the person best able to fill it, someone who can demonstrate the necessary skills. Once in the role they're backed by legal authority (as opposed to the power of their army or charismatic manipulation), but their authority is carefully limited to what's necessary to accomplish the organization's goals.[3]

If this model sounds familiar, that's because most of the institutions we know today are organized on the basis of rational-legal authority. It's a defining characteristic of our modern age. It's the structuring principle of business organizations and government agencies. It's known as bureaucracy.

Max Weber Arrives

The distinction I've laid out between traditional, charismatic, and rational-legal authority is more or less that of Max Weber (1864–1920), one of the pioneers of sociology, writing in the early twentieth century.* His is the canonical analysis of bureaucracy, the citation that appears in every scholarly work on the subject. He emphasized the sociological aspects of bureaucracy, mostly how authority is obtained and exercised, rather than its political-economic or public administration aspects. But his thinking is so clear that his writings are the starting point for almost everything written on the subject.

For Weber, the modern age has been defined by a movement from "magical" ways of looking at the world to more "scientific" or rational ways. Rationalization, to Weber, meant the use of rules and instrumental systems to understand and manage the world, and bureaucracy was simply one aspect of a broader trend[4] toward rationality epitomized by science and engineering. Frolicking gods and angelic intervention would no longer determine business success or national policy now that the world had become "dis-enchanted" (that is, no longer understood as based on enchantment). Instead, the mind would impose order and efficiency on a world that was becoming increasingly complex.

Weber described the archetype or "ideal" form of bureaucracy[†] as a system with these characteristics: (1) division of labor (specialization), (2) hierarchical organization, (3) rules, (4) technical competence, (5) impersonality, (6) formal, documented communications.[‡]

To make it easier to work with, I like to think of Weber's framework in groupings like this:

---

* Though his canonical work, *Economy and Society*, wasn't translated into English until 1947. -au.

[†] Note that many people writing on bureaucracy appear to be confused by Weber's use of the word "ideal" and think he was saying that *bureaucracy* is an ideal way to manage an organization. In fact, Weber is using the term "ideal" in the sense of archetype, or essential characteristics, as in the Platonic ideal of bureaucracy. -au.

[‡] Everyone seems to have their favorite way of summarizing Weber's points in a bulleted list; some have five characteristics, some six, some seven. In *Economy and Society*, 956–958, Weber's actual list seems to be: (1) jurisdictional areas, (2) office hierarchy, (3) written documents ("the files"), (4) office management (technical specialization), (5) full-time working capacity of the official, and (6) general rules. But in Weber's text he restates these in many ways. My list is pretty typical. Other characteristics are sometimes listed as "career orientation," "achievement-focused advancement," "efficient organization," "up-focused or in-focused," and "administrative class." -au.

- **Roles:** A bureaucracy has a formal delineation of accountabilities, organized into a hierarchy and filled with people who have the expertise to accomplish the tasks of their roles.
- **Rules:** The activities of a bureaucracy are determined by rules, which are applied universally and impersonally. A "paper trail" makes the rules self-proving; in other words, one output of a bureaucratic process is a paper flow that proves that the process was followed.

Even more simply: formal, rigid *roles* and formal, rigid *rules*.

Robert Merton, the sociologist best known for introducing the terms "role model" and "self-fulfilling prophecy," emphasized this *formal* aspect of bureaucracy, explaining that in it, "rituals" of communication minimize friction by restricting the interactions between roles to those that are officially sanctioned. With formalized patterns of interaction, officials can work together regardless of their attitudes toward one another, which might even be hostile. Formalities also allow for *calculability* in the sense that each person knows more or less how the other will act in a given interaction.[5]

Impersonality

Impersonality, item five on Weber's list, is worth a deeper look. It implies that the rules of the bureaucracy are applied equally to everyone. Weber used the Latin phrase *sine ira et studio*, "without anger or bias," sometimes translated as "without hatred or passion" or "without affection or enthusiasm." What it really means is everyone is subject to formal equality of treatment.[6]

Impersonality is crucial to the bureaucratic mindset for the following reasons:

- It *separates the official's person from their role*. Officials apply the rules uniformly, and therefore not on the basis of their prejudice, mood, profit, blood sugar level, or whim.
- It promotes *fairness*. Everyone is treated equally. No special exceptions are made for friends, movie stars, Kardashians, or dangerous-looking maniacs with Kalashnikovs.
- It breeds *efficiency*, in that the rules encapsulate the best known practices, and are applied in all cases. Exceptions, which would reduce efficiency, are not permitted.

- It leads to *calculability*. One knows what outcome will result from a request, whereas petitioning a pharaoh or Charles Manson, or the possibility that your competitor is doing so, can lead to surprises.

Bureaucratic Efficiency

Weber and Merton—and many other writers on bureaucracy—emphasize its efficiency, which sounds strange to those of us brought up on stories of bureaucratic waste and ineptitude, and who have likely witnessed it ourselves. In Weber's words, bureaucracy

> is, from a purely technical point of view, capable of attaining the highest degree of efficiency and is in this sense formally the most rational known means of exercising authority over human beings. It is superior to any other form in precision, in stability, in the stringency of its discipline, and in its reliability. . . . The choice is only that between bureaucracy and dilettantism in the field of administration.[7]

Weber saw the modern era as one where specialized technical skills were increasingly necessary. Gone was the time when "dilettantes" could manage business functions. Instead, experts would be accountable for areas in which they were experts, and formalized interactions would be used to coordinate their efforts. Efficiency would result and would be amplified by removing emotional concerns like personal relationships, hostility, anxiety, and the like, leaving only rational considerations.[8]

For both Weber and Merton, *efficiency* was not a single characteristic, but a complex set of attributes. "The chief merit of bureaucracy is its technical efficiency, with a premium placed on precision, speed, expert control, continuity, discretion, and optimal returns on input," says Merton.[9] Or, in Weber's words:

> Precision, speed, unambiguousness, knowledge of the files, continuity, discretion, unity, strict subordination, reduction of friction and of material and personal costs—these are raised to the optimum point in the strictly bureaucratic administration.[10]

So, let me pause and ask, reader, what's your problem with bureaucracy? Why buy a book about how to bust through it? It's hard to see anything objectionable in Weber's definition. Sure, I've got a few reservations: in the IT world we've been finding that generalists ("dilettantes") actually are quite valuable, "discipline" is a heavy-handed word, and I'm not sure efficiency is the right goal (*leanness* is more like it). But Weber is just talking about organizing logically to get good results.

In recent years our view of bureaucracy has diverged a wee bit from Weber's idealized picture.

> The term "bureaucracy" is popularly associated with impersonal hierarchy, rigid rules, predictable procedures, and a pace of decision-making and change that would embarrass a glacier. Emphasizing the disadvantages of bureaucracy in a fast-paced world, theorists have consistently contrasted inflexible mechanistic systems with fluid organic systems, and plodding segmentalist cultures with innovative integrative cultures.[11]

Glaciers are not easily embarrassed.

Over time, Weber's broad understanding of efficiency yielded to a narrower idea of process optimization.[12] Bureaucracies petrified and grew tentacles of red tape that seemed to defy rationality rather than exemplify it.

Business and Government

Modern democratic governments are necessarily bureaucracies. They're based on the rule of law and administered by a civil service chosen by merit, separately from the election of political officials.

But businesses too have been designed as bureaucracies. Mass production demanded strict repeatability and statistical quality control. Global competition demanded cost efficiencies. And the increasing size and scale of business organizations demanded some sort of centralized control over decentralized organizations. In Weber's words, "the very large modern capitalist enterprises are themselves unequalled models of strict bureaucratic organization."[13] "All complex organizations," Wilson says, "display bureaucratic problems of confusion, red tape, and the avoidance of responsibility."[14] It's no wonder that large companies and government agencies looking to digitally transform face similar bureaucratic impediments.

One of the most compelling uses of bureaucracy in today's economy is to support a company's branding. A brand must be consistent; it must deliver a unified, coherent, recognizable experience to customers. And that consistency is a specialty of bureaucracy. McDonald's, for example, has standardized, in minute detail, the operation of its stores and the activities of its employees in an operations manual that is six hundred pages long and weighs four pounds.[15]

Branding guidelines specify how a company's logo should be used, what typefaces are acceptable, the positioning of elements on a page, and the voice and style to be used for communications. Guardrails and reviews ensure that those branding guidelines are followed. Because brands can have tremendous business value—Coca Cola's is said to be worth $59.2 billion and Disney's $52.2 billion[16]—it's no exaggeration to say that a company's bureaucracy can be a critical component of its value.

Just as the government must answer to a diverse citizenry, businesses— at least publicly traded ones—must answer to a diverse base of shareholders. To ensure that employees are doing what those stakeholders want, companies devise governance structures and controls. The larger and more complex an organization is, the more it will see bureaucracy as the solution for aligning its employees with its stakeholders.

The convergence of government and business bureaucracies is noted by Graeber in *The Utopia of Rules*. On one hand, he says, "The rise of the modern corporation, in the late nineteenth century, was largely seen at the time as a matter of applying modern, bureaucratic techniques to the private sector."[17] On the other hand, the bureaucratic techniques of government, Graeber says, originally came from the private sector and then seeped into all aspects of life:

> Americans often seem embarrassed by the fact that, on the whole, we're really quite good at bureaucracy. It doesn't fit our American self-image. . . . If Americans are able to overlook their awkward preeminence in this field, it is probably because most of our bureaucratic habits and sensibilities—the clothing, the language, the design of forms and offices—emerged from the private sector.[18]

In the ultimate twist, private sector bureaucracy actually forces the government to be bureaucratic. Weber draws this connection: "Today, it is primarily the capitalist market economy which demands that the official business of public administration be discharged precisely, unambiguously, continuously, and with as much speed as possible."[19] One reason that businesses demand bureaucracy from the government is the predictability (calculability) it offers. Free markets require transparency and predictability:

> The peculiarity of modern culture, and specifically of its technical and economic basis, demands this very "calculating" of results. . . . Bureaucracy develops the more perfectly, the more it is "dehumanized," the more completely it succeeds in eliminating from official business love, hatred, and all purely personal, irrational, and emotional elements which escape calculation. This is appraised its special virtue by capitalism.[20]

While bureaucracy may seem mechanical and "faceless," the same is true of the "invisible hand of the market." Business decisions today are ultimately out of executives' control—they are made by consumers. The market is relentless, merciless, and foils your best plans. Its decisions cannot be appealed. That is to say, it has many of the characteristics of a bureaucracy.

Customer-Facing Bureaucracy

Bureaucracy goes beyond the organization of work *within* a business; even businesses with a market incentive to provide good customer service can take on the characteristics of bureaucratic impersonality and rigidity in their public personas. Medical insurance companies in the US continue to innovate ways to frustrate their customers with obscure billing codes, arbitrary-seeming rules, surprise requirements for "pre-authorizations," and endless telephone wait times. Graeber relates his experience with a bank when trying to access his account information from overseas, a process that required "speaking to four different representatives, two referrals to nonexistent numbers, three long explanations of complicated and apparently arbitrary rules, and two failed attempts to change outdated address and phone number information lodged on various computer systems."[21]

This bureaucratization of service may partly be explained by a need for formal rules to ensure equal treatment of customers, pressure to standardize processes to control costs, and—in Graeber's situation—the need to ensure security and privacy. But it wouldn't survive without our increasing acceptance, as customers and employees, of this formality and rigidity in customer service. As someone who travels a lot, I'm constantly struck by the scolding, condescending, and mechanical tone airlines use with me.

But a deeper connection between internal and external bureaucracy may be derived as a variation on Conway's Law.[22] Melvin Conway, a computer programmer, observed in 1967 that the structure of an organization's software tends to mirror the organization's communication patterns. In effect, the architecture of its software systems looks a lot like the structure of its organizational chart.

In my bureaucratic variation on Conway's Law, the face that a company presents to its customers is also influenced by its internal structure. When you telephone a company, you're transferred from one customer service agent to another based on their different positions in the organizational chart. You're shifted from phone line to phone line as you cross organizational boundaries. They'll have to look you up in four different IT systems because hierarchical bureaucracies don't put much value on information sharing between silos. Your experience, in other words, mirrors their bureaucracy. Bureaucratic goop seeps through the walls of an enterprise and becomes embarrassingly visible to customers.

Bureaucracy affects even the language enterprises and their officials speak to the public. In Charles Dickens's *Little Dorrit*, a government agency called the Ministry of Circumlocutions circumlocutes and discourages the public from filling out the many forms it requires—on the cogent grounds that nothing will happen with their cases anyway. Chrysler Corp. announced layoffs with a message saying that it was going to initiate a "career alternative enhancement program."[23] Governments, eager to obscure their more questionable actions, find ways to bury us under mountains of verbiage.*

What seems to underlie this type of speech is a denial of agency. Individuals avoid acknowledging their responsibility with the help of vague and confusing language, just as they do by pointing to bureaucratic rules they are obliged to follow. George Orwell famously translated a well-known biblical passage into this anesthetizing exemplar of bureaucracy-speak that avoids using the word "I":

> Objective consideration of contemporary phenomena compels the conclusion that success or failure in competitive activities exhibits no tendency to be commensurate with innate capacity, but that a con-

---

* This is a reference to the story of the Monkey King, as told in Chapter 12. -ed.

siderable element of the unpredictable must invariably be taken into account.[24]

The original passage, from Ecclesiastes (9:11), was:

I returned and saw under the sun, that the race is not to the swift, nor the battle to the strong, neither yet bread to the wise, nor yet riches to men of understanding, nor yet favour to men of skill; but time and chance happeneth to them all.

We at Satanic Airlines are pleased to welcome you to Inferno International Airport, where the local time is . . . eternity. Please remember to take all your personal belongings.

History of Bureaucracy (Part Two): Napoleon to Gaga

As we've seen, bureaucracy has been around at least since Y2K (BCE, that is) when the Old Kingdom of Egypt was building huge stone cats without noses. But something changed in modern times to make it such a deep and disturbing part of our lives. By the time Weber was tossing around *Schimpfworts*, the bureaucratic lifestyle had already progressed enough that he was describing something well established. What had happened?

It's tempting to date modern bureaucracy to the scientific management theories of Frederick Taylor (1856–1915) and Henri Fayol (1841–1925), but really the change was well underway in Europe by the early years of the nineteenth century. The French Revolution in 1789 had replaced a seemingly stable monarchy with the chaos of the mob, thereby initiating a century or so of seesawing between republic and monarchy in an attempt to regain control and structure while also promoting democracy and equality.

Napoleon entered the scene early in the nineteenth century and began bureaucratizing France, restructuring the civil service and introducing his Napoleonic Code. As you know from my last book (*War and Peace and IT*), Napoleon fought his wars on a grand scale. In earlier days, soldiers might have been appointed by a sovereign, drawn from the nobility with little care for whether they knew which end of a rifle shoots the bullets. By the time of Waterloo in 1815, though, Napoleon was managing an army of 200,000 troops against

500,000 British and other allied soldiers. The front at Waterloo was six times the length of that at the battle of Agincourt four hundred years earlier, and Napoleon commanded from a position more than a mile away.*

He was able to manage on this huge scale because the French army had become a professional, hierarchical organization with a well-defined command structure. It had a dozen tiers of rank, at the bottom of which the soldiers were further classified into riflemen, light and heavy infantry, artillery, dragoons, grenadiers, light and heavy cavalry, signalmen, engineers, and scouts.[25] It's a common pattern: with scale, centralization of authority, and specialization come the sparkling adornments of bureaucracy.

France continued to be an innovator in bureaucracy throughout the 1800s. In time, as we've seen, they developed that strange idea of rule by desks, based on the notion of a fair, impersonal, rule-driven society, with continuity provided by a cadre of civil servants. This made sense to Weber, who found it natural that bureaucracy would accompany mass democracy—its universal rules and ideals help create order in an environment where economic and social differences, along with patrimonial authority, are eliminated.[26] Unfortunately, France's bureaucracy was quickly distorted by the petty maneuverings of the appointed officials that Balzac painfully describes in *The Bureaucrats*.[27]

Among the spoils of war that the English seized after Waterloo, apparently, was the idea of rule by desks, for they soon began to vie with France for bureaucratic supremacy. Refusing to be outdone by Balzac, Charles Dickens also took inspiration from the escalating bureaucratic arms race and became a spokesperson for British supremacy. "Britannia," he says in *David Copperfield*, "that unfortunate female, is always before me, like a trussed fowl: skewered through and through with office-pens, and bound hand and foot with red tape."[28] Ugh, sick image, but no doubt sincere. There's the nineteenth century for you.

On the business side, firms became larger as industrialization allowed for economies of scale. With advances in industry and technology—particularly in transportation and communication—and the need for large capital investments to build factories came centralization and standardization.[29] The obvious next step was to apply a science and engineering mentality—the pride of the modern

---

*Waterloo: Napoleon's 1815 defeat by the British and their allies, after which he was exiled to the island of St. Helena. Agincourt: battle in 1415 in northern France wherein the British defeated the French army. One mile away: see Battle of Borodino in Schwartz's *War and Peace and IT*. -ed.

era—to business processes and accountabilities. That's when Fayol, Taylor, and Weber came along and gave us the beginnings of management theory.

Skip a few more decades forward, to the Nazi genocide, a highly engineered bureaucracy applied to unspeakable ends. The Nazis too faced a problem of scale. After 1942, determined to murder all the Jews, they had to figure out how to make it practical. Six million is a lot—and they also had to deal with the Slavs, Romani, homosexuals, and others they'd marked for elimination. They mobilized an unprecedented bureaucratic effort to find, catalog, transport, kill, and dispose of their victims and their possessions.

It was not just in the mechanization of death that the Nazis showcased what bureaucracy can do; they also systematically used the legal bureaucracy to turn Jews into noncitizens and deprive them of their rights. Once the bureaucracy was in motion, it was easy for the perpetrators to overlook their own responsibility; they were simply filling roles in a machine efficiently set up to manufacture Jewish death. As Arendt put it, bureaucracy was conveniently a system where "neither one nor the best, neither the few nor the many, can be held responsible, and which could be properly called the rule by Nobody. . . . Rule by Nobody is clearly the most tyrannical of all, since there is no one left who could even be asked to answer for what is being done."[30]

Nevertheless, by the 1950s bureaucracy had become the everyday lifestyle for corporate men and women in proverbial gray flannel suits.* Cookie-cutter suburbs fed white collar workers into city offices, and large enterprises became larger. Then, in the 1960s, students rioted against coercive authority, later becoming executives so they could exercise coercive authority themselves. Bureaucracy spread like a virus.

Then computers and the internet invented speed, and Lady Gaga began changing musical genres and clothing styles every few days. Which brings us to today's anxiety about the need to move fast while neck-deep in bureaucratic sludge.

Busting Bureaucracy

We hear frequently of attempts at "bureaucracy busting." But bureaucracy turns out to be hard to bust, leading even Weber to despairing exaggeration:

---

*Mr. Schwartz is referring to the novel *The Man in the Gray Flannel Suit* by Sloan Wilson (1955), about the struggles of a military veteran in cookie-cutter suburbia and bureaucratic officedom. -ed.

"The only real way to rid oneself of an established bureaucracy," he says, "is to simply kill them all, as Alaric the Goth did in Imperial Rome, or Genghis Khan in certain parts of the Middle East."[31]

Incoming politicians vow to do away with bureaucracy, but in the end find it essential for exercising power, and instead of destroying it, wind up trying to direct it to their own ends. Frederick the Great's attempts to abolish serfdom were frustrated by his inability to control the bureaucracy, which thought him naive and uninformed.[32] Hitler's genocide, as we've seen, was abetted by his bureaucratic talents. As it was co-opted by trolls looking for sustenance, the US's Paperwork Reduction Act, predictably, produced paper. The Government Paperwork Elimination Act, just as predictably, produced even more.

New CEOs, as soon as they've located the restrooms and the nearest Starbucks, begin promising to do away with red tape and "bloated" bureaucracy, to the wild enthusiasm of shareholders and the press. Paul Adler, Professor of Management and Organization, Sociology, and Environmental Studies at the University of Southern California, cites an article praising the leadership abilities of one new CEO, who "trashed two fat books of policies and replaced them with just 11 important ones," saying that "Those rules, aimed at one percent of employees, handcuff the other 99 percent."[33] There's no reference to the institutional knowledge that might have been trashed in the process, or of what replaced the rules. GE, famously, undertook a transformation intended to reduce its paperwork. "Unfortunately, it is still possible to find documents around GE businesses that look like something out of the National Archives, with five, 10, or even more signatures necessary before action can be taken."[34]

The political scientist and public administration expert James Q. Wilson, in his book *Bureaucracy*, writes about the US government's procurement system, which is governed by the FAR (Federal Acquisition Rule), a monumental* document of six thousand pages. The problem with fighting procurement waste, he says, is that as soon as waste is discovered, more rules get added, resulting in even more waste.

> If despite all your devotion to the rules Congress uncovers an especially blatant case of paying too much for too little (for example, a $3,000 coffee pot), the prudent response is to suggest that what is needed are more

---

* As a running gag throughout the book, Schwartz uses a different synonym for "large" every time he mentions the six-thousand-page FAR. -ed.

rules, more auditors, and more tightly constrained procedures. The consequence of this may be to prevent the buying of any more $3,000 coffee pots, or it may be to increase the complexity of the procurement process so that fewer good firms will submit bids to supply coffee pots, or it may be to increase the cost of monitoring that process so that the money saved by buying cheaper pots is lost by hiring more pot inspectors. Or it may be all three.[35]

He gives a specific example: a case where the army, because of rules intended to reduce waste, had to spend $5,400 and 160 days to get competitive bids for spare parts that cost $11,000. For all that cost and effort, they saved only $100 in the end.[36]

One reason why bureaucracy-busting initiatives have little chance of success is that they're centrally managed, and centralization tends to require more bureaucracy. Graeber even frames an "iron law of liberalism" that says that "any market reform, any government initiative intended to reduce red tape and promote market forces will have the ultimate effect of increasing the total number of regulations, the total amount of paperwork, and the total number of bureaucrats the government employs."[37]

Nevertheless

Nevertheless, I'm going to show you how to bust bureaucracy. More specifically, I'm going to give you some ideas on how to digitally transform your organization even when bureaucracy is holding you back.

By *digital transformation* I mean adopting continuous innovation and change, risk reduction through agility, rapid sensing of market and competitive changes, and business flexibility. Most large enterprises, whether public or private sector, are not set up to move any faster than a glacier. And bureaucracy, as Frederick the Great and GE discovered, melts slowly.

Let's be clear on what we plan to bust. It's not Weberian bureaucracy, per se, that we hate. It is something like this:

Bureaucracy (n): immovable obstacles to what I am trying to accomplish that come from somewhere else in the enterprise and frustrate me. Examples: MD-102, Paperwork Reduction Act, new covers on TPS Reports. Used in a sentence: *I am about to kill myself because of all this* *bureaucracy*. See also: death, waste (human and process), and dung beetles.

Bureaucracies have three characteristics according to this definition: they're stubborn, they're obstacles, and they come from elsewhere.

Stubborn. Constraints are unappealable "no"s. They don't take account of my special circumstances, and probably reflect an earlier understanding of good practices or a reaction to a situation that occurred long ago.

Obstacle. Constraints are frustrating what I'm trying to accomplish. I'm trying to do what's right for the organization, but I'm being prevented.

Elsewhere. Someone *outside* my team is imposing the constraints, and I had no say in formulating them. Someone is wielding power over me, and I don't like that.

Emotionally, this is what we hate about bureaucracy, right? And we tend to label organizational experiences as bureaucracy when we feel these emotions, whether they fit the Weberian definition or not. We're not talking about the Venerable Immortals of the Ten Continents and Three Islands here, who presumably mean us well and try to support us (though being "venerable" and immortal perhaps makes them suspect). We mean the Crabby Trolls of the Nine Audits and A Million "No"s.

CHAOS MONKEY IN THE BUREAUCRACY

So be cheery, my lads, let your hearts never fail, While the bold har-
pooneer is striking the whale!

—Nantucket Song in Herman Melville, *Moby Dick*

At this point the danger arises that he may first exclaim, "Is that any
business of yours, sir? Who are you to me?", and then, if you continue
to pester him, he may raise his fist and land a blow on you. This is an
enterprise that I too was once very keen to pursue, until I fell into such
difficulties.

—Epictetus, *Discourses*

Job Descriptions

An interesting thing you discover when you become a government Chief Information Officer (CIO) is that your job description is a law. The Clinger-Cohen
Act of 1996, Title 40, Subtitle III, Chapter 113, Subchapter II, clause 11315
establishes the role of a government agency CIO and lists the role's duties.
Here's a piece of my job description:

(3) annually, as part of the strategic planning and performance evaluation process required (subject to section 1117 of title 31) under section
306 of title 5 and sections 1105 (a)(28), 1115–1117, and 9703 (as added
by section 5(a) of the Government Performance and Results Act of 1993
(Public Law 103–62, 107 Stat. 289)) of title 31 . . .[1]

This seems a wonder of precision, given that the role of CIO in most enterprises is notoriously difficult to define. Don't let it fool you—government CIOs struggle with ambiguity just as commercial CIOs do, but if we ever needed to establish our authority for a decision, we could refer those who questioned us to Clinger-Cohen's impenetrable text.

My employees had helpfully sent me a copy of Clinger-Cohen and a few other important documents before I EOD'd (Entered on Duty) and was sworn in. Several of my other favorite documents were included in their email: a guide to 180 or so acronyms I'd be seeing every day, some promising-sounding laws called the Paperwork Reduction Act and the Government Paperwork Elimination Act, a thick stack of paper called MD-102, and a map of the Washington, DC, metro system. I scanned quickly through the documents, noted that they had nothing to do with the way anyone runs IT, and put them aside.

Shortly after I EOD'd, I was in a tiny meeting to discuss a tiny project. My memory's probably a tiny bit unreliable on this, but I think it was just a tiny change to the text on a tiny web page. I asked my people how long they thought it would take.

"Eight months," they said carefully, with a side glance at each other.

"Eight months?! How could that little change take eight months?"

"Well, actually, we were going to say something longer, but we knew you wouldn't like it."

"Is our contractor so slow that it will take them that long?"

"No, the contractor is pretty good."

"Well then, why would it take eight months?"

Their enigmatic reply: "MD-102."

Another incident, also early in my time at USCIS: I was at a meeting to discuss the fate of one of our IT systems, something called RNACS. RNACS was just what you'd expect given a name like RNACS—an old mainframe-based IT system, a piece of clunky, cave-dweller technology, expensive to maintain . . . and no longer used. After some discussion we were sure that no one would ever need it again. "Okay," I said, "let's decommission it." Decommissioning meant we'd turn it off, archive any data it held, and stop paying for its upkeep. There was silence in the room.

"Uh, sir?" someone said.

"Yes?"

"You don't have the authority to decommission it."

"Why not? I'm the fu . . . I'm the CIO!"

"MD-102."

Dang. Probably should've read that thing when they sent it to me.

MD-102 was Management Directive 102, a DHS policy used for overseeing the delivery of IT systems. It defined twenty-one distinct roles in the oversight process. In its hundreds of pages of plus thirteen appendices it listed eighty-seven documents that had to be prepared when delivering any IT system and eleven gate review meetings that had to be held to approve its various phases. Each document had to be signed by a giggle* of officials, and each gate review meeting had to be attended by a synod of prescribed voting members and a terafool of nonvoting observers.† At least one of the documents, something called an Analysis of Alternatives, routinely ran to a hundred pages or more and had never taken less than eighteen months to write. A favorite document of mine (with eighty-seven documents, one is bound to have favorites) was something called the Integrated Logistical Support Plan, which explained how we were planning to swab and pilot the new battleship—I mean, IT system. If there was a Louvre or Prado for bureaucratic art, MD-102 would have crowds lining up to view it.

Could there be some connection between MD-102 and the fact that it took years and hundreds of millions of dollars to deliver any IT capabilities?

Enter the Monkey

In 2010, Netflix released a piece of software called the Chaos Monkey, whose purpose was to randomly assassinate‡ other bits of software that were running. This might not sound like a great idea, especially when you realize it's meant to run in a company's production environment—that is, among the company's live IT systems, the ones actively serving customers and employees. The reasoning behind Chaos Monkey is that since today's IT systems are built to be

---

* Gaggle? -ed.

† Apparently, a brilliant meme that a collection of baboons is "a congress of baboons"[2] turned out to be a hoax. But in looking it up I discovered the (apparently legitimate) collective nouns: a shrewdness of apes, obstinacy of buffalo, coalition of cheetahs, business of ferrets, bloat of hippopotamuses, conspiracy of lemurs, unkindness of ravens, and wisdom of wombats. Monkeys, as we know, come in barrels. -au.

‡ Have you noticed that the word "execute," which should mean the same as kill, actually means the opposite in the technology world? Just saying. -au.

resilient, to withstand unexpected failures without any noticeable impact, the Chaos Monkey would just test to make sure they really were. Netflix made its code available as open source so that other companies could practice decimating their own systems with friendly fire, and many do. Eventually, we did too at USCIS, but that's getting ahead of the story.

Chaos Monkey spawned a new field in Information Technology: Chaos Engineering. Software systems have become so complex and interconnected that it's virtually impossible to know what might go wrong. Chaos Engineering is a discipline that uses controlled experiments on running IT systems to find those complex scenarios that might lead them to fail, so that the software can be fixed to handle them. Automated scripts "inject" different types of failures to see what follows—what other sorts of chaos they lead to—so that technologists can make their systems more resilient.

Since organizations themselves are complex and interconnected social environments, the consequences of organizational change sometimes must also be determined experimentally. Christopher Avery, a leadership expert and speaker, in an article on responsible cultural change in businesses, talks about using a "provoke and observe" approach:

> We can never direct a living system, only disturb it and wait to see the response. . . . We can't know all the forces shaping an organization we wish to change, so all we can do is provoke the system in some way by experimenting with a force we think might have some impact, then watch to see what happens.[3]

One tries something out of the ordinary and sees whether there is resistance, and if so, where it comes from and what it consists of. Then one formulates a strategy for dealing with it.

If you look back at my Clinger-Cohen job description, you'll no doubt agree that government IT is a complex environment, with many interacting, networked, and obscure connections to be unraveled. The only way to improve it would be to provoke it, observe the consequences, and adjust. What was needed was a chaos monkey in the government.*

---

*In Chapter 12 you'll learn the Way of the Monkey, the first force for transforming bureaucracy. For now, just watch the Monkey in operation. -au.

Speed and Government

I should probably give you some background. My agency, US Citizenship and Immigration Service (USCIS), is the component of the Department of Homeland Security (DHS) that handles *legal* immigration to the US—green cards, naturalizations, refugees and asylees, foreign adoptions, and about ninety other functions (things like providing some people proof of citizenship and letting others renounce their citizenship). USCIS folks are the nice guys of immigration—they don't arrest and deport people (that's ICE) and they don't sit in the airport and look grumpy (CBP and TSA).

As CIO, I wanted very much to find a way that our IT organization could respond quickly to our agency's needs. It might not be obvious why speed is important in the government, but this was something I'd learned along the way. I'd joined the government in 2010, toward the beginning of the Obama administration. On June 15, 2012, I was at home watching the evening news on TV when the president came on and announced his new immigration initiative, Deferred Action for Childhood Arrivals (DACA). This was the first I'd heard of it. The president also announced that it would be rolled out in sixty days.

The president didn't know, because, er, he hadn't asked us, that our average time to release an update to an IT system was eighteen months. When we analyzed the DACA initiative, we found that it would involve making changes to more than twenty IT systems. The math wasn't encouraging.

We did it, of course. USCIS began accepting applications on August 15, 2012. We had to waive a few requirements here and there, skip steps in our standardized processes, get our contractors on board with the emergency effort, push off other work while we focused on DACA, and . . . it's probably good that I don't know what else. I know there were individual heroics, stressful meetings, and food truck wrappers all over the office.

If it had been a one-time effort, we could have left it at that. But at the beginning of the Obama administration there was talk of comprehensively reforming the immigration system, so we expected plenty of change. We also had a very large and famously "failing" IT project in the works, something we called USCIS Transformation. It was intended to be a five-year project, and after five years it had—at least according to the official records—spent about a billion dollars and delivered nothing. Even by federal government standards, this was considered pretty bad. For a sense of scale, in five years most people could have read MD-102 two or three times, and maybe the introduction to the gargantuan FAR.

The solution to large failing projects and to slow delivery cycle times is well known in the IT community: a combination of what are called Agile techniques, DevOps, and the cloud. The idea is to work in short, fast increments, finishing and releasing pieces of IT capabilities quickly and frequently, then adjusting course based on the results and the feedback obtained from users of the software. But MD-102 prescribed exactly the opposite approach—extensive planning, monolithic deliveries, and strict adherence to plans made before the project was started. Clearly, we couldn't work within the bounds of MD-102 and also deliver speed and agility. But MD-102 was the policy of our corporate overseers, DHS.

Barriers to agility were built explicitly into MD-102's workflows, with steps like a Systems Definition Review (SDR), which "evaluate[s] the readiness of the project to proceed to Stage 3, Design . . . the SDR uses a set of exit criteria to evaluate completion of activities and products for this stage." There are seventy-three exit criteria, including "Have the requirements collected to date been specified in clear, meaningful, and testable format using 'shall' statements?"[4] In translation, that means, "You must slow down until the bureaucracy catches up." It was a way to spend enough time documenting and approving the requirements that you could be sure they were no longer relevant.

Or, the definition of the integration and test phase, which is allowed to begin only after all of the development work has been completed: "The purpose of the Integration and Test Stage is to demonstrate that the solution developed satisfies all defined requirements and to complete the integration of configuration items that have been readied during the Development stage."[5]

DevOps, on the other hand, requires that integration, testing, and delivery start right away, at the beginning of the project, and proceed throughout. It also has as a principle: "Maximize the amount of work not done." That is, try to find requirements that you can avoid implementing.

Not that MD-102 was the only impediment, but it was a handy enemy. If you could make it through all the words, what it communicated was "you must move at the pace of an embarrassed glacier and spend vast amounts of money if you want to be allowed to do anything good for the American public." Arguably there were worse impediments in government—the Paperwork Reduction Act is a good candidate (more on that later)—but MD-102 was the most immediate. It was the leviathan breathing bureaucracy down our necks,* so the battle with MD-102 commenced.

Robot Pranks

MD-102 was not crafted by evil bureaucratic robots playing robot pranks. It was created by dedicated civil servants who wanted to guide projects into delivering good results and effectively using the public's resources, generally the taxes paid by citizens. It institutionalized practices that were considered by many to be best practices when it was written. But IT had changed, and new ideas such as those we planned to implement had shown themselves to be much more effective.

The writers of a document like MD-102 are also not naive. They left open a back door, as most bureaucratic artworks do—an exception process. In this case, something called a Project Tailoring Plan. So, we began there, "tailoring" the process laid out in MD-102 to be exactly the opposite of the process laid out in MD-102.

The snag with a Project Tailoring Plan is that someone has to sign off on it. This is hard because most people are too busy when you ask them to take a personal risk. But we got a signature because (1) several of our projects were frighteningly behind schedule and no one could figure out another way to fix them, and (2) everyone had heard that DHS IT needed to become agile, and this was the one way anyone had thought of to do so.

The moment was right. The DHS CIO had recently written a widely distributed email saying we should try out some new Agile ideas. That sort of email is like a banana to a chaos monkey.

We also had the advantage of the then-recent failure of Healthcare.gov, the president's signature healthcare initiative. When the site was finally launched after extended political battles, it quickly fell apart. I taught my staff to ask "Do you really want another failure like healthcare.gov?" in answer to any questions they received.

So, we were given limited permission to try out something more agile, at least for the technical part of the work. We decided to use a process based on

---

* Actually, whales can't do this. They don't even have noses. -au.

the Agile framework called Scrum,* organizing our work into short iterations, with working software delivered after each one.

Now, an interesting side conversation developed. I said that MD-102 was not agile. The guardians of MD-102 said that it supported agility just fine, because you could get an exception with a Project Tailoring Plan, as we did. I said that since Agile is the best-known way to get results, you shouldn't have to get an exception to use it. MD-102's rules saying that you have to work the old, discredited way unless you get an exception are not actually good guidance, IMHO.

So why, I asked, don't we just make MD-102 say that you have to be agile and fast, unless you get an exception? The rulemakers laughed, because obviously they couldn't be as irresponsible as *that*. A Systems Engineering Center of Excellence had been involved in formulating MD-102, and the Center of Excellence said that it's excellent to have a lot of documents and gate reviews, and they would know, since they are the Center of Excellence.

Anyway, we proceeded with a big project that was now tailored to be agile. We rolled out Scrum,[†] juggled feature backlogs, stood up for a fifteen-minute standup every day, retrospected religiously at the end of each increment, and practiced continuous improvement on our agile process to get better and better.

Agile Amateurs

Matta![‡] A problem arose. Because it was a huge failing project that we were trying to fix, it had the attention of the auditors—in particular, that of the Government Accountability Office (GAO) and the DHS Inspector General (IG).

There was something surreal about their audits. The GAO didn't know that much about IT delivery, much less about Agile practices. I, on the other hand, with the appropriate nose-up arrogance of a digital technologist, considered myself an expert, having used Agile practices more or less since the Agile Man-

---

*Note that I am no longer a big fan of Scrum. Some of my reasons will become evident later in the book. -au.

[†] A popular Agile Software Development framework, which Mr. Schwartz discusses in greater detail later. As he says, it calls for fifteen-minute daily standups and frequent retrospectives. -ed.

[‡] "False start." See the sumo references below. Schwartz is thinking of his struggle against MD-102 as a comical clash between lumbering players, like a sumo bout. -ed.

ifesto was written in 2001, and I had several people working for me who were Agile coaches and thought leaders.

So, it surprised us when we went to a meeting where the GAO presented their findings and told us . . . we were not agile enough. Seeing that we were using Scrum, they had done some research, and they compared our practices to those of the official Scrum framework. It turned out that in our continuous improvement retrospectives we'd decided on a few departures from the rules of Scrum. For example, we'd experimented a bit with Scrum's *product owner* role. Our challenge was that the tremendous scope of our project made it difficult to have a single product owner from the very siloed business operation, and when we had several product owners each was incentivized to maintain a never-ending list of requirements (feature backlog) so that they kept the teams working on their part of the project forever. We tried some experiments to see if we could overcome the problem. We'd also made a few other changes here and there, based on what we'd learned as the project proceeded.

GAO hit us with a fact-based analysis. They listed the points where Scrum practice said one thing and our practice was different. Then, for a kicker, they pointed out that the creators of Scrum, Ken Schwaber and Jeff Sutherland, had said that you can't change anything in Scrum, or it's not Scrum.[6] Ergo, we were not agile.

I explained that the idea of Agile is to inspect and adapt, and that a good Agile practice was to hold retrospectives for continuous improvement. Once again, I was laughed at.

Prosecutorial voice: "So you admit you made changes. According to Jeff Sutherland, then, are you doing Scrum?"

I had to admit that we weren't. Then I thought I had them with a brilliant closing argument that "Scrum is not the same as Agile." Nice try, but I was dealing with bureaucracy professionals. They just drummed their fingers on our Project Tailoring Plan where it said we were going to use Scrum. We were not doing what we said we were going to do.

Fastest-Ever Digital Transformation

What had defeated us? Think about it for a second. It wasn't really government bureaucracy. It was Scrum bureaucracy. Scrum had a bunch of rules, and Jeff Sutherland had said you must follow the rules. Scrum—please don't hit me, Agile IT folks—Scrum is a bureaucratic way of performing IT delivery. It has defined roles—scrum masters, product owners, team members—and it has defined rules—fifteen-minute standups, backlogs, grooming, story points, and something about pigs and chickens that even its adherents are embarrassed to talk about.* I don't mean that it's necessarily bad,† just bureaucratic.

This led to an epiphany. I realized—I had been told this before, but I had never seen such a clear example—that the auditors' real job was to compare what we *said* we would do with what we *actually* did. How to overcome the system then was obvious.

You know the idea of aikido and other Japanese martial arts? You try to use your opponent's strength against them. In a sumo match, the wrestlers push against each other. But if your opponent pushes too hard and you respond by pulling, you can throw them off balance and win the match. A chaos monkey, it turns out, can sow chaos better by mastering sumo.

What if I flexed my own underdeveloped bureaucratic muscle and wrote a policy that said we had to be agile? I could define agility in my own way . . . exactly the way we wanted to run our projects. Then if GAO audited us in the future, they'd be reading my policy and checking to see that everyone was following it! They'd be on our side. A virtuous circle. An *inashi*,‡ a *deashi*,§ a true sumo solution.¶

So, I looked into how I'd go about writing a policy. Unfortunately, I found out that I didn't have the authority to do so, and in any case, it was a long and complicated process. Nor did I have the authority to write a Management Directive, like MD-102. But—I was told by my best bureaucracy savants—I *could* sign a Management Instruction, composed by them in fluent Orwellian,

---

* Pigs and chickens: In Scrum, the project team members are "pigs" and everyone else is a "chicken." The idea is that team members are fully committed, like pigs who provide bacon, and everyone else is only "involved," like the chickens that provide eggs. Scrum says chickens should defer to pigs, as in George Orwell's *Animal Farm*. Knowing Mr. Schwartz, he is probably also thinking of the fact that the pig-leader in *Animal Farm* is named Napoleon, one of Mr. Schwartz's favorite historical figures. -ed.

† It is, actually. -au.

‡ Sidestepping or dodging move. -ed.

§ Constant forward motion. -ed.

¶ A classic paragraph from Mr. Schwartz. He is weaving together threads: bureaucracy, bloated, whale, sumo wrestler. -ed.

as long as it wasn't a policy, and the people who worked for me would still have to follow it. This was becoming fun.

MD-102 had an official-sounding name, so I knew our instruction had to have one too. Not having any examples to draw on, I decided to name it MI-CIS-OIT-001, or Management Instruction, Citizenship and Immigration Services, Office of Information Technology, Number 1. It doesn't roll off the tongue . . . so it seemed perfect.

Our non-policy carefully defined what we meant by agile. It prescribed eight practices for every IT initiative, and it described five more that were optional. For example, it mandated frequent delivery of code, time-boxed iterations, retrospectives, and continuous testing. There (finger snap)—we had a lack of "policy" that said everyone had to be agile. Fastest Agile transformation ever! We were provably agile the day I signed the non-policy.

Later, when we learned about DevOps, my experts wrote me a new MI with the equally catchy name MI-CIS-OIT-003.[7] On the day I signed that one we'd transformed all of our IT activities to DevOps. This is why bureaucracy is wonderful.

(If you want to transform your organization in just two days, you'll find MI-CIS-OIT-003 in Appendix A to this book.)

Be Right a Lot

Now there *were* a few problems with this approach. The first was that my policy conflicted with MD-102, which had been signed by someone much higher in the organization. The second was that when my employees saw my policy, they whispered to each other, "What is the CIO talking about?" They had no idea *how* they were going to do what I said they had to do, and besides, they said, it was impossible because of MD-102. But I was still congratulating myself on my bureaucratic sumo move, so I figured we'd deal with those things later.

In my mind the conflict with MD-102 was just a small impediment—yes, my employees still had to comply with it while they also complied with my policy, but since it was an impediment and I was a servant leader, I could just tell them not to worry because I would deal with it.

"Go ahead and follow my policy, and I'll deal with MD-102," I said. See? That fixed it with one sentence. How did I deal with the impediment? Mostly I asked the DHS CIO for help. I had his banana memo to refer to.

This put all the risk on me, and that was okay. We have a leadership principle at Amazon that goes like this: *Be Right a Lot.** That helps when you're taking risk in a bureaucracy as well: it's less risky when you do the right things.

I knew that our agile approach at UCIS was going to lead to great results. All we needed was a bit of time to prove it. Good news—big bureaucracies move slowly enough that we had plenty of time to show results before anyone got around to questioning us. Again, bureaucracy made things easy for us.

The second problem, as I said, was that my IT employees had no idea how to be agile. Here again bureaucracy came to the rescue. I have to be a bit immodest again to explain this. The government bureaucracy is extremely hierarchical. And I was rather high in the bureaucracy. As a member of the Senior Executive Service, I was technically the equivalent rank of a two-star general or admiral in the military.[8] Now, I had no military experience and would never have made it to that sort of rank if I did. I'm about as fit as you'd expect someone to be whose chief forms of exercise are giggling and lifting a Starbucks venti to my lips. But in the federal bureaucracy, people—largely—treated me as if I were worthy of respect. So, when I puffed my chest, summoned all of my command-and-control authority, and nicely asked everyone to be agile, they said, "Yes, sir!" Of course, that's also what they said when I told them that they should read my favorite short story by Herman Melville. Side note: read "Bartleby the Scrivener."† What a great story.

But they were motivated to figure it out, after they got tired of telling each other that I was as crazy as a sumo-wrestling monkey. I arranged training for them and paired them with technologists who already knew what they were doing, and the transformation proceeded.

Another technique I used to great effect: I met with our contractors (we used a lot of contractors), and put on my serious face and said to them something like this: "I expect your people to know more about DevOps than I do, and that's a high bar. If you have talented people working on other government projects, take them off those projects and put them on mine." Then I would scowl and walk out of the office like I imagined a two-star general might.

---

* This principle is more nuanced than it would appear. It also means that the leader should seek out other opinions and data and be willing to change views if warranted. -au.

† In Melville's short story of bureaucratic rebellion, Bartleby is a clerk in a legal office. Any time his boss asks him to do something, he replies, "I'd prefer not to." -ed.

By the time we got to writing MI-003, we'd learned a lot. Instead of defining what good practices were, we defined ten *outcomes* that we wanted. They were things like "Frequent delivery of valuable product" and "Work that flows in small batches and is validated." Then we wrote an addendum in which we listed what we considered *today* to be good practices but noted that the addendum would change often. So, we essentially wrote a policy that said "this policy will change often, and that is a good thing."

Wrong Again

As you can tell, I was proud of my newfound bureaucratic savvy. But GAO and the IG raised the bureaucratic stakes. When they heard about my new policy, they dinged it again. The problem, they said, was that I hadn't set up any mechanism to *make sure* my people were doing what my policy said they should do.

That was a pretty clever maneuver, because, you see, MD-102 *had* such a mechanism. It was called independent verification and validation (IV&V). The idea was that an objective, independent outside party would come in at the end of each project and check against the initial requirements to make sure every feature in it had actually been delivered, whether it turned out to be necessary or not. It was a check to make sure that the project had not done anything that risked flexibility or agility, and that every unnecessary bell and whistle* in the requirements document had been rung and blown so that the government had wasted as much money as possible.

Well, they had me again. No matter: we now knew enough to release MI-CIS-OIT-004, our non-policy on Independent Verification and Validation. We mandated a role for IV&V that was exactly like MD-102's, with a few exceptions. While MD-102's IV&V made sure the full, or maximum, amount of IT work had been done, MI-004's made sure that the *minimum* had been done, that teams were finding as many things as they could *not* to do from the original requirements while still getting the same business outcomes. IV&V would also do as little auditing as possible given the project's risk, and it would make sure that the teams were doing DevOps well and were happy and motivated.

---

* According to https://www.phrases.org.uk/meanings/bells-and-whistles.html, the expression "bells and whistles" originally did refer to things that made a lot of noise, as you'd think. Today it refers to what government contractors often deliver instead of useful software for the billions of dollars they're paid. -au.

Enter the Razor

William of Occam* was a medieval Christian philosopher. Like many philosophers, he's most famous for saying something that he never said. In a principle called *Occam's Razor*, he proposed (he didn't) that simpler explanations are better than more complicated ones, other things being equal. Or he said that explanations that posit fewer entities are better than explanations that posit more. He might have not said either one. In any case, Occam is given credit for a principle of "ontological parsimony" that said you shouldn't add extra stuff you don't need. Newton's Law of Gravitation, Occam's rule would say, is to be preferred over a law that says apples fall because massive objects like the Earth cause a chorus of invisible bureaucrats to write a policy instructing apples to fall or else, and apples, being law-abiding, follow the rules.

My bureaucratic variant on Occam's Razor says "Don't add extra work that doesn't add value" or "Choose the process that is leanest, given an equal amount of value delivered" or, in the case where the value to the business is risk reduction, "Don't do extra risk-reduction work that doesn't reduce risk." It's a principle of *bureaucratic* parsimony.

Applying the razor, we devised a new tailoring plan to accompany MI-003 that shaved MD-102's eleven gate reviews to two, and the number of documents from eighty-seven to fifteen. We continued looking for ways to get an even closer shave. We also trimmed our procurement times from six or more months—sometimes as long as three years—to thirty days in some cases. We whittled down our up-front business case-building to as little as a month, and pared the time it took us to procure computing infrastructure from nine months to just a moment in the cloud.

By mastering the ways of the Monkey, the Sumo Wrestler, and the Razor we'd not only transformed IT, but we'd also set up checks and balances to make sure it stayed transformed. We'd gone from releasing new IT capabilities once every eighteen months to three times a day for some of our IT systems. We'd taken a project that had been "underway"—writing documents but not doing anything—for four years, and in just six weeks begun deploying new IT capabilities that had measurable, meaningful business impact.

Now, that's what bureaucracy can do!

---

* So that there shall be no confusion, know that our preferred spelling for this name at Exothermic Press is "Okham" but we have made an exception for Mr. Schwartz. -ed.

A Brief Moment of Reflection and Self-Awareness

All right, it wasn't all as smooth as that might sound. It was more a matter of stumbling around in bureaucracy-land until we found some tricks that worked. We inspected and adapted, and in the end had some good successes and also some notable failures. We never did get MD-102 to mandate agile practices, though it was changed to explicitly say that sane practices were acceptable.

Checking back in with USCIS a few years after I left, it appears that many of our changes have stuck, especially the cultural change that left employees willing to try new things and advocate strongly for them. Other areas that were important to me have seen some backsliding, as later management considered them less important. And I'm not sure anyone actually read "Bartleby." But USCIS stands as a strong example of how change is possible in a resistant bureaucracy.

Though I tell the story with some snark—meant in fun—the most important thing I learned was that virtually everyone involved cared deeply about the agency's mission and wanted desperately to do the right thing. We succeeded best when we unlocked that motivation. Bureaucracy is the mechanism for accomplishing mission outcomes in the government. It won't go away. But it can't remain an impediment to accomplishing that mission once the passion of employees is stirred and directed to the right ends.

Estimating Costs

There was another complication I should tell you about. MD-102 required that we calculate Life Cycle Cost Estimates (LCCEs) for our planned projects. The very reasonable idea of the LCCE was that project teams should disclose not just the cost of building or acquiring a new technology, but also the cost of maintaining it over time. According to the scholars charged with interpreting MD-102, our LCCE should assume that our new immigration software system, ELIS, would be in operation for twenty years once it was completed. So, calculating our cost estimate would involve estimating IT costs for the next twenty years.

That's difficult, since a twenty-year estimate would include, ahem, a bit of uncertainty. Like how much prices might change for our cloud infrastructure, how much labor costs might increase, what new technologies we'd need to incorporate into it, how many immigration applications we might need to process in the future. (We could perhaps hedge a bit by buying Red Bull futures.)

And a big uncertainty—how much immigration laws might change over the next twenty years. The guardians of MD-102 insisted that an estimate could be prepared with good statistical rigor by paying contractors a whaleboat of money to use simulation techniques. We were pretty sure that no simulation could give an accurate estimate with that kind of uncertainty and wanted to keep our whaleboat of money. But we complied and paid contractors to do the calculation, which came to $2.1 billion as the twenty-year cost.

A year or two later, the scholars of MD-102 told us that their interpretation had changed and that now our estimate should project costs for *thirty* years in the future. There's a good amount of uncertainty about what IT costs might look like thirty years into the future—after all, thirty years in the *past* almost no one had a PC, let alone a notebook, a tablet, or a smart phone. But we changed the cell in our spreadsheet model from twenty to thirty, and dutifully reported a new estimate of $3.1 billion for the thirty-year LCCE.

The Inspector General then wrote a report saying that our project was doing so badly, that our costs were planned to jump from $2.1 billion to $3.1 billion—we were going to overspend by $1 billion! We protested that nothing had changed. The difference between the two numbers was just that it was a thirty-year estimate instead of a twenty-year estimate. The IG put that into a footnote in their report.[9] The press apparently doesn't read footnotes, because the articles they wrote said that our project was going over budget by $1 billion.

Score one for the bureaucracy.

The Paperwork Reduction Act (PRA)

I mentioned that one piece of bureaucratic art that slowed us down was the Paperwork Reduction Act (PRA) of 1995, 44 U.S.C. 3501 et seq. The "Act" in its name tells you that this was a law, passed by Congress. A bureaucracy-busting law! It was intended to reduce the amount of time the public had to spend filling out forms for the government. That's a brilliant idea. I've recently filled out applications for visas to other countries that ask for information like my father's cousin's children's names and occupations and my favorite brand of chewing gum. Even better, Congress set up a concrete metric to measure the PRA's success—multiply the time it takes to fill out a form by the number of people who fill it out, and that gives you the total burden on the public. The PRA's goal was straightforward—to minimize burden.

I know this sounds like a good thing for those of us trying to modernize government IT by making application forms electronic. The first sign of trouble is that there is also another act called the Government Paperwork Elimination Act (GPEA). The Knight of Occam asks: "Why would we need both a Paperwork Reduction Act and a Paperwork Elimination Act, and why is there still so much paperwork?" All will become clear.

Congress made the mistake of specifying the precise process that would be used to implement the PRA, and Congress, for the most part, is not filled with experienced process managers. The PRA was to be overseen by a small team of bureaucrats in the White House called OIRA (Office of Information and Regulatory Affairs), and any new form a government agency wanted to release to the public would first have to be approved by them and given a control number. You've seen these on the bottom of government forms. To get approval from OIRA, you had to send them a mock-up of the form, along with an explanation of each data field and why it was needed, and an estimate of the burden. Then, after OIRA's critique, you would improve the form, publish it for sixty days to gather the public's comments, work with OIRA to improve it again based on the feedback, and then republish it for another thirty days for more public comments. And then OIRA would decide whether to approve it.

Now, this process probably makes sense if you're Congress. But given that OIRA is chronically understaffed, it sometimes took as long as eighteen months for a form to be approved. And OIRA later determined that the process would apply not just to newly created forms, but to any change to an existing form. That's *any* change—including changes whose purpose was to reduce the paperwork burden. So it might now take eighteen months to reduce public burden, and more effort and cost than most agencies wanted to spend. You had to think carefully before doing anything of the sort.

Furthermore, OIRA decided that electronic forms were also subject to the process. If we at USCIS wanted to offer an online version of one of our ninety or so paper forms, we'd have to go through the entire approval process again, even though the paper version had already been approved. If we later decided to change it based on applicant feedback, we'd have to do it yet again. And our plan was to make all ninety forms electronic.

They added a bonus rule that there had to be "parity" between the electronic form and the paper one—we couldn't do anything that gave an advantage to people who chose to use the electronic form. Now, it's common in electronic forms for the software to fill "default" values into some of the fields based on what it already knows about an applicant, and to validate what an applicant types to make sure they haven't accidentally listed their age as negative ten or their favorite TV show as *Real Housewives of New Jersey*. But, of course, paper doesn't do that, so it was (in theory, at least) prohibited.

One more thing. It's an IT best practice to do A/B testing when designing a form. That means that for each design decision that has to be made, several versions of the form are created to see which option works best when people use it. With the PRA we obviously couldn't do that, because the form had to be fully approved *before* we let people use it.

Ah, you're wondering what the Government Paperwork *Elimination* Act is for. The GPEA of 1998 (1998!) required federal agencies, by 2003, to provide electronic rather than—or in addition to—paper options for the submitting of information *where practicable*, and to accept electronic signatures rather than paper ones, *where practicable* (my italics).[10] Although we wanted to accept electronic signatures on our forms, the Justice Department apparently thought that in our case *it wasn't practicable*, so we set up a process where our digital applicants signed a paper form when they came to our offices to give us their fingerprints.

Why We Do This to Ourselves

MD-102, the LCCE, and the PRA (and GPEA) exist for very good reasons. You could say the same for most bureaucratic processes in the federal government. The federal hiring process, for example, is highly formalized because it must make sure that hiring is done fairly and without bias, and because it implements a policy that favors military veterans for government jobs, which is a policy goal. The procurement process takes six thousand pages to describe in the massive FAR because it's carefully designed to make government procurement fair—to avoid bribery or even unconscious biases on the part of the procurers. In a way, the government is striving for perfection in how it serves its citizens, and the bureaucracy I've made fun of in this chapter is their well-meaning, passionate attempt to do so.

In the business world, formal rules and accountabilities also exist for good reasons. One can always ask, "What is the control objective of this rule?" There invariably is, or once was, such an objective. Sometimes a rule serves to reassure investors that the company has control over its reporting (an explicit goal of Sarbanes-Oxley, for example) or control over its spending. Sometimes the rules and authorities are put in place to mitigate risks or perceived risks. Sometimes they're there to prevent problems from recurring, as in the case of the missing corkboard diagram. Sometimes they're intended to promote consistency within a brand. All these rules must be applied universally, or they lose their meaning. You can't convince investors you have control over spending if employees are sometimes allowed to bypass the spending rules.

In any social organization, there's tension between freedom and constraint, and a bleeding edge where the two rub up against each other. That's the territory where the bureaucratic Chaos Monkey, Razor, and Sumo Wrestler operate, probing the frontier, investigating where freedoms may lie and readjusting the guardrails to achieve both control and creativity.

IT: THE BIGGEST, BADDEST BUREAUCRATS

Reason furthers unity, but nature furthers diversity; both lay claim to man.

—Friedrich Schiller, *On the Aesthetic Education of Man*

Nothing so tires a person as having to struggle, not with himself, but with an abstraction.

—José Saramago, *All the Names*

IT Bureaucracy: Not Fooling Anyone

Among the biggest, baddest, bullyingest bureaucrats in a large enterprise are the IT folks. Yes, us, the very IT folks who so hate bureaucracy when we find it imposed on us. Your password, we say, must be in a format that guarantees you'll never remember it, and you must change it every few nanoseconds, and you need to remember your old password in order to change it to something else you won't remember. If you notice a problem in our IT systems, you must fill out a trouble ticket; if you want a new feature or some help, fill out another ticket. Or write something called a user story card in the format "As a bureaucrat I want to force people to use the ticketing system so that they will grind their teeth with frustration." Everything we touch turns to standards. Then, once we've set them, we put trolls in everyone's way to enforce them. We make employees sign Acceptable Use Policies before we let them use the company network acceptably. Never, we say, connect your personal device to the company network, and be sure to lie to us when we ask if you're using your personal device for company business.

If you're an IT person, you're probably sputtering, "But! But! We have no choice! These are best practices! Hackers are trying to steal our cat videos!" Quite so, quite so. See my point? For the rest of the enterprise, these policies are handed down by purported experts, IT people, the cave dwellers who don't care about getting the real work of the company done, and they are endlessly frustratingly bureaucracy.

When we discover better ways to use technology, it's natural for us to want to force people to use them. If we notice there's inefficient duplication of IT systems across different lines of business or office locations, we want to centralize purchasing and architectural decision-making. We need governance mechanisms to control our technologies because . . . well, there are lots of good reasons.

Digital transformation forces us IT folks to confront our standardize-and-govern mentality. Will technology free us from bureaucracy, or will it entwine us further in it? It's worth some thought as we manufacture our bureaucratic goo.

Mechanization

The connection between technology and bureaucracy goes deep. Weber understood that there was a mechanical, nonhuman aspect of bureaucracy:

> The professional bureaucrat is chained to his activity in his entire economic and ideological existence. In the great majority of cases he is only a small cog in a ceaselessly moving mechanism which prescribes to him an essentially fixed route of march. The official is entrusted with specialized tasks, and normally, the mechanism cannot be put into motion or arrested by him, but only from the very top.[1]

With that quote, we see the core tension of bureaucracy before us. Bureaucracy is what we get when we think through the best way to perform each operation, then set up rules to make sure employees always do it exactly that way. But once we do, it seems like we'll have mechanized employees' activities, and we might just as well replace them by machines. What role can individuals play in a system that moves under its own logic and power?

As I've suggested, bureaucracy echoes many of the intellectual developments of the modern era. Just as Napoleon was organizing his army into logical ranks and files and creating the Napoleonic Code, the German philosopher G. W. F. Hegel was publishing his major work, *The Phenomenology of Spirit*,* arguing that history represents the development and unveiling of an "absolute idea," or *Geist*, and that we as individuals are caught up in that larger development which proceeds inexorably around us. Karl Marx, one of the "Young Hegelians," picked up on this idea and wrote about history as an inevitable progress toward communism, with individuals essentially relevant only to the extent that they play a part in that drama. After Hegel and Marx the role of an individual in this "machine" of society and history became a focus of philosophy in the works of, among others, Kierkegaard, Nietzsche, and the existentialists, and in Melville's vision of an uncaring, hostile natural world in which we are tossed about. Bureaucracy, in other words, was hardly original, just a recapitulation of what was already going on in academia.

Weber says: "The fully developed bureaucratic mechanism compares with other organizations exactly as does the machine with the non-mechanical modes of production."[2] There's a deep ambiguity in Weber's conception of bureaucracy. On one hand, he talks about it as "domination by knowledge" and a meritocracy—that is, a *human* effort. On the other hand, he talks about an impersonal application of rules, a *mechanical* effort.

A good deal of our discomfort with bureaucracy comes from our anxiety at being treated like expendable parts in a machine. It's a legitimate fear, since bureaucracy is motivated by the assumption that, left to themselves, people will screw everything up. Bureaucracy is used to make sure recalcitrant workers actually work; to restrict employees who would otherwise pad their expense reports; to stop government officials from taking bribes. Because it's based on a fundamental distrust, bureaucracy feels like it exists only because there's no way to fully eliminate people. Alfred Krupp, the munitions manufacturer, said it bluntly:

> What I shall attempt to bring about is that nothing shall be dependent upon the life or existence of any particular person; that nothing of any importance shall happen or be caused to happen without the foreknowledge and approval of management; that the past and the determinate future of the establishment can be learned in the files of the management without asking a question of any mortal.[3]

---

* 1807 to be exact. -au.

We should be particularly sensitive to this in our era of digital transformations, for bureaucracy, in this view, is about using an algorithm to guide human behavior. In Weber's day, computers didn't exist; the closest he could conceive was an organizational system where people execute algorithms themselves.

A Very Geeky Analogy: Part One

Allow me to elaborate this analogy, because I'm going to suggest that (1) the thought pattern behind bureaucracy is very close to the way technologists think, and (2) perhaps counterintuitively, this suggests a way that we can minimize the torments of bureaucracy by literally automating them away.

In my geeky analogy, the roles in a hierarchical, bureaucratic organization are like the microservices of an IT architecture.* Just as each microservice has a well-defined and bounded role in the architecture, so each role in a bureaucracy is bounded through a division of labor and technical specialization. As roles in a bureaucracy interact through formalized patterns, so do microservices through their formal interfaces (APIs), which represent a contract that the microservice "agrees to," thereby lending calculability to its activities. Officials in a bureaucracy enact only their roles; their human biases do not affect their performance. Similarly, as long as a microservice fulfills its contract, its internals don't matter; this is the principle of loose coupling, or the separation between interface and implementation. As microservices are orchestrated to perform a business function, each having a place in an algorithm that delivers an IT capability, so bureaucracy orchestrates the roles in its organizational chart to deliver on the goals of the enterprise.

Bureaucracy, then, is the algorithms (rules) and their authorized users (roles) that control the behavior of an enterprise. Bureaucracy is an organization's software.

Bureaucrats by Nature

It turns out that the "alphas" of *Homo bureaucraticus* are the software engineers, those who've learned to control others by standardizing processes and

---

* A *microservice* is an independent piece of software code that performs a simple piece of functionality and can be integrated with other microservices to perform complete tasks that are relevant to a user. Each microservice can be used in multiple complex tasks. Mr. Schwartz is talking about best practices for designing such microservices, which is an important topic in the digital world. -ed.

roles and providing automation that essentially forces everyone to do things their way. In Adler's words:

> Technology is know-how that has been objectified and thus rendered relatively independent of the skills of specific actors. Know-how can be objectified in equipment and associated software programs; it can also be objectified in organizational procedures and structure.[4]

Consider again my keynote story in the introduction (the case of the corkboard's disappearing diagram). Software developers, in trying to improve a process, effortlessly found a bureaucratic solution. The mechanism they chose was a formal, defined set of steps that would apply to all team members, whether they're forgetful or not. It's an algorithm; a technologist's solution to social interaction.

From another angle, software code *itself* is a kind of bureaucracy. A rule-maker—called a programmer—writes code to represent rules that will be followed by the computer and the user, constraining the behavior of both. "Code" is a "codification" of expected behaviors. It uses "validations" to restrict user behavior and allows employees access only to functions that fall within the boundaries of their job descriptions. It is embedded in a business process that may be specified in a user manual, an SOP document, a tradition of how the software is used, or instructions from a pointy-haired manager.

Code happens to be a special kind of rule that is "executable"; that is, a policy which is detailed and formal enough that we can build a machine to execute it. If we didn't have the machine, it could be executed, mechanically, by a person . . . which would make the connection to bureaucracy more evident.

If this seems like a stretch, spend some time with software users. You'll find that for them, code enforces arbitrary or strange "features" and restrictions on them, which seem to come from some hidden corner of a bureaucracy. They do things *this* way and not *that*, because that's how the software is set up. They're forced into strange workarounds, perhaps entering values into fields that were clearly not designed for their purpose, because it's the only space available. If they need a change to the code, they enact formal rituals and sacrifice budget dollars to gain a position in a product backlog.

The backlog, by the way, is a truly ingenious piece of bureaucracy—a last in, nothing out queue that imprisons requests until some inscrutable process grants them a hearing. Like Joseph K. in *The Trial*, the user never finds out what their feature request is accused of or when and how justice will be rendered.

Standards, Centralization, Greek Names

It's been a commonplace that IT must standardize. We just must, because—you know—otherwise bad stuff would happen. Without standards, independent parts of the organization might make duplicative or inconsistent choices. We might spend money on several pieces of technology where a single one would do; we might have to train our people to support multiple platforms; we might introduce security risks as employees use tools we haven't vetted. Software engineers might go off and write code in a programming language like Ruby or Malbolge or Khepri or something other than a standard CIO-soothing-language like Java.*

If it's not clear that standards are a kind of bureaucracy, consider an employee who's not allowed to use a piece of software or hardware they've used in a previous job that's better than the one IT has standardized in their current job. Maybe they're told they must use an iPhone instead of an Android phone, or vice versa. If technologists want to make up names for their server computers, they must choose names from Ancient Greece rather than Ancient Rome.†️ Or they're stuck with an old version of an operating system because it's still the company standard.

In many cases, the benefits of standardization outweigh the costs; it's a great idea. The standards that enabled the internet—well, they enabled the internet. But knee-jerk standardization often neglects the costs it imposes, for bureaucracy has a cost. We might not be able to take advantage of new technology (say, functional programming languages, which are becoming increasingly valuable), we might not be able to hire programmers who want to program in MobYdIck,‡ or we might frustrate our excellent technologists who know that a better way lies outside the standards.

---

*Ruby is a real language, Malbolge is a real language (sort of), and Khepri is an Egyptian god. -ed.

†️ This actually was a standard in one of the companies I worked for. -au.

‡This is not a real programming language. -ed.

Closely related is the question of centralization versus decentralization. To Weber, the need for centralization was what drove the introduction of bureaucracy in the first place.[5] But as James C. Scott, a political scientist teaching at Yale, shows in *Seeing Like a State*, centralization results in a loss of important local details as higher-level abstractions are imposed.[6] He talks about a centralized government's need to "make a society legible, to arrange the population in ways that simplified the classic state functions of taxation, conscription, and prevention of rebellion."[7] But such simplifications lose fidelity; the representation they create "always ignores essential features of any real, functioning social order."[8]

IT suffers from this same oversimplification and loss of detail when it centralizes. Apparently minor differences between two business units cause problems when their ERP systems are consolidated. Shared services and centralized management add overhead by demanding formal interactions between the center and the periphery: ticketing systems, periodic status meetings, contentious prioritization, budgets, chargebacks.

At DHS, we watched a dynamic of centralization and decentralization play out. DHS, remember, was formed through a merger of agencies with very different goals, practices, and cultures. It includes among its twenty-two component agencies FEMA (which has to respond quickly and flexibly to disasters), USCIS (primarily an application-processing agency), ICE (a law-enforcement agency), the Coast Guard (a military organization), and the Secret Service (the agency which guards the president and fights counterfeiting).

Despite this diversity of missions, "corporate" DHS must oversee the whole. It had to devise a framework that would apply equally to all of the component agencies and all of their activities, ensuring that their investments were productive and directed at the right mission needs, that projects were well executed, and that infrastructure remained secure. They had to answer to Congress and the public for runaway investments, and cope with budget limitations when Congress reduced appropriations. This is how MD-102 arose.

Because the overseers were so far removed from our day-to-day activities, their oversight had to be conducted through formal mechanisms and documentation. Each project disaster—and there were plenty—was answered with the creation of new formal controls to reassure Congress and OMB (the Office of Management and Budget) that it would never happen again. But how could there be an alternative? DHS was, itself, overseen.

Joseph K.[*] Files a Ticket

There are many good reasons why IT departments have inflicted ticketing systems[†] on their colleagues, but there's no denying that they're a piece of IT bureaucracy that inspires our coworkers with dread and loathing. Tickets are impersonal and unpleasantly formal. They require information to be entered that is only occasionally relevant. They create a formidable "paper" trail, as email follows email with the ticket's status changes. They trigger predetermined workflows of approvals and handoffs from which deviations are difficult.

Tickets make employees feel like they're making requests of a machine. The ticket management process is opaque—who knows when someone will next take an action on the ticket or what they're busy with now that prevents them from doing so? For all the requestor knows, trolls in a cave somewhere are waiting until they finish barbecuing the last requestor who tried to get their ticket processed faster. A ticket winds its way through organizational silos on its way to fulfillment, with each silo given a seemingly arbitrary SLA (service level agreement) that specifies how slowly it can process the request. I've had tickets auto-cancel because no one had taken timely action, and then been directed to a survey asking if I was happy with how my problem was solved.

Imagine what Kafka would make of this process. Joseph K. might fill out a ticket asking what crime he was accused of and would periodically receive status messages: "Your request has now been given the status of 'pending'!" or "Your case has been routed to the appropriate authorities. Please click here to answer a few questions relating to your case that will help us improve our customer service." It's an IT equivalent of "All lawyers are currently helping other defendants. Please continue to wait as your case is very important to us."

Ticketing systems grew, I think, from the idea that IT is a service provider to the rest of the business.[‡] Their intention was to formalize the interactions between the business and IT so that IT could show that it was providing predictable levels of service. But what a great tool for implementing a siloed, specialization-of-labor bureaucracy!

---

[*] From *The Trial*. -ed.

[†] Those are the software systems that force you to create a database "ticket" whenever you have a request, and then track the progress of your ticket as it is ignored. -au.

[‡] See my previous books, particularly *A Seat at the Table*. -au

Security, Mom

Imagine you're a non-IT employee in an enterprise. You're given IT's Acceptable Use Policy to sign and told you must take an online security training every year. If you don't, automated reminders threaten to escalate to your manager. You're told never to click on an email that looks "phishy": that is, any email that has misspellings, strange return email addresses, comes from Nigeria, or is absolutely ordinary and appears to come from your mother. Never click on an attachment, the mandatory training tells you, unless it is from someone you trust and not from someone *pretending* to be someone you trust.

What you see, simply, is a security bureaucracy. The rules come from people you don't understand, are a barrier to what you want to get done, and can't be appealed. You're set up to fail, since you can't distinguish between an email from a friend and an email pretending to be from a friend. Hide from the trolls—you're probably already guilty of noncompliance. Good luck.

Compliance Audit

IT enforces company bureaucracy. It helps the enterprise ensure compliance and achieve clean audits. That's convenient, because today enterprises are subject to an acronym soup of compliance regimes—one part HIPAA to several parts GDPR, FISMA, KYC, and PCI-DSS, salted with SARBOX to taste. These frameworks assign formal accountabilities to particular roles in the organization. To satisfy these frameworks the company must show that formal controls are in place and effective. If there is any way to do so without bureaucracy, I can't imagine it.

Since all work flows through IT systems, it is IT that plays the role of bureaucratic troll, essentially posting the signs saying "if you push this door an alarm will sound" and then making sure that the sound is loud and annoying. not only enforces compliance but can also demonstrate through its electronic audit trails that compliance has occurred. An automated DevOps pipeline tracks every change made to code. The company can tell who made a change and when, and what follow-on tasks were triggered. When tests are run, their results can be recorded automatically; when deployments are made, it's a matter of record who did the deployment, when, and what code was deployed. This is bureaucracy made effortless and invisible. Nevertheless, it's still bureaucracy. The trolls have just found a new home, inside software code.

Agile Bureaucracy

Recall that in Chapter 2, the Chaos Monkey was defeated at one point not by government bureaucracy, but by Scrum bureaucracy. Scrum is a popular Agile IT framework. It provides a structure that incorporates Agile principles within which delivery teams develop and deploy IT capabilities. It's sometimes considered a transitional phase between traditional and more agile ways of working; while it incorporates Agile principles, it's nevertheless palatable to established enterprises. Of course it is: it has all the feel of an authoritarian bureaucracy.

Ken Schwaber and Jeff Sutherland, the creators of Scrum, command, for example: "the Development Team *isn't allowed* to act on what anyone else [other than the product owner] says."[9] Requests for features, according to the Scrum scriptures, must be written as user story cues ("as an alien I want to enter the Earth's atmosphere and abduct a human so that I can learn about their bureaucracy"), then placed into a product backlog where they're sorted by a spreadsheet master occupying the role of product owner. The team must stand together for fifteen minutes each day to ask each other precisely three questions: What have you done since yesterday? What will you do by tomorrow? Do you have any impediments? They must estimate story points (what?) and calculate their work velocity by counting those story points (what?), and then flagellate themselves for not accomplishing enough story points (what?). And, as the government auditors pointed out to me, if you change any element of Scrum, you've sinned. Here's the relevant text from Scrum's inventors: "Scrum's roles, events, artifacts, and rules are immutable and although implementing only parts of Scrum is possible, the result is not Scrum. Scrum exists only in its entirety."[10]

Verdict: IT—Human, Annoying

If you're an IT geek, don't fool yourself into thinking that because you love to get things done quickly and effectively, and because you rebel against rules imposed on you, you're free from the bureaucratic urge. No, it's more likely that you have an impressive ability to optimize processes and implement controls by turning people's freedom into constraints. You, *mon semblable, mon frere,** are probably a bureaucracy savant.

---

* "My likeness, my brother." This is a reference to the dedication in Baudelaire's *Les Fleurs du Mal*. -ed.

WHY BUREAUCRACY IS BAD

Pleasure was separated from work, means from end, effort from reward. Eternally shackled to one small fragment of the whole, man imagined himself to be a fragment, in his ear the constant and monotonous noise of the wheel that he turned . . . he simply became the impress of his occupation, his particular knowledge.

—Friedrich Schiller, *On the Aesthetic Education of Man*

The greatest hazard of all, losing one's self, can occur very quietly in the world, as if it were nothing at all.

—Søren Kierkegaard, *The Sickness Unto Death*

Metaphysical Pathos

Whence flows our deep hatred of bureaucracy? It seems strange, does it not? Bureaucracy is just a way to structure social interactions, particularly in a large enterprise. True, it's a way that others impose their wills on us, but we all understand that when we sign up to work for a company we give them the power to tell us what to do. Our time belongs to our employer. Why should we be bothered if our employer wants to waste it by making us feed the trolls with plates full of unnecessary paperwork? Yet bureaucracy is somehow nightmarish, something that disturbs us at a deep level.

The sociologist Alvin Gouldner, in *Patterns of Industrial Bureaucracy*, talks about a "metaphysical pathos" surrounding bureaucracy.[1] Where Weber saw a rational management technique, the rest of us see a way of life, deeply troubling and anxiety inducing. This, perhaps, is what distinguishes modern bureaucracy—it's hard to imagine the ancient Egyptians or Romans suffering metaphysical anguish over a simple hierarchy and a set of rules. After all, they'd already ceded authority to a ruler; bureaucracy was merely the ruler's tool.

Once again, it helps to look at the context in which modern bureaucracy arose. At 9:40 a.m. on November 1, 1755, just as the bureaucratic age was dawning, Lisbon was struck by one of the most deadliest earthquakes in history: a magnitude 8.5–9.0 convulsion that killed as many as 100,000 people and bounced Europe into the modern age. The earthquake was deeply troubling to intellectuals, who struggled to explain how its indiscriminate destruction of both good and evil could possibly have been the work of a just and benevolent God.* Where before people had believed that they could control their fates by pleasing a personal God, the world now appeared impersonal, hostile, or at best indifferent, implacable . . . mechanical.

Bureaucracy, rising immediately in its wake, was not just an administrative system, but indicative of the indifferent, mechanical world around us. It replaced God as the prime mover of a hostile world. It's in that sense that *Moby Dick*, a fight against dumb, brute nature by a human who knows he can't win, is a novel about bureaucracy, with harpoons and rope in place of offices and desks.

Bureaucracy as Nightmare: Literature

Gouldner's "metaphysical pathos" is revealed in the way writers have chosen to write about bureaucracy. Their literature is largely about a world that operates according to its own bizarre nightmare logic—what we call surrealism. To choose a few examples:

Kafka's protagonists live in a world both familiar and unfamiliar to us, one that seems logical, but logical in a way we don't recognize. Joseph K. is accused of a crime and the authorities won't tell him what it is. When one of his prosecutors says to another, "You see, Willem, he admits that he doesn't know the Law and yet he claims he's innocent," we understand just what he means . . . sort of.

Ismail Kadare's vision of *The Palace of Dreams* is a map of the unconscious, with dark, dusty corridors that branch off in all directions, unlabeled, with no way other than chance to stumble on what you're searching for. Mark-Alem

---

* Susan Neiman's book *Evil in Modern Thought* provides a great description of how the earthquake affected the intellectual history of Europe. -au.

finds himself working at the palace and promoted for reasons he doesn't understand—he's only told that he "suits" the organization. Eventually, activities at the Palace of Dreams prove disastrous for his family and destabilizing for the Palace itself, after which the bureaucracy somehow reconfigures itself, now with Mark-Alem at its head.

José Saramago, in *All the Names*, paints us a dark, dusty archive into which Senhor José enters late at night to search for records. He works in a government bureau that rigidly controls all of its employees' activities, both through tradition and coercion. Though the clerks are processing intimate records about human beings, their work lacks any connection to the people themselves. Senhor José rebels by trying to find someone whose record he has stolen from the archive.

In Thomas Pynchon's *The Crying of Lot 49* even the postal bureaucracy is the source of paranoia and violence, and yet a mystery you want to understand. *Catch-22*, humorous and lighthearted through most of its chapters, somehow works its way up to a surreal scene where Yossarian walks the streets of Rome only to find a series of bizarre, dreamlike scenes. And David Foster Wallace's unfinished novel *The Pale King*, about clerks at the IRS (Internal Revenue Service), includes unexplained moments where a character levitates from his chair.

"Metaphysical pathos" is an apt term for a literature of rebellion against—and inevitably defeat by—a bureaucratic order. Bartleby, in Melville's short story "Bartleby the Scrivener," enacts a gloomy rebellion against—what exactly?—refusing the work he's assigned with "I'd prefer not to." Ultimately, he starves to death in debtor's prison. In Akira Kurosawa's film *Ikiru*, Watanabe's rebellion against bureaucratic unhelpfulness, told through a series of flashbacks, leads his colleagues to a brief and fleeting realization that they must rebel against the bureaucratic order . . . an insight that fades with hangovers and daylight the day after his funeral.

Immovable obstacles. Odd laws. Weird logic. Futile rebellion. Inevitability. Paranoia. Bureaucracy.

I Got That, But Why Exactly Is It Bad?

A critical point to remember: a digital transformation blocked by bureaucracy does not have to address any of this metaphysical pathos. We don't have to reach Kafka's castle, navigate the Palace of Dreams, or figure out who's undermining the postal system. Frustrating as it may be, the kind of bureaucracy we want to fight is simply an administrative system. It means us no harm.

To overcome bureaucracy, we need to separate those of its aspects that are problematic from those that are not, and focus our efforts on the former. We must disengage from the metaphysical pathos and reengage in a practical way. Let's now identify the actual bad stuff.

1: Surprise!—It's Inefficient

Despite Weber's unbounded enthusiasm for bureaucracy's efficiency, those of us who encounter it today are less keen. James Q. Wilson, speaking of government agencies but intending his words to apply to businesses as well,[2] says that to citizens and taxpayers,

> bureaucrats are lethargic, incompetent hacks, who spend their days spinning out reels of red tape and reams of paperwork, all the while going to great lengths to avoid doing the job they were hired to do. Their agencies chiefly produce waste, fraud, abuse, and mismanagement.[3]

To Stewart Clegg, a sociologist teaching at the University of Technology in Sydney, Australia, "bureaucracy is synonymous with inefficient business administration, pettifogging legalism, and red tape."[4] I enjoy that term, *pettifogging*,* a word I've never used in my own sentences. *Red tape* I'll take to mean excess process, waste, a lack of leanness, so these authors' comments amount to one thing—bureaucracy, Weber's views notwithstanding, is not actually effective at doing what it sets out to do. It's *not* a rational way to organize.

Indeed, that's why those of us who write about IT leadership today object to it. We see today's business environment as dominated by rapid change, uncertainty, and complexity. To cope with it, organizations need speed: short lead times, unconstrained experimentation, and fast feedback, all of which bureaucracy resists. Bureaucracy's division of labor by function—what we often call *siloing* today—is one culprit, since work must be passed from one group to another (from software development to testing to operations, for example) with delays compounding at each handoff.

---

* It's actually derived from the word "petty" and an archaic word "fogger," or huckster. The German root is also written as "fucker."[5]

According to von Mises, bureaucracy is *necessarily* inefficient, since it's the system that's used for management when there's no market value for the services produced. Since nonprofits and government agencies can always spend more trying to deliver better service, their spending must be checked by rules and people who can say no—that is, a bureaucracy.[6] Even in market-serving, profit-seeking corporations, areas like compliance, risk management, human resources, and administration don't directly touch customers. Only bureaucratic controls can determine how much compliance and risk management and workplace snacks should be produced.

2: Its Goals Are Displaced

Even if the rules and hierarchy are set up to further the goals of the organization, over time, the aims become less important; all that remains is adherence to rules and process. There is, as Merton says, a *displacement of goals* to the rules themselves rather than to their desired outcomes.[7] Rules are fetishized; they "become symbolic in cast, rather than strictly utilitarian."[8]

Over time, goal displacement becomes more severe as new hires are trained in the rules rather than in their purpose. And since officials are admired for their knowledge of the rules' subtleties and their ability to recall the rules' minutia, enforcement of the rules becomes entwined with an official's self-worth. In our government environment, employees take immense pride in knowing the details of the elephantine six-thousand-page FAR—more pride, it often seems, than in how fairly they managed procurements themselves.

3: It Stifles Innovation

In "Bureaucracy and New Product Innovation," James D. Hlavacek argues that because innovation always seems inefficient, it can have no place in a bureaucracy—which, as we know, is designed for efficiency (that idea again! Damn you, Max!).[9] Companies have optimized their processes for doing what they did well in the past; new ideas are inefficient because they disrupt those processes and demand, at least for a time, practices that are not yet finely tuned. In fact, bureaucracies are designed for precisely the opposite of innovation— they routinize what the company has done to make it repeatable. Innovation requires a sudden leap, a movement outside today's roles and rules, and as such is resisted.

Ideally, the market would determine whether an innovation should be pursued. But in a bureaucracy, it's a *proxy* for the market that makes decisions—the bureaucratic hierarchy, through its budgeting or capital investment mechanisms. Entrepreneurs in a capitalist system are free to try out new ideas even if everyone thinks they are crazy; ultimately, only their success or failure matters. But in a bureaucracy, an entrepreneur has to convince those higher in the organization, often those who were responsible for promulgating the status quo.

Employees in a bureaucracy have well-defined tasks. Since they're assessed on their performance of those tasks, innovation is just wasted effort with no reward. Wilson sums this up as a bureaucratic principle: "Never do anything for the first time."[10]

4: It Fosters Blind Spots

Safe within a framework of rules that legitimize their actions, employees become passive and stop trying to do what they know to be best. After a discussion of new techniques in software development, an employee at USCIS might say, "Yes, but none of that's possible—DHS will never let us do it." Or I'd be asked to "be practical and stop talking about things we just can't do."

What an official has been trained to do in the past becomes a blind spot in the face of change.[11] Functionaries develop "special preferences, antipathies, discriminations, and emphases" that over time take away their ability to adapt the rules to new circumstances they encounter.[12] Various terms have been used to capture this phenomenon: *trained incapacity*, *occupational psychosis*, or *professional deformation*.[13] Again, it's important to take note of our context today: with the rapid change we experience in the digital world, trained incapacity is a serious problem.

5: It Dehumanizes

Bureaucracy substitutes mechanisms for ordinary human interaction. In its striving for impersonality—application of rules without regard to human considerations—it loses sight of the individual. Bureaucracy requires the high levels of discipline and the loss of individuality characteristic of an army. Because it considers human choice to be a danger, it demands that officials refrain from using their judgment.[14] Clearly, bureaucracy values conformity and reliable behavior;[15] otherwise, how could it deliver "calculability?"

Antibureaucrats dream of a future where positive human interactions once again matter, a future where work involves the whole person, and where organizational relationships are based on influence, persuasion, and collaboration rather than just exercises of hierarchical authority.

6: It Oversimplifies

To make its rules general enough to apply in all cases, bureaucracy simplifies by abstracting only those characteristics that are relevant to a rule. If you must be over twenty-one to drink in Missouri, your only relevant attribute is your age; in particular, whether it is over or under twenty-one. It doesn't matter if you're from a European family that's used to drinking wine with every meal. It doesn't matter if you're mature for your age. The rule simplifies by placing you into one of two categories. In doing so, it disregards the true complexity of life as it is lived.

Merton explains that general categories are essential to bureaucracy:

> The activities of "trained and salaried experts" are governed by general, abstract, and clearly defined rules which preclude the necessity for the issuance of specific instructions for each specific case. The generality of the rules requires the constant use of categorization, whereby individual problems and cases are classified on the basis of designated criteria and are treated accordingly.[16]

The extent of categorization often depends on the extent of centralization. This is at the root of James Scott's case in *Seeing Like a State*, where he argues that a state's tendency toward categorization and generalization loses important practical knowledge that is held closer to the activities they are governing.[17] The same, as I said, was true at DHS. Utopian planners like Le Corbusier* often take a bureaucratic, rationalist, simplifying, distant approach. The cities designed on this basis, Chandigarh (Le Corbusier) and Brasília (Lúcio Costa, Oscar Niemeyer, and Joaquim Cardozo), are notably cold and inhospitable environments because, though they were rationally designed to meet social

---

* Le Corbusier (1887–1965): a Swiss-French architect and urban planner. Among his sayings: "To create architecture is to put in order. Put what in order? Function and objects." And "Modern life demands, and is waiting for, a new kind of plan, both for the house and the city." -ed.

and economic objectives, they were laid out in the absence of the practical wisdom and natural impulses of the people who would eventually live in them.

While this sounds like a good argument for decentralization, there are nuances to consider. Although the US began as a commonwealth of self-governing colonies, it eventually became a union with a large amount of centralized control. Though the amount and the nature of that control is very much under debate today, Americans have found it useful to have a central authority that manages at least defense and foreign relations and applies the principles of a national constitution. Or, taking enterprise IT organizations as an example, centralized control may help by promoting information security and by negotiating contracts, even while other functions are decentralized.

Categorization leads to the frustration we often feel in the presence of bureaucracy. In Merton's words:

> Since functionaries minimize personal relations and resort to categorization, the peculiarities of individual cases are often ignored. But the client who, quite understandably, is convinced of the special features of his own problem often objects to such categorical treatment.[18]

7: It's Not Enough

Bureaucracy, somehow, misses the point. By laying down in law exactly how the company should operate, it leaves out the part of business that has to do with inspiration and strategy. Somehow a company has to create itself; it has to find a niche by satisfying customers. Even if it never innovates again thereafter, it still needs to respond to competition, devise strategies for minimizing its taxes, design the office cafeteria, figure out how best to hang motivational posters on its walls. And how did that very first innovation happen? It seems like bureaucracy leaves out the critical part of business success.

I know, traditional bureaucracy presupposed that those things happen among top management of the company, and bureaucracy is the tool they then use to control their workers once the creative work is done. But in the white-collar service economy, inspiration and creativity are more likely to be needed throughout time and across levels of the hierarchy.

Even in those more controlled parts of an enterprise, rules can never cover enough details to fully run the business. That's why unions have sometimes used a work-to-rule protest rather than a strike. Unionized employees are told to follow the rules exactly, which turns out to be an exceptionally efficient way to get nothing done.

8: It's Coercive

Bureaucracy is a way to control employees based on the assumption that left to themselves, they'll do the wrong thing. In a factory, bureaucratic rules may specify when employees can take breaks, what penalties will be imposed for absenteeism, and where they may eat their lunches. There might be quotas for production, and it's likely there are forms to be filled out to track performance.

Our typical encounters with bureaucracy are big "no"s. We submit our expenses for reimbursement and are told that they're a dollar over the allowable threshold. We try to get an employee some computing equipment they need and are told that it is nonstandard, nonacceptable, and non-going-to-happen. We try to build software to solve a business problem and are told that we haven't written our requirements in enough detail.

Graeber says that "bureaucracy represents an inherent flaw in the democratic project."[19] "In principle," he says, "all of these stuffy functionaries in their offices, with their elaborate chains of command, should have been mere feudal holdovers."[20] And there is something feudal-seeming about it; what Weber saw as a rational division of responsibilities can also be an irrational distribution of power to officials who hoard and exercise it coercively.

The rules of MD-102 are rules about what you must or must not do. The real purpose of its gate reviews is to *stop* a project from proceeding: the possible outcomes of a review are "bad" or "acceptable"—never "good." Permission to continue is given grudgingly, if at all, rather than with an enthusiastic offer of support. Safeguarding the public interest is viewed as saying no to things that might threaten it rather than incubating things that will advance it.

There's an interesting parallel to IT practices. For many years, we built IT systems that deliberately constrained users. Each input field on a screen had its purpose; anything a user typed was "validated" and rejected unless it met restrictive criteria. We spoke of "idiot-proofing" our systems, meaning that we forbade users from doing just any old thing they might find useful. Users were discouraged from using the system in any way other than what was specified in a user manual. In the British TV comedy *Little Britain*, a bank worker responds to every customer request by entering it into her computer and reporting "Computer says no!"[21]

Today this paradigm is changing. It has to, because the people who use company IT systems have gotten used to the flexibility and convenience of smartphones and the other devices they spend their days with. IT systems have begun to allow users to enter free text to initiate searches, rather than limiting them to checkboxes and required fields. They may see "type-ahead" dropdowns (those boxes with helpful suggestions that appear as you are typing text) to help them along. Analytic tools and data lakes make it easier for users to follow their own trains of thought. Instead of constraints, IT systems are increasingly designed to present possibilities. In the words of John Brady, CISO of FINRA, they lower the cost of curiosity.[22]

9: It Petrifies

As value is displaced from goals to the rules themselves, the rules become a tradition and a bond that holds the community together. In von Mises's words, "Formalism, even ritualism, ensues with an unchallenged insistence upon punctilious adherence to formalized procedures."[23]

Our gate reviews at USCIS were religious ceremonies—QA reassuringly began each by formally calling the roll to make sure all the signatories were present, laying out ground rules that were the same every time ("Please pay careful attention as the flight attendants demonstrate the use of the safety equipment"), leading the meeting through a standardized series of reports, and in the end asking me, "Do you approve?" and then asking each of the signatories in turn, "Do you concur?" Amen. Then everyone around the table stood up and shook hands.

Once rules become rituals, changing them is tantamount to breaking apart the community. The rigidity with which rules are *applied* becomes a rigidity in *the rules themselves*. Our idea that MD-102 should be changed to actually encourage—rather than just permit—the new best practices was not just dismissed but viewed as bizarre and dangerous. Even those who accepted that our new practices might work better resisted making them into a new rule, because the old rule was still the rule, even if not the practice.

Perhaps in Weber's day the pace of change was slower, allowing him to assume that an efficient process would remain an efficient process indefinitely. Or perhaps it's just an instance of the old philosophical conflict between *rationalism* and *empiricism*. Bureaucracy is a rationalist enterprise: it uses logic, rather than experience, to find the best processes. Once you've done that, empirical experience is irrelevant—you already know the best way. But that puts you in an inconvenient position when the PRA just doesn't do what it was meant to do.

10: It's Risky by Being Risk-Averse

Bureaucracy is a way to mitigate the risk of trying out newfangled ideas. Its slow, careful, managed pace of change is based on defining repeatable processes and refining them to the point where they're emptied of risk and institutionalized as commandments. In a fast-changing environment, however, this makes them all the more risky. Efficiency is the wrong goal if you are risk averse today; what you really want is flexibility, the ability to sense change and respond creatively to it. The problem with bureaucracy is not that it is risk averse but that it is risky.

Verdict: Bureaucracy, Meh, Okay

Bureaucracy is inefficient, wasteful, dehumanizing, coercive, oversimplifying, and risk averse. It leads to a focus on means rather than ends, trained incapacity, and petrification. All true, at least for the bureaucracies we typically find blocking our way. But is it possible that there are bureaucracies around us every day that we don't notice because they aren't in our way? And are these characteristics essential to bureaucracy, or might they just happen to accompany it?

Assuming we accept, more or less, Weber's definition of bureaucracy—in my handy oversimplification, rigid rules and rigid roles—the answer is a bit of both. Bureaucracy does indeed require simplification, abstraction, and unfreedom. Simplification, however, can be good or bad. Just as abstraction is needed in mathematics and science to make possible higher-order discoveries, it's needed in active organizations to make possible coordinated activity.

Petrification, however, was never part of Weber's conception. The hierarchy was to be filled with experts—professionals—who would stay up to date in their fields of expertise. Through their experience in the bureaucracy, their skills and knowledge would also increase day by day. Bureaucracy was to be "domination through knowledge," capturing institutional learning and repurposing it into efficient rules for action.

As for the obsession with means over ends and the trained incapacity, these are simply management challenges. Bureaucracy is not unique; in any organization, it's up to managers to help their employees overcome cultural "psychoses."

Bureaucracy is dehumanizing to the extent that it's mechanical and imposed from the outside, a leviathan that bats humans about now and then with its tail. There's no way to persuade Moby Dick to cooperate with his hunters and stop destroying boats. But to Weber, "impersonality" meant only that rules were to be applied without bias or caprice—not that people would be made to feel helpless.

WHY BUREAUCRACY IS GOOD

The man who is guided by reason is more free in a state where he lives under a system of law than in solitude where he obeys only himself.

—Baruch Spinoza, *Ethics*

In limitations he first shows himself the master,
And the law can only bring us freedom.

—Goethe, *Was Wir Bringen*

What's so terrible about bureaucracy, then, aside from a bit of dehumanization, inefficiency, learned helplessness, and metaphysical pathos? Alright, those aside, is there something about bureaucracy that we actually like, something that is useful to us? What would an advocate of bureaucracy—if such a person existed—say, not in its defense, but in its praise?

The following are some aspects of bureaucracy we might want to borrow as we design our digital organizations.

Ethical Considerations: Bureaucracy Is Fair

A particular ethical attitude is required of bureaucrats, a willingness to put their own beliefs and biases aside and proceed purely on the basis of what benefits the organization.

> The ethical attributes of the "good" bureaucrat—strict adherence to procedure, commitment to the purposes of the office, abnegation of personal moral enthusiasms, and so on—represent a remarkable achievement.[1]

Weber spoke of a *Lebensordnung*, or ethical life-order, implicit in bureaucracy.[2] Procedural fairness is built in, preventing officials from giving special treatment based on past allegiances, or on personal or family relationships. An official's duty is *to the role* and to fulfilling it in the way it was designed, not to their own interests. According to Clegg, "One way of reading Weber's account of bureaucracy is as a treatise on the formation of a particular type of moral character bounded by an emotionally strong sense of duty as a vocation."[3] As Professor Paul du Gay of Copenhagen Business School relays, Weber believes the bureaucrat:

'takes pride in preserving his impartiality, overcoming his own inclinations and opinions, so as to execute in a conscientious and meaningful way what is required of him by the general definition of his duties or by some particular instruction, even—and particularly—when they do not coincide with his own political views.'[4]

This ethic of self-abnegation is simply *not* a consideration in systems of leadership by notables. Kingship is necessarily the practice of nepotism. Aristocrats have special privileges rivaling even those of Diamond Medallion frequent flyers. To be admitted to the Tower of London one needed only to be disliked by the king. Charismatic leaders such as Hitler and Charles Manson had no need for fairness when choosing their victims. To Weber, on the other hand, an ethic of fairness was essential to any system that would be based on rationality rather than emotion and arbitrariness.

In the government, we were constrained by the procurement process of the colossal six-thousand-page FAR. We weren't allowed to just choose a vendor that we "knew" was best; we had to give others a fair chance to compete for our business. If we'd been allowed to choose based on our preferences—whether we intended it or not, whether we were conscious of it or not—our choices would have been influenced by our preconceived ideas, our incomplete knowledge, our prior relationships with vendors, or our comfort in working with incumbents. To avoid such biases, the FAR required us to clearly define the requirements of each procurement, decide in advance how we would evaluate the bids, let the vendors know, and then make sure that we applied exactly those criteria when making a decision. It was a pain in the neck, and it took a lot of effort—that is to say, it was costly and slow—and didn't always lead to the best result. But the ideal of equal treatment overrode those problems.

We should *want* bureaucrats not to treat us as individuals, because impersonality prevents arbitrary, discriminatory, and abusive treatment.[5] Employees are protected from their managers because both are constrained by rules and formal interaction patterns.[6] Someone who is unhappy with the way a bureaucracy is treating them is presumably someone who thinks they deserve special treatment; they'll inevitably find that special treatment at the very least requires paperwork, red tape, sign-offs, and frustration.[7] And so it should be, no?

A bureaucracy is also meant to be a *meritocracy*. It standardizes the requirements for each role and thereby makes the role available to anyone who qualifies. By formalizing recruitment, application, and selection, and by using standardized tests or other assessment criteria, it extends that fairness into all its hiring-related activities.[8] Compared to technology companies, government IT employs a rather diverse workforce. Could this be because the hiring and promotion process is set up for fairness, while the commercial sector has conscious or unconscious biases that prevent it from becoming diverse?

To be honest, I'm a fan of neither the mountainous six-thousand-page FAR nor the government's hiring process, because I believe their goals can better be met by simpler and less wasteful processes. But, for the most part, they're honest attempts at equal treatment and fairness (I say *for the most part* because they're influenced by lobbying, and because the procurement process tends to exclude small companies that can't afford the costs of the burdensome process). And let's not forget that the hiring process might inadvertently discriminate against certain groups, and that the culture of a particular government agency might not promote inclusion. But the *intention* is to use standard criteria to reduce the effect of personal biases. If anything, the problem is not that the FAR and the hiring process impose bureaucratic rules—it is that they may be the wrong rules.

Its ethical basis makes bureaucracy consistent with the modern world's humanistic principles. "To oppose bureaucracy," Clegg says, "is to oppose a particular conception of modernity as rational, legal, meritocratic, and universalistic."[9]

Formality and Role Definitions

The literature of IT is a literature by and for creative knowledge workers; its discomfort with bureaucracy might not be shared by everyone across an organization. Even if the business world is digitizing rapidly, there are still many jobs that require discipline, routinization, and process efficiency—repetitive work in mass production, clerical processing, and routine service operations, for example. It's not that those roles don't require innovation, but their innovation is generally related to efficiency and to continuous improvement of cost, quality, and timeliness.[10] Bureaucracy may be ideally suited.

Even knowledge work includes routine tasks that can be handled more smoothly and with less frustration through bureaucratization. Studies have found that the more routine the tasks, the more acceptable a formalized, standardized approach is to employees.[11] Other studies indicate that employees don't mind routinized processes as long as they're designed well,[12] are consistent with their values, and can be seen as furthering their goals.[13]

In fact, there are many cases where employees ask for more bureaucracy. I'm talking about those moments we all experience when we get frustrated with vaguely distributed responsibilities or disappointed in how other employees are contributing and ask, "Can you please tell me exactly what my responsibility is?" or, "Can you clarify what my job description is?" or, "Can you tell me who's accountable for this?" or, "Isn't there some kind of lethal injection for people like my coworker?"

It shouldn't surprise us, then, that increased formalization of roles tends to increase job satisfaction and commitment.[14] Hugh Willmot, a professor of management and organization studies at Cass Business School in the UK, speaks of "the distinctive capacity of bureaucracy to clarify responsibilities, ease role stress, and thereby enable employees to work effectively."[15] Edgar Schein considers corporate culture, his field of study, to be a mechanism for making the world meaningful and predictable, thereby reducing employee anxiety.[16] If that is so, bureaucracy contributes to corporate culture by delineating and formalizing those aspects of roles that are routine. Fewer things for employees to stress over leads to more areas where they know for sure they are performing acceptably.

Perhaps most telling is that when unions advocate for workers, their goal is to increase the formalization of rules and roles. Collective bargaining agreements (CBAs) might include clauses along the lines of "employees shall be granted fifteen-minute breaks after each three hours of work time" or establish formal grievance procedures. Our CBA at USCIS included precise measurements for cubicle size depending on an employee's level in the hierarchy, and requirements that seniority be considered in assigning employees to tasks, giving promotions, or deciding whom to lay off in the event of reductions.

Size and Scale

Bureaucracy helps coordinate activities across units of a large enterprise by formalizing the interactions among them. Schein says that

> with increasing organizational size, people can no longer remain functionally familiar with others, so they have to resort to more formal processes of contracting, monitoring each other, and in general substituting processes and procedures for personal contact.[17]

Interestingly, he's not saying that bureaucracy makes processes impersonal and formal, but the opposite: that the increasing size of the enterprise causes the need for impersonal and formal interactions, which we then label bureaucracy. Here again, Schein's description of corporate culture comes startlingly close to ours of bureaucracy: "Every organization that succeeds develops a way of structuring work; defining the production and marketing processes; and creating the kinds of information, reward, and control systems it needs to operate effectively."[18] Bureaucracy, in this sense, is an aspect of corporate culture that provides—dammit—those efficiency benefits.

As an example, my team at AWS accepts requests for our participation in customer meetings from around the AWS enterprise. Our wiki explains how those who want our services should proceed. In some cases we ask them to fill out a ticket in our ticketing system, where they answer a set of questions that helps us prioritize their requests. The wiki explains how we'll respond to those tickets and under what conditions we'll accommodate the requests. This bit of bureaucracy both formalizes a process and helps clarify our role in the division of labor. It brings order to a process that was becoming chaotic and difficult to manage as the enterprise grew.

Compliance and Grimaces

In an era where compliance frameworks are proliferating, bureaucracy provides an effective way to cope with them and keep auditors smiling.* "Bureaucratic management is management bound to comply with detailed rules and regulations fixed by the authority of a superior body," says von Mises.[19] Bureaucracy

---

* I'm pretty sure I've seen an auditor smile, though it could have been a grimace. -au.

is compliance, so no wonder that it can help us survive compliance audits. "Even where bureaucratic behavior is not so routinized that it can be conveniently prescribed by rule, we insist on rules when there is a significant risk of an impermissible outcome."[20] The key word is *impermissible*—in this case, falling out of compliance. Bureaucracy, in this sense, is a factory within the organization whose product is compliance. That product has value: it lets the company operate in a regulated environment. It is a foundation for all of the other value the company produces.

Persistence of Memory

In the corkboard example I gave in the introduction, a team tried to introduce a formal process to solve a problem they had experienced. They were turning their learning—that a diagram posted on a corkboard might get misplaced—into a rule that would prevent the problem's occurring in the future. Bureaucracy is a "vast organizational memory of best practices"[21] that helps us avoid constantly reinventing the circular block of rigid material that spins around an axle.*

When we optimize processes or solve problems, we memorialize our findings in a documented process, an SOP, or a manifesto. Formalized processes are precisely the specialty of bureaucracies. They're also—no coincidence here—the specialty of information technologists, who, as Adler noted, "objectify" know-how in equipment and software.[22]

In one of the classic works that fueled the Agile IT revolution, Hirotaka Takeuchi and Ikujiro Nonaka argued that "knowledge is [also] transmitted in the organization by converting project activities to standard practice. . . . Naturally, companies try to institutionalize the lessons derived from their successes."[23] Companies naturally, in other words, turn successful practices into bureaucracy. Formalized processes can be examined, improved, benchmarked, and agreed upon, where informal processes cannot. Du Gay adds, "Process is care and thoroughness; it is consultation, involvement and co-ownership; it is (as we were reminded by the failure of international process in the run-up to the Iraq war) legitimacy and acceptance; it is also record, auditability and clear accountability."[24]

---

* The wheel. Schwartz has a passionate hatred of clichés. We've spent months trying to help him find an alternative to "cog in a wheel" and have concluded that there isn't one. -ed.

Rational Results and Capitalism

Markets require a type of transparency and predictability that is well served by what Weber called the "calculability of results" of bureaucracy.[25] A broadcaster needs to know what FCC rules it must satisfy in order to be allowed to do business. A company incorporating in Delaware needs to know what the requirements will be and whose approval it must seek.

On their part, commercial entities need to satisfy investors by providing transparency into their operations. The bureaucracy that is a company's budgeting process, its spending and procurement processes, and its operational SOPs all contribute to the predictability that capital markets require. Sarbanes-Oxley was created to reassure investors that they could trust the information provided by companies; it's a compliance bureaucracy that lubricates the capital markets.

It's the very impersonality of the market that makes entrepreneurship possible. For entrepreneurs and investors to risk their time and capital in new ventures, they must have some measure of security such as that provided by laws and—perhaps predictability is not the right word—they must know that their efforts will have rational results.[26]

Green Eggs and Meaning

Rules are the background to our creative activity; they're guardrails and frameworks that structure our efforts but don't fully constrain them. Creativity is not only allowed; it's facilitated by rules that provide a structure within which experts can exercise their skills.

Art—which we imagine as the height of creativity—is also highly constrained. A painter works with paint and canvas, not with dance and song. Western music is made with the twelve notes of the scale. The composer Igor Stravinsky once said that "the more constraints one imposes, the more one frees one's self. And the arbitrariness of the constraint serves only to obtain precision of execution."[27] The meaning of an artist's work is found partly in its context in the history of art and the cultural milieu in which it is created; yet artists do not choose their circumstances. Rebellion rebels against something.

There's a technique in literature called constrained writing, where authors accept an arbitrary set of rules within which to work. In lipograms, for example, a particular letter is avoided; in an acrostic, the first letters of successive words or sentences form another word or sentence. Sonnets and haikus have exacting structural constraints. And Dr. Suess wrote all of *Green Eggs and Ham* using only fifty different words on a fifty-dollar bet he'd made.[28]

In IT, software engineering remains a creative discipline. It does not become less so if we surround it with guardrails to make sure that the code is secure, resilient, and scalable, or if we apply some enterprise architecture standards. In fact, those guardrails can take some of the weight off software engineers and leave them free to focus on the creative aspects of their work.

Creativity, innovation, practice of a professional specialty—these all happen within formal frameworks that give them meaning. Structure—in itself—does not oppose innovation or human interaction—it is the background against which they appear.

Verdict: Bureaucracy Not Evil

Bureaucracy is a reasonable path to accomplishing certain types of goals—say, guaranteeing fairness or establishing compliance. It can institutionalize best practices and give comfort to employees with highly routine jobs. For Adler, the problem with bureaucracy is the coercive manner in which it is often applied.[29] To me, the waste that typically attaches to bureaucracy is the main evil. In Part II, I'll combine these ideas and lay out a path to making bureaucracy workable, and even in some cases desirable, in a digital enterprise.

Even for von Mises, a determined critic of bureaucracy, the problem isn't bureaucracy itself, but how and where we choose to use it.[30]

> The assertion that bureaucratic management is an indispensable instrument of democratic government is paradoxical. Many will object. They are accustomed to consider democratic government as the best system of government and bureaucratic management as one of the great evils. How can these two things, one good, the other bad, be linked together? . . . To these objections we must answer again that bureaucracy in itself is neither good nor bad. It is a method of management which can be applied in different spheres of human activity.[31]

Even within a framework of rules and authorities, officials can approach their jobs with energy, rigor, integrity, inventiveness, and attention to efficiency and effectiveness.[32]

PART II

BUILDING
A BETTER
BUREAUCRACY

WE'VE BEEN DOING BUREAUCRACY WRONG

And then we say, "Lord God, how can I break free of anxiety?" Can it be that you have no hands, fool? Perhaps God didn't make any for you? Then sit down and pray that your nose doesn't run! Or rather, wipe your nose and stop making accusations.

—Epictetus, *Discourses*

Look ye, pudding-heads should never grant premises.

—Herman Melville, *Moby Dick*

Technology Changes Bureaucracy

A lot has changed since Weber's day. Manufacturing, which accounted for only about 12% of jobs in 1840 but trended steadily upward through Weber's time to about 38% in the 1950s, fell to less than 20% by 2010. On the other hand, the services industries now make up over 75% of jobs.[1] The type of bureaucracy we see today is primarily meant to control service workers, not factory workers. Digital technology has taken hold and become central to the way businesses compete and public sector organizations accomplish their mission objectives. Efficiency and productivity look very different in a digital and knowledge-work world: the goal is not to produce more lines of software code per hour or to manufacture better formatted PowerPoint presentations.

What today's organizations need, primarily, has more to do with speed and short lead times. Businesses are caught up in an environment of rapid and continuous change, complexity, and uncertainty, driven in part by the actions of their competitors—some of which are startups bent on undermining traditional industries. It's driven as well by the fickle preferences of consumers, who might suddenly race to a competitor in as little time as it takes to read an inappropriate tweet from a CEO or hear of a new style of yoga. The business environment is subject to sudden political change, regulatory change, and geo-political instability; coronaviruses and trade wars; terrorist actions and new installments of *Fast & Furious*. Consumer expectations have risen as technology has put empowering tools in their hands (and on other body parts)—smart phones, tablets, wearables, virtual reality headsets, gaming consoles.

And bureaucracy is still with us. That seems strange. Bureaucracy works best, Weber acknowledged, in situations of routine, repetitive work. It locks in routines and formalizes processes so that they are well-known and repeatable . . . forever and ever. When the world calls for speed and agility, fastness & furiousness, bureaucracy just doesn't seem rational. Formal rules and roles lend stability—but stability in the face of disruptive change is what makes Blockbusters and Kodaks of previously admired companies.

I'll suggest in this chapter that we can use bureaucracy to gain speed and support innovation. It's a tool available to us for situations where it fits. It can accelerate and routinize repetitive work and provide guardrails that relieve worry. It can help us satisfy external demands—like compliance frameworks and pressures from bad-guy hackers—that would otherwise interfere with our delivery of value and our pleasure in our work. I know, claiming speed as an advantage of bureaucracy sounds a bit unhinged. But much of what we've learned in delivering digital IT capabilities can help us change the way we practice bureaucracy, for the better.

We'll have to shear off many of the bad practices that have attached themselves to bureaucracy. We'll have to eliminate bureaucracy that's not adding value, limiting its scope to where we really need it. And then, we'll be able to use techniques we've learned from DevOps and Agile IT to make our bureaucracy lean, learning, and enabling.

The problem is that we've been doing bureaucracy all wrong.

Bureaucracy: Annoying, Necessary

Admit it—Weberian bureaucracy is not the stuff of nightmares. The *other* stuff we've added, stuff outside of Weber's bureaucratic "ideal" of rigid roles and rigid rules, is what made Kafka's reputation. Bureaucracy is just a tool, a way to add formality where formality is helpful, a way to rigorously specify processes when rigor matters. It's a solution to problems organizations face as they grow and personal contact is lost among employees or between employees and the public. It's neither good nor bad, just as the law of gravity is neither good nor bad. We shouldn't have nightmares over gravity, but, then again, we should use it only when we want to descend toward the Earth or attract massive bodies, not when we're leaving Earth to return to our home planet after abducting bureaucrats for study.

Unfortunately, the way we usually practice bureaucracy *is* a nightmare—the trolls-in-caves, carbon-copying, weigh-'em-down-with-sludge school of bureaucracy that menaces our productivity and elevates our stress levels. But what if we could tease apart these strands, separate bureaucracy as benefactor from bureaucracy as tormentor—and somehow make the Sadean part go away? Look—we don't really hate bureaucracy, we just hate big cockroaches like Gregor Samsa.*

In fact, we need bureaucracy, at least in the Weberian sense. And we're stuck with it because the traditional division of labor between Marketing, Sales, Finance, and Operations is still with us, even if other functional delineations are being erased. To achieve the fastest lead times, we need it to streamline those repetitive, mechanical activities that Agile frameworks refer to as "toil." Large enterprises need some formal patterns of interaction. Even innovators like Amazon and Google, as we'll see in later chapters, impose structure to rationalize their operations. And there will always be some sort of formal "governance" to convince investors, regulators, and customers that particular controls are in place. At some level of abstraction, every large enterprise is a bureaucracy.

During my time in the government, I realized that no amount of digital transformation would eliminate government bureaucracy. And we wouldn't want to have it any other way. The US government has, as a fundamental principle, an institutionalized lack of trust. We have a system of checks and balances because we do not trust any one branch of government. We have formal mechanisms that prevent government officials from bringing their biases to roles that are meant to be in service of the public. We give hiring preference to those who have served our country in the military. We implement rules that constrain how we award contracts to make sure vendors are treated equally. In other words,

---

* Gregor Samsa is the protagonist of Kafka's "The Metamorphosis." Mr. Schwartz's tongue is firmly in cheek, as he earlier said that Samsa turned into a dung beetle, not a cockroach. -ed.

bureaucratic structures are used to satisfy the public that the government is acting in their interest.

I found that government bureaucrats are on the whole well-meaning and devoted to mission success. Their activities are tightly constrained in ways that are hard to imagine until you face them every day. But bureaucracy per se is not what constrains them: it is *our* wishes, as expressed through Congress, the president, and the free press that, when translated into the syntax of bureaucratic rules, control the behavior of federal employees. Bureaucracy is an *answer*—the answer to the question, How can we set guardrails and controls that make sure that government employees do what we want them to do?

Businesses are no different. The capital markets do not just naively trust the management team of a company. Management does not just trust employees. The government does not just trust businesses. Unions do not just trust management.

Bureaucracy does not just tell people what to do—it provides proof that they are doing the right things. The red tape we hate so much yields a paper trail to show that the rules were followed. That's how bureaucracy addresses an institutional lack of trust.

Adler puts it nicely:

> We need bureaucracy for the discipline it affords, but we don't want it because it brings a host of negative consequences. . . . My research suggests that the negative consequences of bureaucracy—rigidity, alienation, and low commitment—may be widespread, but they are not inherent in bureaucracy. They are the result of poor choices in the specific form given to bureaucracy in too many organizations.[2]

Digital Bureaucracy

While everyone can see that technology has changed, what's less obvious is that the way technologists work has also changed—dramatically. And since technology is increasingly central to businesses, it's also changing the way businesses operate and are led. The innovative management styles developed by technology-centered companies are beginning to influence more traditional enterprises. As DevOps, user-centric design, and machine learning have entered businesses, silo boundaries have been crossed. Businesses are learning to focus on product rather than their own processes, to enter markets incrementally and refine their products and services iteratively, and to make decisions based on real data rather than projections and assumptions.

To the extent we use technology to refine our bureaucratic approach, we can harvest bureaucracy's advantages—fairness, simplification, optimization, transparency, and compliance—but with a tad less metaphysical pathos. Digital transformation does not need to sidestep or eliminate bureaucracy. Instead, it needs to realign bureaucracy, turn it from an impediment to an ally, make it not just *allow* speed and joy, but *foster* it. In a transformed digital organization, bureaucracy is given its proper place, while creativity, innovation, values, and shared humanity leap to the foreground.

There's my new formula for digital transformation—that vague goal for which bureaucratic bobbleheads are bobbing support.* Our story starts in the IT world at about the turn of the millennium when Agile methods began to catch on . . .

Enter Agile and DevOps

At first glance, Agile and DevOps seem like the opposite of bureaucracy.

Agile IT delivery is based on inspecting and adapting. It's best contrasted with what was called a plan-driven approach, where requirements were amassed and approved, a project plan was assembled, and a project team tried to deliver exactly those requirements exactly according to that plan. Success meant that the plan's milestones and budget were met. An Agile project team, in contrast, looks back frequently to assess what they've learned and what's changed, and incorporates those learnings and observations into its plans. Success is measured by results; the plan is expected to change with circumstances. Feedback and adjustment are guiding principles.

Since Agile delivery accepts and values change, it's perfect for environments where complexity and uncertainty dominate. That is, everywhere, at the moment. To maximize feedback and learning, it's practiced by small teams who deliver IT capabilities quickly and in small increments, learning with each one.

DevOps entered the scene in about 2009 and is today's preferred approach to delivering IT. It combines Agile and Lean ideas and organizes technologists into collaborative, cross-functional teams. Each team has all the skills it needs

---

* See Schwartz, *War and Peace and IT*, for an explanation of the bobbleheads. -ed.

to create, test, secure, deploy, and operate code, and takes ownership for doing all those things. (In *A Seat at the Table* and *War and Peace and IT*, I suggested we add non-IT business expertise to DevOps teams as well, and make teams responsible not just for delivering technology, but also for getting business results.)[3] DevOps relies heavily on automation to deliver results extremely frequently in tiny increments—sometimes as often as hundreds or thousands of times every day—thus maximizing learning as the enterprise gets to see the results of each small piece of work.

Where bureaucracy emphasizes following the rules, DevOps emphasizes getting results; the displacement of goals common in bureaucracy is not seen in DevOps. Where bureaucracy would have a division of labor based on functional expertise, DevOps has cross-functional teams; where bureaucracy pushes accountability down a hierarchy of organizational chart roles, DevOps holds teams, as a whole, accountable. And while bureaucracy defers to experts higher in the hierarchy, DevOps relies on an experimental approach to support data-driven decisions.

DevOps, you'd think, couldn't be more different from bureaucracy.

DevOps Is Bureaucracy

Those surface differences obscure the many deeper connections. DevOps is in fact a brilliant implementation of bureaucratic ideals. Like any Weberian bureaucracy, DevOps is full of rules—and they are rigorously and impartially enforced, without anger or bias or whim or caprice. Some are cultural norms (the team wears the pager), some are rules of thumb (automate all the things; if something is painful, do it more often; always make your changes to the master branch), and some are automated (code cannot be deployed unless it has passed all its tests; code only becomes part of the build after it receives a peer code review).*

DevOps regiments those aspects of IT delivery that are repetitive "toil" through a bureaucracy that is enabling and lean. For example, code is tested and deployed through automated scripts that enforce security and quality con-

---

* "Wears the pager": software developers respond to emergencies (operations specialists used to); "automate all the things": DevOps jokey language for "automate everything"; "master branch": don't delay before merging different programmers' changes together; "peer code review": all code gets reviewed by another programmer before it can move forward. -ed.

trols. Those automated rules keep us secure and compliant and let us optimize our practices to where we can deploy code thousands of times per day.

Functions that were once handled by human bureaucracy—reviews by change control boards, say—are now taken care of by automation and standardized practices, but that doesn't make them any less bureaucratic. More so, perhaps. There are no exceptions and the rules are applied impersonally—*very* impersonally, because they're applied by machine.

DevOps is a culture and a process. And the culture reinforces the belief that the process is one which . . . thou *shalt* follow. Thou had damn well better— DevOps is bureaucracy functioning as institutional memory. It incorporates the practices that our collective experience has found to be most effective. Check in code often. "Prove" that your code does the right things by writing tests and showing they pass. Deploy often, but only if your tests have passed. If you break the build, you must fix it right away. Automate your infrastructure. Make sure absolutely everything, including infrastructure, is checked into source control. Use a testing pyramid; focus mostly on unit tests. Its processes are rigid, well defined, and impersonal. DevOps, you might say, is a reference implementation of Weber's bureaucratic ideals for the digital age.

DevOps is automated bureaucracy—and so what? It's still a humane approach to IT delivery, joining together the former silos of IT development and operations behind a single goal. In the next chapter I'll distinguish between bureaucracies that are enabling and those that are coercive. DevOps works so well because it's enabling. Does it also have coercive aspects? Perhaps. Do you find it suspicious that so many teams are adopting DevOps when we tell them it's the right thing to do? Would a technology team not feel plenty of peer pressure if they decided to adopt "blameful retrospectives"?[*][†]

I consider DevOps to be a revolution in how we deliver IT capabilities. My books have presented it as the solution to many decades of dysfunction in how companies use technology, in particular how they've traditionally thought of IT as separate from something called "the business," and as a result have treated their technology departments as if they were an arms-length contractor outside their corporate walls. DevOps gives us a way to bring technology into the heart of an enterprise by dissolving the wall that shuts it out.

---

[*] DevOps teams use "blameless" retrospectives, which encourage all team members to find the root causes of problems without blaming themselves or others. -ed.

[†] With all due respect, -ed, I think that's what "blameless" means. -au.

And that's why I want to force everyone to use these best practices. I mean, *enable*.

Reconciling Weber to DevOps

There are a few tweaks we'll have to make to Weber's ideas to make him happy with DevOps.

Although Weber speaks of a division of labor based on technical specialization (which contrasts with the cross-functional teaming of DevOps), what is truly central to his framework, I think, is the division of *accountability* along precisely drawn lines. Well-defined accountabilities in Weber's model ensure that there are neither gaps nor overlaps when the work is orchestrated into a whole.

Division of accountability is also a core principle of DevOps, in that teams are fully committed and responsible for the IT capabilities they deliver. DevOps principles say "run what you build." The point—an important cultural difference from previous ways of doing IT—is that a team doesn't toss its work over to someone else to manage when it claims to be "finished." Instead, the team takes full responsibility for the code's entire lifecycle and the business results obtained with it.

DevOps lends itself to a product-based organizational model. Such a model is just as rational as Weber's hierarchy of technical functions, and more rational today: just as Weber was overwhelmed by advances in technology and thus made technical specialization the basis for his division of labor, enterprises today are overwhelmed by the potential for customer-centricity and deeper engagement in the digital world, and make customer-facing products the basis of their rationalized hierarchies.

Another tweak we must make to Weber's model is that accountability in DevOps is at a team level rather than an individual one. Essentially, some nodes on the organizational chart are filled by teams rather than individuals. This, frankly, goes against Weber's thinking: he dismissed "collegiate" organizations—those with group accountability—as inefficient.[4] Instead, he took as his model the "monocratic" variety of bureaucracy, where every role is occupied by an individual, which, he says, allows for the highest degree of efficiency.[5] But in our digital world of fast-spreading memes, hacker toolkits for script kiddies, stealth startups, and high-spending venture capitalists, it's more rational to value short lead times over process efficiency.

Oddly, Weber doesn't see this. Speed—interpreted as fast response and short lead times—must have meant something very different in his time, because he's adamant that his monocratic variety of bureaucracy provides it:

> The extraordinary increase in the speed with which public announcements are transmitted, whether about economic or even purely political matters, has in itself created nowadays a continuous and intense pressure in the direction of the maximum possible acceleration in the time taken by the administration to react to situations as and when they arise: the best results in this respect are normally only achieved by strict bureaucratic organisation.[6]

Weird, huh? He seems to be talking about today's digital economy, and he's suggesting that bureaucracy fits. He's so close to getting the digital world right . . .

The lean principles of the Toyota Way didn't start to be formulated until 1930, after Weber's *Economy and Society*, and the details of the Toyota Production System didn't come together until sometime between 1948 and the 1990s, when they began to influence American Lean Manufacturing. With them came the idea of minimizing lead times by eliminating the eight kinds of *muda*, or waste. I can only conclude that Weber did not know real speed. He believed that it followed from scientific process efficiency improvements, including higher capacity utilization, which is viewed as a potential source of waste in Lean. We'll disagree with Weber and stick with the Lean view on this one.

A Schimpfwort in Hierarchy-Space

DevOps and Agile practices like Scrum may be instances of Weberian bureaucracy, but in execution they're very different from the gnarled forms of bureaucracy we encounter every day and think of when we hear our favorite *Schimpfwort*.

DevOps is a model bureaucracy because it's empowering while structured and controlled; lean as a matter of principle; and set up to learn through feedback loops and monitoring. It's also designed as a bureaucracy that doesn't inspire metaphysical pathos: it lets employees innovate and test their ideas at low cost, low risk, and high speed; it automates red tape so that employees can focus on work that motivates them; it enforces controls required by compliance frameworks and security objectives, but does so behind the scenes through automation rather than through gatekeeping trolls; and it increases organizational agility rather than reinforcing the organizational sluggishness that we know to be dangerous in a disruptive environment, and which traditional bureaucracies have generally exacerbated.

As an example of how DevOps changes the game for bureaucracy, in the next chapter I'll explain how security teams can enforce their security rules in DevOps through automated tests and guardrails and through early participation in design and engineering. When they do so, they're still experts occupying roles in Weberian hierarchy-space, and they still impose bureaucratic controls on the DevOps teams—it's still *their* automated tests an IT system has to pass—but they no longer need to act as gatekeeping trolls who leap out of the shadows at the last minute to croak "no!" Or, using the language of the next chapters, they provide lean and enabling bureaucratic controls to empower the developers, and a process by which their bureaucratic controls could be continuously improved.

Bright Empty Terms

Some management theorists suggest we've entered a postbureaucratic world where new forms of organization are better suited. They speak of "fluid organic systems" and "innovative integrative cultures."[7] They emphasize competition or collaboration between parts of the business rather than rigidly delineated roles and predefined rules.[8]

Other management theorists argue that these postbureaucratic models are actually just bureaucracy in another guise.

> Organizations in which, for example, there is reliance upon a set of core norms, rather than a detailed set of rules and procedures, may be more intensively "bureaucratic"—in the Weberian sense of being dominated by a logic of formal rationality that deploys these norms instrumentally, with a view to streamlining the means of established ends. From this perspective, "post-bureaucratic" features and forms of organization are, perhaps, better characterized as "hyper-bureaucratic."[9]

These theorists are disturbed by the shiny, propaganda-like, bureaucratic-feeling language in which neobureaucracy is often couched. Graeber, for example, notes "a peculiar idiom that first emerged in such circles, full of bright, empty terms like vision, quality, stakeholder, leadership, excellence, innovation, strategic goals, or best practices."[10] Wilmot goes further:

> Phrases such as "moving away from a silo culture", "putting customers as the heart of all decision-making", "decentralizing into neighbourhood teams" are redolent of "post-bureaucracy"-speak. As argued earlier, they are potentially consistent with the drive of formal rationality to calculate improved means of attaining existing means. But, when the underpinnings of bureaucratic ethos and principles are neglected, a likely outcome is an escalation of the pathologies of bureaucracy—in the form of paralysis and disorganization—without remedial virtues.[11]

Some write of businesses as complex networks that constantly reconfigure themselves.[12] In my previous books I've drawn on sources like Joseph Clippinger III's *The Biology of Business* to present the idea of businesses as complex adaptive systems (CASs). The idea of a CAS is based on biological systems that continuously adapt to survive natural selection. Managers in a CAS set up "fitness" parameters and then leave the business free to evolve, expecting that the processes most fit to deliver successful results will naturally survive. Agile IT approaches are consistent with such postbureaucratic views of the business enterprise: they're based on team accountability, informal networks, customer-centric design, and rapid adjustment through feedback, controlled not top-down but through evolution and adaptation. At the same time, they often follow very structured frameworks; bureaucracy, you might say, still lurks in the background.

Perhaps this debate is missing the point. These "postbureaucratic" approaches may be equally bureaucratic—but they may all the same be *better* bureaucracy. Today's digital techniques, while they erect bureaucratic structures, change the nature of bureaucracy by eliminating or attenuating its disadvantages. For example, many bureaucratic controls that were previously enforced by mechanizing human behavior can now simply be mechanized.

Doing so eliminates the soul-deadening work of administration and the petty exercises of power that enter, unbidden, into bureaucratic administration. We can separate the mechanical, bureaucratized part of what employees do from the creative, satisfying part, and let the employees focus on what motivates them. Bureaucracy, through automation, becomes background to the real work of delighting customers or citizens; it can stop being coercive, bloated, and petrified, and start being enabling, lean, and learning.

Risk and Outcomes

Bureaucracy is often not the right tool to use. There are many areas (most areas?) where control should be loose and informal or where there's a risk that rules, rather than results, will become the focus. Areas where principles and values and good management skills can substitute for heavy-handed governance. Places where we want employees to bring themselves—their personalities and perceptions—to their role.

The tools of the digital age can help us narrow the scope of bureaucratic controls in an organization in at least three ways. First, they reduce risk; with lower risk, we can substitute less onerous controls. Second, they allow us to put controls on outputs rather than process; this is a key area where today's knowledge-work economy differs from Weber's manufacturing-centric milieu. And finally, management through values, a practice highly refined by companies like Amazon, makes it possible to widen the spaces between bureaucratic controls.

A combination of DevOps and the cloud is powerful for reducing risk. The cloud reduces business risk because with it infrastructure can be replaced at any moment, whereas outside the cloud the hardware purchased upfront might turn out later not to meet the company's needs. Infrastructure can also be scaled up or scaled down without penalty as a company's needs change. Organizations using the cloud can try out new business ideas inexpensively and with no commitment; for example, we can use machine learning, augmented reality, or virtual reality to design new customer experiences. DevOps reduces business risk further by frequently delivering small, incremental features so that the company can continually check to make sure it's getting the right results and, if necessary, adjust course or discontinue investing before much damage is done. As risk is lowered, bureaucratic red tape can be peeled off.

At the same time, speed and lowered risk mean that controls can be placed on outputs and outcomes rather than on the processes that produce them. In MI-CIS-OIT-003, for example, our requirements were at the level of "deliver frequently" and "work backward from the customer" rather than at the detailed execution level of MD-102's demands like "write an analysis of alternatives with the following sections." We could measure whether a project team was "delivering frequently" or "working backward from the customer" because results were quickly and frequently being delivered.

In manufacturing, it makes sense to streamline the activities that produce the product through rules and well-defined processes. In knowledge work, however, doing so is rarely effective. You can't tell people how to think; even telling them how to prepare an outline or a mind map is probably not going to improve a company's competitive position. Instead, you'll do better to put controls on their output—making sure their code is secure or that their external communication follows branding guidelines. Of course, this has led to troll-keeping behavior in the past, but through automation, fast feedback, and the shift-left technique I'll describe in the next chapter, we can repurpose our trolls.

Values and Principles

As DevOps has arisen, a new management style has also emerged that reduces the need for formal bureaucratic structure: the use of agreed-upon values and principles to align employees' activities. Employees are expected to use their judgment in applying the principles to each of their decisions; managers oversee their work by giving them feedback on how they do so. The principles are a common language across the enterprise, so employees can coordinate their activities and arrive at joint decisions consistent with the principles yet formed through their diversity and interaction.

In his study of bureaucracy at the gypsum factory, Gouldner noted that bureaucracy took hold in one part of the factory—the part that produced gypsum boards—but not in the mining operations. His explanation was that the miners shared a strong set of values and cultural norms that determined their actions. In Gouldner's words, "The informal group and its norms, then, constituted a functional equivalent for bureaucratic rules to the degree, at least, that it served to allocate concrete work responsibilities and to specify individual duties."[13]

Amazon similarly uses shared values and shared mechanisms to avoid heavy-handed bureaucracy. The company is grounded in a set of fourteen leadership principles that guide hiring, employee development, work activities, and decision-making throughout the enterprise.* They include values

---

* Here's the complete list of principles: (1) Customer Obsession, (2) Ownership, (3) Invent and Simplify, (4) Are Right, A Lot, (5) Learn and Be Curious, (6) Hire and Develop the Best, (7) Insist on the Highest Standards, (8) Think Big, (9) Bias for Action, (10) Frugality, (11) Earn Trust, (12) Dive Deep, (13) Have Backbone; Disagree and Commit, and (14) Deliver Results. -au.

like "Customer Obsession," "Bias for Action," and "Have Backbone; Disagree and Commit."

Because employees are expected to act based on these principles, they can largely be left free to make decisions on their own. They can have productive discussions asking each other, "What's the most customer-obsessed way we can do such-and-such?" Managers can coach their employees on better applying the principles, thereby fostering continuous improvement.

In places where standardized processes are important, Amazon has introduced mechanisms, tools that they've found effective in executing on the leadership principles. Chief among them is the mechanism of the PRFAQ—a combination of a press release and Frequently Asked Questions (FAQ) that's used to frame discussion about new products and services. The author of a PRFAQ begins by writing a press release, pretending that the proposed product is already complete and is being launched, making clear its benefits to customers. The FAQ section includes answers to questions the author would expect from within Amazon and outside. The PRFAQ is read and discussed as a sort of business case, with others contributing ideas and asking questions, until it is perfected or discarded.

The fourteen leadership principles together with mechanisms like the PRFAQ guide employees' activities in a way that accomplishes much of what bureaucratic rules would do. But they fail some of the tests for Weberian bureaucracy: role distinctions are mostly erased because decisions are made by arguing about the application of the principles, and anyone who can present a case that their solution is more customer-obsessed or more biased for action will likely win, regardless of their organizational position. They also fail as rules to be applied rigidly and universally, since rather than *determining* actions they're used to *support* proposed actions. One could also argue that they are not "impersonal" as in a Weberian bureaucracy; instead, they are meant to be inclusive. Employees bring their unique points of view, the things that make the company diverse, to the process of generating and assessing creative ideas that implement the principles.

The principles don't eliminate the need for traditional bureaucracy: Amazon still has expense reimbursement policies, codes of conduct, nondisclosure agreements, security reviews, brand guidelines, and plenty of other formal and "impersonal" processes. There's a weekly operations review to ensure that our services perform to our high standards, and a standardized process for making and reviewing budget requests.

The rules and standardized process are just background support for what really matters to Amazon: innovating on behalf of customers and remaining the world's most customer-centric company. Customer Obsession, Bias for Action, and the other leadership principles keep employees focused on the objectives and provide a basis for judging ideas while giving them room to innovate and continuously improve customer services—opening a space between the bureaucratic rules, so to speak.

Bureaucracy provides guardrails and repeatable, simple processes for the administrative tasks that employees don't want to spend time on. Principles provide a flexible context that establishes the goals toward which the employees should direct themselves. The actual day-to-day work is innovation, expert technical execution, continuous improvement, and changing the world for the better.

How to Fix Bureaucracy

There are three things we must do to eliminate bureaucracy's Kafkaesque aspects. We must make it *lean* by removing waste and shrinking lead times. We must make it capable of *learning*; that is, changing as the environment changes and as better ways are found to accomplish goals. And we must make it *enabling*—that is, helpful as a way to get things done rather than a no-saying, gatekeeping, troll-controlled impediment.

Lean Rather Than Bloated

Think of MD-102, with its eighty-seven documents and eleven gate reviews. It asks employees to fill out templated forms, wait for approvals, produce status reports, and sit in meetings. There's a goal to all this busy work: risk reduction. But isn't it possible to accomplish that goal equally, or even better, with a less costly and less time-consuming process? One that is leaner and speedier? We can find out by applying the Lean toolkit, the discipline that is used in Lean Manufacturing, Lean Six Sigma, and the other Lean practices that descend from the Toyota Production System.

Learning Rather Than Petrified

Bureaucracy requires that we apply rules universally and fairly. Its roles and rules are necessarily rigid in the sense that they are *applied* without exceptions and by following a formalized process. But this says nothing about how the rules are *made*. It's not an essential characteristic of bureaucracy that its rules don't change, only that once they're *set* they're applied rigorously.

And that's precisely what we must do: make our bureaucracies capable of learning. That, in turn, requires that we set up feedback loops that tell us how well the rules are working, sensing mechanisms that let us know when new "best" practices exist, and mechanisms for continuously improving the rules.

Enabling Rather Than Coercive

Is the primary purpose of the rules to control employees' activities by restricting them, or to empower employees by giving them a structure within which they can innovate and be productive? The distinction may be subtle, but it makes all the difference between Kafkaesque nightmare and Blakean pleasant dreams.

Weber's idealized bureaucrats use reason to efficiently accomplish objectives. That, in itself, is enabling: it supports employees in working together to get things done. Unfortunately, bureaucratic structure can also be used by officials to control others for their personal satisfaction. Or it can establish well-tested protocols for getting work done and set guardrails that allow employees to work safely, quickly, nimbly, and with confidence. We'll prefer the latter option—to make bureaucracy enabling rather than coercive.

A Very Geeky Analogy (Part Two)

If we can make bureaucracy lean, learning, and enabling, we can use it to organize a company effectively, at grand scale. In the analogy I introduced earlier, bureaucracy can be like an IT architecture that makes extremely complex systems possible by orchestrating the activities of microservices—bureaucrats and workers—through formal and logical activity patterns.

To push the analogy even further, in a well-formed bureaucracy we use loose coupling as a design principle so that each component—microservice, team—can innovate independently, knowing that the result of their combined activities will be the ultimate goal of the organization as a whole. Each component can be individually optimized, as can the overall algorithm that orchestrates their activities—that's the principle of *leanness*. Each is checked into version control where it can be refined and improved and refactored—that's the principle of *learning*. And each provides capabilities that can be used by the others and can rely on the overall design and the tooling to take away stress and toil—that's the *enabling* part.*

You might object that formal design is a good practice for code but not for human interactions. That's often true—which is why we should restrict the use of bureaucracy to those cases where it helps us. But there are many cases where formal interactions between people are helpful, especially when you try to coordinate the activities of many diverse people toward a defined goal, or where routines can reduce anxiety. When you walk into a restaurant, you know more or less what to do—tell the host at the front desk you have a reservation, get shown to your table, look at the menu, order your steaming bowl of strozzapreti.† For most of us, a stressless experience.

Verdict: No Sniveling

Willmot says that it's not "simply a matter of reducing the number of forms or files but, rather, creating and processing those forms and files in such a way that is consistent with the bureaucratic principles of fairness, justice, equality, and so on."[14] Our next task is to examine what bureaucracy looks like when it is lean, learning, and enabling. Then we'll bring back the Monkey, the Razor, and the Sumo Wrestler to teach the bureaucracy how to get there.

When bureaucracy is in your way, you'll have to do something about it. You have a few choices: (1) you can accept its impediments with an attitude of learned helplessness, whining like Epictetus's pupil in the epigraph to this chapter; (2) you can try to make the bureaucracy go away, which is rather like telling Moby Dick to stop thrashing against your tiny whale boat; or (3) you can try to fix the bureaucracy by making it into a better bureaucracy. For the rest of this book, we'll focus mainly on option three, with only a small bit of whining and whaling.

_____

* "Loose coupling": the "inside" of a microservice doesn't matter to other microservices; "checked into version control": code is stored in a database that keeps track of changes; "refactored": improved without changing its functionality; "toil": repetitive, unrewarding work. -ed.

† Strozzapreti, which literally means "strangled priests," is a kind of Italian pasta. Beginning in *A Seat at the Table*, Schwartz has been referring to it often, probably because he enjoys the name. By coincidence, it is also the name of my university in Milano. -ed.

TOWARD AN ENABLING BUREAUCRACY

Purely in your interests, not in mine, I must make it clear to you that you would be making the biggest mistake of your lives if you were to consider the fact that I have spoken to you with an open heart and mind a sign of personal weakness or a diminution of official authority.

—José Saramago, *All the Names*

To think is easy. To act is hard. But the hardest thing in the world is to act in accordance with your thinking.

—Goethe, *Faust*

Which Way, Max?

A crucial assumption has snuck its way into our real-world implementations of bureaucracy: the assumption that employees are recalcitrant and therefore must be coerced into doing what is right. Bureaucracy is a natural and rational way to get results *despite* employees' normal inclinations. But Adler argues that employees often are and certainly can be motivated to share the company's objectives, and that bureaucracy can therefore be designed to be enabling rather than coercive.[1]

The tension between coercion and enablement can be traced back to Weber, who on one hand speaks of bureaucracy as "domination based on knowledge" and on the other hand as "authority derived from occupying a role."[2] Which is it, Max—do bureaucrats have authority because of their expertise, or authority because of their placement in the organizational chart? A doctor has authority over us because we believe the doctor is competent and is acting in our interests—that is domination by knowledge. A factory supervisor, on the other hand, may have authority because it comes with the role. Both sources of authority, apparently, are possible.

Remember that modern bureaucracy arose along with scientific management. Frederick Taylor, one of the pioneers of the field, used time and motion studies to analyze and reconfigure every movement of employees on the assembly line. Look at how Taylor explains what he was doing:

> It is only through the *enforced* standardization of methods, *enforced* adoption of the best implements and working conditions, and *enforced* cooperation that this faster work can be assured. And the duty of enforcing the adoption of standards and of enforcing this cooperation rests with the *management* alone.[3]

I didn't add those italics—they're Taylor's own. He assumes that employees will resist standardization and process improvement unless it's forced on them. He also assumes that managers are better able to plan and optimize employee activities than the employees themselves.[4] Those are *big italicized assumptions*.

In the bureaucracies of ancient Egypt and ancient China, Weber points out, employees could be coerced through the use of physical violence—that is to say, they were slaves who could be tortured. But such coercion, says Weber, is not the best way to achieve efficiency. Modern bureaucracies do even better by offering a guaranteed salary and a career that's furthered by good performance rather than subject to the whim of a superior. Even just strong but empathetic management, coupled with respect, can have better results. As he says,

> Taut discipline and control which at the same time have consideration for the official's sense of honor, and the development of prestige sentiments of the status group as well as the possibility of public criticism also work in the same direction. With all this, the bureaucratic apparatus functions more assuredly than does legal enslavement of functionaries.[5]

There's a vicious circle in coercive bureaucracies: coercion demotivates employees, so they become more recalcitrant, so more coercion becomes necessary. According to writers like Adler, this circle can be broken: employees begin with a certain level of motivation, and if the bureaucracy is designed to support and intensify that motivation, a *virtuous* circle ensues. He cites Motorola as an example of a company that has used bureaucratic mechanisms "to provide a common direction and to capture best practices in ways that supported high levels of commitment and innovation."[6]

Most companies use a common, very structured piece of bureaucracy— their annual budgeting process—as a way to control and constrain employees. The Beyond Budgeting movement argues that control through budgeting is not actually effective because it takes away decision-making power from the employees who would otherwise be in the best position to seize opportunities as the year progresses. Since there's considerable uncertainty in the business world, locking managers into cost targets that were set as far as eighteen months in advance interferes with their ability to create value for the company.

The mistaken assumption, say Beyond Budgeting proponents—similar to that of recalcitrant employees—is that without centralized control of spending there will be anarchy. They show that it's possible to set up rigorous control structures that do not take away the soupçon* of managerial judgment needed to achieve full efficiency and take advantage of market opportunities. Bjarte Bogsnes, who implemented Beyond Budgeting at Statoil Hydro, a large energy company, says:

> There are, however, two other types of control that we want less of. The first one is controlling what people shall and shall not do, through detailed budgets, tight mandates, detailed job descriptions, rigid organizational structures. The second type of control, we probably never had to begin with. That is the perceived control of the future, the one we think we get if we only have enough numbers and details in our plans and forecasts.[7]

Bureaucracy requires rigor and scientific planning, but it does not always require a heavy-handed, restrictive control over employees without their consent. Instead, it can provide structure, frameworks, guardrails, and tools to build on the good intentions of employees. It can involve employees in the creation of rules and workflows, and make them willing participants in finding good ways to accomplish the organization's goals.

---

* A soupçon is just a trace of something. You might have thought it has something to do with soup and maybe a little spoon, but actually it comes from the Latin "suspectio" and has more to do with the word "suspicion." -ed.

My corkboard story in the introduction has a subtle piece of enabling bureaucracy. While requirements for an IT system often appear in a coercive guise—programmer, you "shall" make the system produce strozzapreti recipes—requirements can also be an *enabler* for the programmer. Someone else has already done the work of thinking through a useful system feature and documenting it, which saves the programmer effort and research. In the corkboard story, the team asked me to draw them a state transition diagram because that would help them understand the application processing flow and be a useful reference for them as they created their system. I was working for the team, you might say, by giving them a bureaucratic artifact when they wanted it.

Gypsum

In *Patterns of Industrial Bureaucracy*, Gouldner criticizes Weber's account of bureaucracy on the grounds that it presents a static picture that leaves out the important dynamics of how bureaucracy is introduced into a company and changes it. In his analysis of the gypsum factory he describes the motivations of the people involved and shows how the cultural context—different between the mining operation and the board factory—affected how and to what extent workers accepted bureaucratic management.

As I said in the Introduction, this book is mainly about the kind of bureaucracy that resists digital transformation—the kind that holds back white-collar knowledge-work initiatives. Gouldner's book reminds us that factory bureaucracy can be rather a different thing. At the gypsum plant, much of the bureaucracy is dedicated to making employees work harder, or at least up to a predefined standard, on the assumption that they'll slack off, or "goldbrick," in its absence. Middle managers are treated with suspicion as well; red tape is used by central leadership to enforce their policies on workers directly so as to bypass the "shirking" managers. The gypsum factory's bureaucracy includes prohibitions against absenteeism, "write-ups" of problems with employee performance, and disciplinary processes.

There are also some interesting similarities to the bureaucracy we see in knowledge-work settings. Governance controls in IT, for example, come from a central authority but are applied to all employees—in other words, they bypass "shirking" managers who might not effectively be managing their employees. While IT bureaucracy usually does not assume that employees are lazy goldbrickers, it does assume that employees are liable to spend the company's money foolishly. The manner in which the bureaucracy is applied—say, by the ARB in the Chaos Monkey chapter, is equally paternalistic and mostly punitive.

Gouldner concludes that several distinct patterns of bureaucracy are possible. A *disciplinary* or *punishment-centered* bureaucracy institutes rules because of a lack of trust. It limits the employees' discretion, legitimates any punishments that may be imposed, and establishes *minimum* levels of performance.[8] Rules in a disciplinary bureaucracy are equivalent to orders that are given directly by a supervisor; they're a crutch for management.[9] Disciplinary bureaucracy is closest to that side of Weber's model where authority comes from incumbency in a legally defined office.

Gouldner notes that disciplinary bureaucracy can be imposed not just by management, but by employees as well, in which case it has the characteristics of a *grievance-based bureaucracy*.[10] A union agreement, as I mentioned earlier, is a set of formal bureaucratic rules imposed on management. At the gypsum factory, workers won rules that restricted management's discretion in awarding promotions by requiring that seniority be considered.[11] Just as management-initiated bureaucracy addresses management's lack of trust in employees, employee-initiated bureaucracy reflects a lack of trust in management.

Closer to Weber's idea of expertise-based authority is the pattern Gouldner called *representative bureaucracy*, where workers participate in crafting the rules. An example from the gypsum factory is the complex of practices related to worker safety.[12] It was bureaucracy for sure: it called for rules and red tape, paperwork, meetings, and reports. But it was concocted jointly by management and workers, and was continuously improved in meetings between them, based on reviews of safety findings and incidents. Management provided a safety and personnel manager, whose authority was based on his expertise in factory safety.[13] Management and workers both agreed to abide by the safety rules, as each saw it as in their own interests.

Adler accepts Gouldner's typology, referring in his work to coercive (disciplinary) and enabling (representative) bureaucracies. A coercive bureaucracy, in his sense, is one that mandates compliance, punishes violations, and enforces adherence to standards. An enabling bureaucracy, on the other hand, provides rules that help amplify the effectiveness of people, and does so in part by allowing flexibility and dynamic change in its rules.[14]

Motivation Revisited

The IT community has been heavily influenced by books like Daniel Pink's *Drive*, which argues that intrinsic motivation through autonomy, mastery, and purpose is much more powerful than extrinsic motivation like financial incentives. Mastery and purpose can certainly live in a bureaucratic environment (at least in the Weberian meritocratic ideal, where roles are occupied by masterful employees who exercise their mastery for the organization's good). On the other hand, bureaucracy limits autonomy, or rather allows autonomy only to the extent that the employee stays within the rules.

But Adler cites research showing that autonomy is not the most important motivator—that "when authority is subordinated to common goals, efficacy seems to be more important in determining motivation levels," and autonomy becomes merely a matter of "hygiene."[15] Employees who are motivated by the goals of the organization are willing to accept limitations on their autonomy in service of those goals. The plausible implication is that purpose, motivation by goals, is by far the strongest motivator of Pink's three.

It's easy to think that all organizations are coercive because they co-opt individuals to work toward the organization's goals rather than their own.[16] But studies show that employees adopt an organization's goals as their own, and can be motivated by them. Adler notes that "work can be fulfilling, rather than a disutility, and that organization can be experienced as a cooperative endeavor rather than as an abrogation of autonomy."[17]

Enabling rules are templates that have been found to work well and to support employees who are, in fact, committed to the success of the organization. Coercive rules, on the other hand, become a substitute, rather than a complement, for employee commitment.[18]

Why, then, are bureaucracies so demotivating? It's a question of how they are designed. Employees react better when *routine* tasks are formalized.[19] They also—unsurprisingly—prefer what they consider *good* rules rather than *bad* ones.[20] In Gouldner's representative bureaucracy, employees are comfortable with the rules because they participate in developing them.[21] Other studies have shown that rules that are positively associated with *commitment* reduce alienation.[22] And, finally—again, no surprise—rules are accepted better when they're perceived to be in the interests of both management and employees (safety rules in Gouldner's example) rather than punishment-centered (for example, rules against using company equipment for personal purposes).[23]

Innovation

It's conventional wisdom that bureaucracy interferes with innovation. That notion has been tested in research, and the results are surprising. As Adler puts it,

> the commonly hypothesized negative relationship between innovation and formalization held for most studies of service and not-for-profit organizations and for innovations of higher scope, but the preponderance of the evidence pointed to a positive, not negative, correlation between formalization and innovation in manufacturing and for-profit organizations and for both product and process innovations.[24]

One possible explanation is that by capturing the results of previous work—in its function as institutional memory—bureaucracy provides a head start and a focus for new innovative efforts. Another is that by formalizing the interactions between different groups within the company, it establishes ground rules for how services might be obtained and coordinated, especially for large-scale innovation initiatives. Or, possibly, the existence of guardrails in bureaucracy allows for faster innovation because it occurs in a safer environment.

In IT, we innovate partly by recombining reusable software services in new ways. It helps to have guardrails in place so that innovative ideas can be tried out quickly and validated without much worry about security and operability. It's a similar matter with innovation in a bureaucracy. The crucial matter is that the bureaucracy is applied to controls and tools, but not directly to the innovative ideas, which then would easily be shut down under bureaucratic scrutiny.

We tend to focus on the proclivity of bureaucracies to shut new ideas down, but we should also consider the factors that create conditions under which new ideas are generated. Adler lists a set of conditions he believes are necessary for innovative behavior:

a) a minimum of employment security
b) a professional orientation toward the performance of duties
c) established work groups that command the allegiance of their members
d) the absence of basic conflict between work group and management
e) organizational needs that are experienced as disturbing[25]

Bureaucracy can satisfy these conditions. Why not? It provides employment security, hires professionals, organizes into a hierarchy of work groups, establishes formal interactions that avoid basic conflict, and certainly can disturb employees when necessary.

Another interesting twist is reported by David Buchanan and Louise Fitzgerald in an article on health care bureaucracy. Although most people associate inflexibility with bureaucracy, research has found that intensifying bureaucracy has actually *increased* the flexibility of professional service workers.[26] The mechanism might be the same: the availability of guardrails and tools to draw on for what is routine may allow the employee to approach the distinctive aspects of each situation more flexibly.

Atul Gawande's writings on medicine also demonstrate how a kind of bureaucracy can support innovation and craftsmanship. In *The Checklist Manifesto*, he promotes the use of checklists, even in knowledge-work environments such as surgery. Not only do they drastically reduce errors, but they also provide a sort of comforting safety net for medical providers, since they'll help catch flaws of memory, attention, and thoroughness.[27] While checklists are a bureaucratic device, they nevertheless support the surgeon in what is clearly a highly skilled and creative activity. Gawande says, "[People] require a seemingly contradictory mix of freedom and expectation—expectation to coordinate, for example, and also to measure progress toward common goals."[28] Checklists—and certain other types of bureaucracy—give employees autonomy by pushing decision-making and innovation to the periphery while still providing centrally determined guardrails.[29]

Security as Enabler

In earlier chapters I talked about the deep and surprising relationship between bureaucracy and IT. I claimed that DevOps is an extremely enabling type of bureaucracy that frees technologists to be creative and solution minded. It takes good practices, standardizes them, then automates them to make them repeatable and reliable. In doing so, it turns what would otherwise be intrusive bureaucratic ceremony into tools that engineers can use. It adopts bureaucratic mechanisms to remove toil—the dull, repetitive, nonthinking work—and lets the technologists focus on what motivates them.

To illustrate, I'll describe in some detail how DevOps handles the bureaucratic aspects of security. Because information security does require deep technical expertise that's constantly refreshed, large enterprises generally have a dedicated team of security experts who formulate security policy, engineer security solutions, test IT systems for security vulnerabilities, and respond to security incidents—those frightening moments when monitoring software indicates that a hacker is trying to or succeeding in breaking into the company's IT systems. This is the team that tells you not to use your pet monkey's name as your password, and frowns at you when you click on an email that says you've won a million dollars in the Nigerian lottery.

Security is a classic IT example of Weberian bureaucracy. The security team must know its functional area well, and its knowledge becomes even deeper over time as it accumulates experience through its role in the hierarchy. Security "dominates by knowledge," since others in the company are unlikely to have Security's deep—and important—understanding. Since keeping the company secure requires employees to behave in ways that are not natural to them, Security must formulate rules and enforce them. Their rules are viewed as an imposition by other employees—and customers, as Graeber's anecdote about dealing with his bank reveals*—and may therefore be resisted, and as a result require coercive enforcement. And because Security is carefully audited and plays a big part in many compliance regimes (for example, compliance with payment card industry requirements formalized in PCI DSS), security controls must be carefully documented.

Before DevOps, security teams would review new IT systems just before they were deployed to users and would invariably find vulnerabilities. This was a kind of bureaucratic gatekeeping that was imposed on software developers, who were eager to deploy the products of their hard work to the people who would use them. Sometimes the vulnerabilities were bugs in the code; sometimes they were a matter of required security controls that the software engineers hadn't implemented. In the government, security for a "moderately" sensitive system required 303 controls and system "enhancements."[30] There was ample opportunity for the security team to identify problems and reject the code. Their security review was about compliance and enforcement.

With DevOps, though, security experts participate earlier in the design and coding process, lending their expertise to make sure each system is secure when built. (DevOps practitioners call this "shifting left," referring to the

---

* See Chapter 1. -ed.

time sequence on a Gantt chart.) They provide reusable security software components that developers can incorporate into their code, standardizing authentication, authorization, and auditing functions, for example. They put automated guardrails in the cloud to keep an eye on what's happening in the live systems. If a developer deploys something dangerous, Security can be notified to take action or can just arrange to have it automatically disabled. Compared to their traditional gatekeeping role, these techniques put security teams in the position of enablers and contributors rather than enforcers.

What most directly takes the place of traditional enforcement is the use of automated security tests. The security team can prepare automated tests for developers to use to check their code for compliance and security. The tests can be run every time a developer makes a change to their code, and a test can report back *to the developer* immediately if it finds a problem. Sometimes the security test platform helps the developer further by providing information on how to avoid the security flaw in the future. The tests are tools, in other words, for the developers—and yet they apply Security's controls.

The result of all this enabling bureaucracy is that developers can do a better job of delivering secure code quickly. The security team acts as experts in their domain and are respected for that expertise; they no longer have a confrontational relationship with the development teams. At the same time, all of Security's objectives are met—even better than they could be through gatekeeping reviews and cranky enforcement.

Has the security bureaucracy been eliminated? Not really—the software development process is still constrained by the same security controls and still requires approval by the security authority. It's just that the rules are now automated, and the security authority has put its hierarchical powers into the automation as its proxy: they've agreed that if the code passes the automated tests, then it meets their definition of secure.

These DevOps principles work not just for security, but for virtually all aspects of IT delivery that require compliance. For example, financial controls can be implemented in the cloud by tagging cloud resources with cost-accounting labels that show which budget category should be charged and what the resource is being used for. Reports can then be generated to analyze this information along various dimensions. Automated scripts can shut down infrastructure that doesn't include such tags; the finance department can be notified automatically when spending thresholds are exceeded—you get the idea. Automated controls replace verbal troll reprimands. The IT delivery teams can move quickly and take matters into their own hands, within the constraints of the automated rules.

Automated functional testing of code is also an instructive case. One of the characteristics of bureaucracy, as I've said, is that it's self-documenting; that is, you not only comply but provide evidence that you have complied. Thus the reliance on paper forms—filling one out is not only a step in a workflow, but a way to prove that the required process has been followed simply because the paper exists. It's an audit trail.

Developers must prove that their code works and that it implements the "required" functionality. They do so by writing automated tests and showing that their code passes the tests. In the old days, tests were something used by a separate QA organization to catch programmers before they deployed faulty code—they were an excuse for angry troll foot stomping. Today, tests are a way for developers to demonstrate that their code meets requirements and complies with quality standards. It's a reversal of the bureaucracy; a way to turn a gatekeeping enforcement task into a proactive, enabling tool for developers.

Self-Service Bureaucracy

The ideal DevOps working environment is self-service, where one team never needs to wait on another to get what it needs. In IT, delivery teams used to wait for infrastructure engineers to procure and set up infrastructure for them, or for other development teams to update code they relied on. In a self-service model, they get the building blocks they need, subject to certain rules and formalities, as if they were buying cups of ramen noodles from a vending machine. The bureaucrats still play their part: they decide which brand of ramen noodles to make available in the machine—say, after checking to make sure it has the appropriate nutritional content. But the hungry customer doesn't have to place an order and wait for someone who's already eaten and therefore feels no urgency to approve it before they can slurp their noodles.*

A DevOps organization will often have a special team that creates, maintains, and manages a standard platform and set of tools for all the product teams to use. They usually build it in the cloud, where there's a great variety of tools available that can be provisioned or deprovisioned at will. Because the

---

* Note that Schwartz is back on the subject of pasta here, as in *A Seat at the Table*, though he has diversified from Italian pastas to East Asian. -ed.

platform is self-service, developers use it to speed up their work. But the platform team can also satisfy the need for bureaucratic controls by vetting the tools they make available in the platform, configuring them with security features, or tagging them with cost categories. They can fill the vending machine with only operating systems that have been security-tested, hardened, and approved; when the development teams pop their slugs into the machine, out comes compliance.

Self-service is also an elegant solution to the annoying bureaucracy of ticketing systems. Instead of launching a request into the unknown and waiting for the Heavenly Immortal of the Great Nomad from the Eight High Caves to do something about it, the software engineer in need can just help themselves from the communal punchbowl.*

Earlier (in Chapter 3) I mentioned a trend in IT toward allowing users more freedom in how they use IT systems. This too is enabling bureaucracy, as Adler notes:

> The distinction I propose to make between enabling and coercive designs of organizational systems parallels the distinction between equipment designed for usability and to enhance users' capabilities, and equipment designed to foolproof the process and to minimize reliance on users' skills.[31]

Agile Enablement

The shift from a coercive to an enabling bureaucracy is a large cultural change, as managers give up the prestige and comfort of being able to compel behavior from employees. Adler provides a few handy charts for distinguishing the designs of coercive and enabling bureaucracies.[32] The similarity of enabling principles to Agile IT principles is striking. Then again, we shouldn't really be surprised. As I explained earlier in this book, Agile frameworks provide a bureaucratic structure within which agility can be practiced. It happens to be a good—and enabling—structure. I've combined and paraphrased several of Adler's tables and added the corresponding Agile principles in Table 1.

---

* This is exactly what the Monkey King does at the Empress's party. -ed.

Table 1: Coercive versus Enabling Design (with Corresponding Agile Principles)

Coercive Design	Enabling Design	Agile Principle
Have experts design systems and management enforce them	Involve employees in design to encourage buy-in	User-centric design and full-team participation
Focus design on technical features	Focus on flexibility and enablement	Reduction of technical debt; simplicity of design
Establish clear upfront goals and design carefully to accomplish them	Test successive prototypes with employees	Iterative, incremental design
Get it right the first time so it rarely needs revision	Encourage continuous improvement through suggestions from employees	Feedback and continuous improvement
Focus on performance standards to highlight poor performance	Focus on best practices to improve performance	Blameless retrospectives; best practices built into process frameworks
Standardize systems to eliminate game-playing	Focus on end results to allow for improvisation and application of employee skills	Diversity of skills in a cross-functional team; delivering value rather than implementing requirements

Enforce management control over employees	Give employees tools and insight to control their own activities	Give teams business goals and let them self-organize to find the best way to deliver them
Systems are instructions to be followed	Systems are best-practices templates to be improved	Continuous improvement

Enabling bureaucracy turns out to be the Agile version of bureaucracy. It includes participation by the "users" of the bureaucracy, design for agility and learning, and fast feedback loops for iterative improvement. These may just sound like the best practices of nonbureaucratic organizations, but with enabling bureaucracy we're still talking about a system with well-defined accountabilities and rules that will be enforced impartially. It's bureaucracy by definition, but applied with a view toward self-service empowerment rather than punishment and control. It's no less bureaucracy for that.

TOWARD A LEARNING BUREAUCRACY

There will be those who consider us to be ridiculously frozen in time, who demand of the government the rapid introduction into our work of advanced technologies, but while it is true that laws and regulations can be altered and substituted at any moment, the same cannot be said of traditions, which is, as such, both in form and sense, immutable.

—José Saramago, *All the Names*

It is a working principle of the authorities that they do not even consider the possibility of mistakes being made. The excellent organization of the whole thing justifies that principle, which is necessary if tasks are to be performed with the utmost celerity.

—Franz Kafka, *The Trial*

Bureaucracy Goes to School

Bureaucratic rules are inflexible and impersonal—that's their nature. But that's a matter of how they're *applied*, not how they're *formulated*. There's no reason they can't be formulated based on lived experience and no reason they can't be changed often as experience teaches new lessons. In a stable environment we'd expect relatively little change; rules are composed rationally, optimized, and then stay put. In a less stable environment we expect the rules to be revisited more often and adjusted. And in the digital world, which accepts continuous change as a given, the rules—to remain "efficient" in Weber's sense—have to be adjusted more or less continuously. Not just the rules: in a changing environment, role definitions and the formal relationships between them also need to be adjusted regularly.

Agile IT approaches are designed for continuous improvement through feedback, incremental change, and retrospection. DevOps emphasizes fast feedback—each unit of work is small so that it can be finished quickly and given to employees or customers to use. Based on the results, the code can be tweaked and improved. The same idea can be applied to bureaucratic rules or indeed any practical framework for taking action in the world.

For example, if we were to apply DevOps to the goals of the Paperwork Reduction Act,* we might proceed as follows: we'd set up monitoring tools to measure how long it would take an applicant to fill out, say, an I-90 form (a green card renewal). Then, we'd code a small change to the form, deploy it, and see if it reduced the burden. If it didn't, we'd investigate why and try a different change. If it did, we'd keep the change and move on to the next. We'd learn in small steps, but continuously. Each change would be treated as a sort of hypothesis—"I believe that if we make this change it will reduce the burden"—and then tested scientifically.

Incremental adjustment of rules is the essence of a learning bureaucracy. Its rules still have the characteristics we (now that we've read Chapter 5) admire in bureaucracy. They still enforce auditable controls, generate evidence that they've been applied, and are formalized and documented so that they can be optimized for efficiency. They're still fair, and their effect is calculable. A learning bureaucracy has both the advantages of bureaucracy and the advantages of agility, strange as that might sound.

I'll use a few government examples to illustrate why bureaucracies must learn to learn, but don't think for a moment that business enterprises are different. Has anyone in your company stopped to test the hypothesis that the annual budgeting process adds enough value to justify its costs? Or that a company wouldn't get better business results by using a different, and perhaps less heavyweight, process for controlling spending? How often do you eliminate legacy bureaucracy that's no longer needed or that could be replaced now by better bureaucracy?

---

* Schwartz talked about the PRA in Chapter 2. The irony of a paperwork reduction law that increases paperwork is a bit like that of a lean sumo wrestler or bloated process like MD-102 that is supposed to improve efficiency. -ed.

PRA: Better If It Reduced Paperwork

The Paperwork Reduction Act (PRA) is a masterpiece of good intentions. Its goals are achievable and compelling. It's a noble effort to reduce bureaucratic paperwork, and its guardians in OIRA are well-meaning and diligent. Unfortunately, it doesn't work very well. The workflow mandated by the Act sounds plausible, at least, I assume, to congressional representatives sitting in the Capitol and legislating. But for Congress to ensure that the law worked well, it needed to insert a feedback and refinement mechanism that would tweak the law to improve its effectiveness.

Every year, OIRA duly reports on the impact of the PRA, as Congress requires. In 1996, when the Act and its amendments were finalized, the country's paperwork burden was 6.9 billion hours. By 2017, even under the watchful eye of the PRA enforcers, it had increased to 11.6 billion hours.[1] And that's in an era when electronic forms make possible a whaleboat-full of simplifications—for example, providing default values for input fields and saving user information to be reused from one form to another. Plenty of us government folks know from our experience exactly how the PRA gets in the way of reducing burden, as I described in Chapter 2. But in the years since 1996, with the burden continuing to increase, with a vast amount of potential digital simplification not taking place, and with government employees aware of just what is going wrong, still no one has changed the PRA's workflow.

Although Congress gets its report from OIRA every year, that report is not true *feedback*—a term that implies a cycle in which new information causes process changes which then result in new information. It's one thing to mandate that paperwork be reduced each year. It's a very different thing to figure out how. In a complex environment like the federal government, figuring out how requires the humility to listen and learn, not the hubris of thinking you can write down a bureaucratic mechanism on one piece of paper that will unfailingly reduce the number of other pieces of paper fluttering through government offices.

MD-102 and Reality

MD-102 helps DHS report to Congress and the public on the status of its projects. What it doesn't do is report on its *own* effectiveness in getting better outcomes for those projects. Since it adds considerable overhead and cost to projects, DHS should be asking: Is it successful? Do projects actually return more value to the public than they would without it? The same questions can be asked at a more granular level—Does requiring every project to have an Integrated Logistical Support Plan actually improve outcomes?

It's possible that MD-102 results in *worse* outcomes. It adds cost. It takes time and therefore delays the delivery of value. It locks in decisions that would better be made as the team learns during project execution. In effect, it requires that teams use antiquated IT delivery practices. It takes focus away from good execution and places it on documentation and a "checkbox" approach. And it leads to large, risky projects, because no one wants to go through its cumbersome process more often than necessary, so they do fewer, but bigger, projects.

I say that MD-102 doesn't report on its own effectiveness, but there's certainly anecdotal evidence that DHS should be concerned. According to the former DHS Inspector General in his testimony to Congress in May of 2019, "Most of DHS's major acquisition programs continue to cost more than expected, take longer to deploy than planned, or deliver less capability than promised."[2]* Although I don't believe those are the right success measures, they are the success measures that MD-102 was designed for.

The inspector general is understating the case—those failures include, for example, Customs and Border Protection's ACE program, primarily a software development effort begun in 2001 and finally completed seventeen years later at a cost of over $3 billion.[3] I'm choosing ACE as an example to distract you from USCIS's own distressing Transformation program, which spent a billion dollars or so before producing anything useful.

These programs were overseen using MD-102, as were all of the other troubled programs the inspector general referred to. You'd think it would be taken as a sign that MD-102 is the wrong approach, but there's a serious risk of confirmation bias. When a project succeeds, its success is attributed to MD-102. When a project fails, it's attributed to not following MD-102 carefully enough, or to gaps in MD-102 that must be remediated by adding more overhead and administrative effort.

Even for projects that are successful, DHS should still ask whether they would have been even more successful without MD-102, or with less of it. But here they face another cognitive bias. If DHS were to consider removing one of

---

* This is the same IG that put the critical fact that he was comparing a twenty-year cost to a thirty-year cost into a footnote in his report, so take his testimony with more grains of salt than perhaps he has budgeted for. -au.

the eighty-seven documents—that is, making a marginal change—it would be met with the argument that doing so could only increase the risk of the project. Since the purpose of MD-102 is to reduce risk, that would be unacceptable. The document stays.

There's no rigorous learning mechanism built into or applied to MD-102, aside from anecdotal evidence or the gut feel of its guardians and an occasional pile-on of more heavy-handed controls when something goes wrong. From the point of view of a CIO overseen by it, it seemed clear to me that many of its costs weren't justified—it could have been changed in ways that would have resulted in better outcomes for the public. I knew that in writing an ILSP, we spent our time trying to figure out how to write an ILSP that would be acceptable to the reviewers rather than making and documenting decisions that were important to a project's success. I was also pretty sure that in projecting the costs of an IT system thirty years into the future we were playing a game with numbers rather than doing anything actionable or relevant to decision-making.

The problem is not just the mechanisms of MD-102 but the fact that those mechanisms could not be tested to see whether they were valuable and to modify them to make them better. If bureaucracy is to serve as a storehouse of good practices, a kind of institutional memory, then how can it not change when its practices are found to work poorly?

MI-CIS-OIT-003

This realization led to our unusual design of MI-CIS-OIT-003, which I described earlier. Instead of requiring particular practices or workflows in the policy, we stated the goals and principles, and then referred readers to an addendum that listed what we believed to be current best practices. We wrote explicitly that although those were considered best practices at the moment, the addendum should remain a living document and should be adjusted periodically. In MI-CIS-OIT-004 we solidified that idea by saying that when a project was audited, the auditors should review the project against the goals and principles, *and also* against whatever was considered at that moment to be best practices. In other words, we tried to build a learning loop into the bureaucratic rules.

It was moderately successful. It helped us create a culture that was comfortable with change and understood that change was to be expected. On the other hand, since I left the agency, I don't think the addendum has been updated. The next time I try this experiment I'll probably strengthen its bureaucratic aspects by *requiring* that it be reevaluated and changed at least annually, and setting up a formal process for doing so. More bureaucracy here would result in more learning.

Checkmating Erosion

In *Seeing Like a State*, James Scott provides some examples where governments have used feedback and learning to overcome the loss of important detail that accompanies simplification and categorization. He talks about water management in Japan, comparing it to a game of chess. The engineer makes a move, sees how nature responds, and then determines his next move. Through this incremental, feedback-based approach the engineer "checkmates" erosion.[4]

Such an iterative process must be used, he says, in any realm where there are considerable uncertainties or complex interactions that make it hard to predict outcomes.

> Virtually any complex task involving many variables whose values and interactions cannot be accurately forecast belongs to this genre: building a house, repairing a car, perfecting a new jet engine, surgically repairing a knee, or farming a plot of land. Where the interactions involve not just the material environment but social interaction as well—building and peopling new villages or cities, organizing a revolutionary seizure of power, or collectivizing agriculture—the mind boggles at the multitude of interactions and uncertainties (as distinct from calculable risks).[5]

When rules are devised centrally or at the top of a hierarchy, they aren't based on the practical knowledge and detail that frontline experts have access to. This isn't necessarily a terrible thing—as long as the policy is tentative and continuously improved as it encounters the real world. This is no more than what Agile IT theorists have been saying—that IT is complex and uncertain, and that we therefore must take an empirical approach, inspecting and adapting, fluidly changing plans.

The California Division of Highways

Steve Kelman, a professor at the Harvard Kennedy School of Government and formerly the US government's head of procurement policy, relates another powerful example from Kevin Starr's *Golden Dreams: California in an Age of Abundance, 1950–1963*. The California Division of Highways in the 1950s, Starr says, was an almost paramilitary, bureaucratic organization, "model conformists, working in a standardized environment, paid at standardized rates, motivated by the same retirement package, living in tract housing, driving similar makes of automobiles."[6] In the early days of highways, and in their careful, systematic, bureaucratic way, they worked to improve traffic safety. They did so by generating hypotheses about what might cause accidents and what might help avoid them. Each hypothesis was carefully tested, and if they found it to be valid, they incorporated it into a rule.

For example, they experimented with signage on the highways. When they found that the typeface used on signs at the time was too small for fast-moving motorists to read, they mandated that larger text be used. When they saw that signs in all-capital letters were harder to read, they switched to mixed upper- and lowercase letters. They chose the background color of green for signs based on their experiments, and they required that the signs be lit at night. They discovered that lane divisions with bumps that caused the car to rumble were effective at keeping cars in their lanes. With each improvement, they reduced highway accidents.

Kelman speculates that bureaucracies might be even better than other organizations when it comes to learning, at least in cases where this kind of systematic inquiry is appropriate.[7] In any case, his example makes clear that the hypothesis-testing paradigm used in digital delivery is in no way counter to bureaucratic structures. Bureaucracy provides the framework, the background, against which the ingenuity of employees can be applied.

Interestingly, in the context of our discussion on motivation in the last chapter, Kelman claims that their success was due to "an evangelical zeal born of their profession and of their belief in freeways and in California's future."[8] The structure of the bureaucratic organization gave them a way to come together in a shared vision and goal.

NUMMI

Adler's study of NUMMI's car factory taught him the power of learning bureaucracies. NUMMI, a joint venture between General Motors and Toyota in Fremont, California, replaced an earlier GM factory that had—by almost any criteria—been a terrible failure. It had the lowest productivity of any GM factory, consistently poor quality, and an employee absentee rate of over 20%.[9] The NUMMI joint venture that replaced it had an absentee rate of only 2% and the highest productivity of any GM facility, twice that of its predecessor.[10]

It pulled off this miracle by instituting a highly structured bureaucracy that operated along the lines of Taylorist process improvement. It obsessed over process standardization. It broke down all of the actions of employees on the manufacturing line into their component movements, optimized them, and then required those optimized movements of all employees. No improvements were allowed unless they could be adopted across the entire organization.

What was special about NUMMI was that it made its teams of factory workers responsible for its Taylorist process improvement. The workers were trained in Toyota's techniques of work analysis, description, and process improvement. It was the workers themselves who timed their team members and proposed process improvements. Because employees didn't fear for their jobs—NUMMI guaranteed lifetime employment—they were comfortable doing so. In 1991, employees proposed over ten thousand suggestions, of which some 80% were implemented.[11]

The teams were trained to find and deal with problems as well. NUMMI's practices made it

(1) difficult to make a mistake to begin with; (2) easy to identify a problem or know when a mistake was made; (3) easy in the normal course of doing the work to notify a supervisor of the mistake or problem; and (4) consistent in what would happen next, which is that the supervisor would quickly determine what to do about it.[12]

Now that's learning and enabling bureaucracy.

As process improvements were proposed and their effectiveness was confirmed, they were then standardized across employees and teams. This had a number of benefits. It gave workers a basis for their continuous improvement, since they always had a baseline process whose efficiency they could measure. It improved safety because each process was documented and could be examined carefully for risks. Inventory control became easier for just-in-time provisioning of resources. Job rotation became easier and fairer. And finally, the entire system became more agile, because workers could quickly reskill and immediately begin improving processes. They became, over time, experts in continuous improvement.

This all took place within a traditional management hierarchy, well supplied with layers of middle management. Managers, however, were taught to view themselves as problem-solvers whose responsibility was to help the floor workers realize their process improvements. They were valued for their expertise, and it was through this expertise that they become managers. It was Weberian "domination through knowledge."[13]

Adler concluded that NUMMI was able to learn through a synergistic combination of its formal, standardized work process and various informal cultural aspects, including the facts that it cultivated broader skill sets among its employees and that it widely shared principles such as continuous improvement.[14] Just as with Amazon's fourteen leadership principles, shared values empowered employees to make decisions knowing that they would be consistent with management's intentions.

Verdict: Learning Bureaucracy Is Agile Too

A learning bureaucracy is bureaucracy as a storehouse of institutional knowledge, knowledge that is added to and refined over time. It's bureaucracy that keeps employees engaged and committed and uses their abilities to improve processes, not just their abilities to turn wrenches or fit car parts into place. It employs the more likable characteristics of Weberian bureaucracy: rules and standards that provide shared knowledge and comfort, and a hierarchy of roles that is truly meritocratic and uses the talents of its managers and workers.

Once again, the parallels with today's IT practices are notable. Both the California Division of Highways and NUMMI based their continuous improvements on hypothesis-testing—just as digital practices, often derived from Eric Ries's book *The Lean Startup*, treat system requirements as hypotheses and insist that they be tested. They both built cultures that encouraged employees to feel comfortable proposing innovations and process improvements, just as DevOps uses blameless retrospectives and supportive small-team interactions. These are not just surface similarities, but deep cultural affinities.

TOWARD A LEAN BUREAUCRACY

In relation to their systems most systematisers are like a man who builds
an enormous castle and lives in a shack close by; they do not live in their
own enormous systematic buildings.

—Søren Kierkegaard, *Journals*

No one, wise Kublai, knows better than you that the city must never be
confused with the words that describe it.

—Italo Calvino, *Invisible Cities*

Bureaucracy Adds Business Value

The sequence of activities, forms, and approvals of a bureaucratic workflow
make up a value stream, like any other. It's a manufacturing process that produces compliance, which the organization believes has value. It may or may not;
if that compliance is a product that the markets (including capital markets)
have no real desire for, or if it's too expensive to produce, then the company
should stop producing it. But a bureaucratic workflow *does* often provide business value: perhaps compliance with PCI DSS, which allows the company to
accept credit card payments; compliance with a manufacturing process that's
been finely tuned for efficiency and inventory management; compliance with
Marketing's branding guidelines, which makes the brand more valuable; or
transparency for the public into how the government is spending its money.
These products of bureaucratic activity are valuable, perhaps essential.

Even if its bureaucratic workflow is adding value, an enterprise can still
work to optimize the bureaucratic value stream by removing waste, thereby

reducing lead time. In other words, it can use the standard toolkit of the Lean disciplines—Lean Manufacturing, Lean Six Sigma, the Toyota Production System—on its bureaucratic mechanisms themselves. It can examine the steps that go toward manufacturing compliance—the documents that must be written, the meetings that must be held, the signatures that must be gathered, and the rubber stamps that must be stamped—and ask itself whether those steps are necessary, and if so, whether they can be streamlined while still producing compliance.

We can make bureaucracy lean.

Is It Possible?

Yes.

Required Waste

We've overlooked this option because we're so used to hearing the noise of politicians, press, and think tanks describing bureaucracy as "bloated" and "wasteful." But waste is not an essential characteristic of bureaucracy, if we understand waste to be activity that does not add value—in the case of bureaucracy activity that doesn't contribute to producing compliance, reducing risk, or precisely repeating optimized workflows. Once we accept that bureaucracy can add value—let's say, by ensuring fairness—then we can speak of making it lean by removing steps that don't contribute to manufacturing fairness.

There's nothing in Weber's definition that requires waste. He wanted *efficiency*, after all. The closest candidate to "required" waste in Weber's framework is the red tape of the last of his list of bureaucratic characteristics, the requirement for formal paperwork. I interpret that as the need for bureaucracy to be self-proving, a need for paper—in some cases a lot of paper—to verify that the appropriate policies were followed, that the right signatures were obtained, that the workflow directed the paper into the right inboxes and trash receptacles. Without this, bureaucracy can't do things like demonstrate compliance with regulatory frameworks.

But paper is no longer paper. In the digital age, there are better ways to produce an audit trail that shows compliance, without adding unnecessary steps.

When we find unnecessary activity in the bureaucratic value stream, we apply the Principal of Parsimony, the bureaucrat's Occam's Razor: given two processes that accomplish the same control, prefer the one that has the shortest lead time or involves the lesser effort.

The PRA Again: Noble, Silly

Back to my favorite bogeyman, the PRA. Its goal is noble: reduce burden. Here are the steps of its current process. I've borrowed some of the wording—including the revealing use of the passive voice in almost every one of the instructions—from guidance issued by the Office of Personnel Management (OPM).[1]

1. Agency employees assemble the PRA package and get it reviewed and approved internally by the agency. (Ten months.)
2. Agency employees enter the package into their internal PRA system, where it is processed by the agency's PRA coordinators. A sixty-day notice is approved. (Sixty days.)
3. The 60-day notice is published in the Federal Register. (Four days.)
4. The public has sixty days to comment. (Sixty days.)
5. The public's comments are processed, changes are made to the form, and the agency's PRA coordinators approve a 30-day notice. (Sixty days.)
6. The 30-day notice is published in the Federal Register. (Four days.)
7. An ICR (OIRA's database) package is assembled and entered into the OIRA system. This can occur in parallel with the thirty-day public comment period. (Ten days.)
8. OIRA waits until the thirty-day period ends, then analyzes the package and the public's responses. There is discussion between OIRA and the agency. In the end, OIRA issues a Notice of Action (NOA) either approving or denying the package. (Sixty days from publication of the 30-Day Notice.)

That totals 248 days for the approval process, plus the ten months at the beginning for preparation of the original package. Even that understates the total lead time, however. OIRA generally asks for changes during the passback period, and calendar time passes as the agency makes those changes and resubmits the package. Also, OIRA is chronically understaffed, so the desk officers are often delayed in assessing the package. At USCIS, we assumed eighteen months for review and approval, plus the preparation time.

The PRA's process must be followed not just for new information collections, but also for any *changes* to them, including changes intended to reduce the public burden. So, let's say we wanted to streamline the application form for replacement green cards (I-90s), intending to radically simplify it to reduce the public burden. In the past, the paper I-90 form asked applicants for pretty much all the information we already knew about them—name, address, nationality, and so on. A lot of this we *had* to ask for so we could match the paper application with the right green card in our database. But now, with an electronic application, we could associate them with the right green card when they logged in, display their old green card on the screen, ask them if anything has changed, and if not, just prepare the new one. Since about 700,000 people renew their green cards each year, this would be a considerable reduction in the public burden and much less effort and cost for the government.

With the PRA, assuming we wanted to put in the effort and cost to meet its requirements, it could still take several years before the simplification could take effect, and in that time the public would continue to be burdened. And the overhead of the PRA process creates a hurdle—a cost that has to be factored into the business case for making the improvement.

The PRA is not the leanest way to accomplish its worthy goal. I could, even with my outdated software engineering skills, delete the code for the unnecessary input fields in ten minutes; but the PRA would require me to sit, hands poised over the keyboard, for eighteen months while OIRA decided that it was okay.

I can think of a few ways to restructure the PRA's process to be more effective and leaner—at least for digital forms:

1. **A/B testing:** *If this is a form already in use*, time how long it takes applicants to fill it out (not in a laboratory setting, but as applicants are actually filling it out online). That's a baseline. Now make the proposed changes. If they reduce the burden from the baseline, then the form is automatically approved, although the agency should continue to see if it can reduce the burden still further. *If this is a new form*, require the agency to submit a simplified package justifying the data collection and have a desk officer briefly review it. Release an initial version to serve as a baseline. Then conduct experiments to reduce the burden as much as possible from the baseline.

2. **Sanity testing:** If this is a modification to an existing form and the only substantive change is that it's being simplified and the burden reduced, then it's automatically approved.

3. **Usability studies:** Require each agency to have trained usability experts who work with a selected group of users to optimize the user experience. Once this is done, the form is approved. Even though usability studies are now standard in software development, they're not part of the current PRA process.

4. **Default to yes:** The agency can go ahead and introduce the new form but must still announce it in the Federal Register. The public is invited to comment while the form's actually in use. The comments go to OIRA, and if they see something that must be corrected, they work with the agency to do so. The public isn't limited to a sixty- or ninety-day comment period, but can request changes at any time. While this risks briefly increasing the paperwork burden, it more than makes up for it by getting good changes out more quickly and avoiding lots of administrative expense and slowness.

5. **Eliminate the PRA process entirely:** But have auditors (inspectors general, for example) periodically audit the agency's information collection forms and release findings if they think a change is necessary.

Each of these replacement processes would dramatically reduce the cost and delay of the process and provide better results for the public. They would also give agencies better data to work from in reducing the public burden, as they could see how the forms are actually being used and gather exact timing information instead of using estimates prepared beforehand.

Doing and Watching

There are two ways to oversee initiatives: bottom-up, starting from the concrete details of the activities to be overseen and improvising a framework to evaluate them; or top-down, beginning with classifications, generalized rules, and consistently applied mechanisms into which the activities can be slotted. The latter is the way of traditional bureaucracy.

I've talked about the literature of bureaucracy, the novels that directly or indirectly take bureaucracy as their *subject*. There's also a style of literature that adopts bureaucracy as its *form*: a literature of "cataloguing" authors, who begin with a grand, all-inclusive structure and apply it to their subject matter—a sort of top-down approach. For example, James Joyce, in writing *Ulysses*, famously said that he wanted to write a book from which a reader could reconstruct all of Dublin on June 14, 1906. Later, with *Finnegan's Wake*, his plan was to represent the history of the entire world. Dante, in *The Inferno*, gives us a complete catalog of sins and where in the underworld they lead to. Balzac, in *The Human Comedy*, wanted to "compete with the Civil Registry" to record all of the people of France.[2]

These authors strived for completeness. They developed templates into which they could slot characters and activities. They were masterful observers and cataloguers. Their frameworks are an essential part of their works, a structuring principle for their unique view of the world.

The creators of organizational bureaucracies are often less masterful. Their *Human Comedys* are often funnier and their *Infernos* are more realistic, but their efforts to categorize and classify can result in books that are longer and denser than *Finnegan's Wake*. A great deal of bureaucratic activity in an enterprise consists of observing and classifying, ensuring that applicable rules are applied.

How much waste, in a business or a government agency, comes from people watching other people's activities to make sure they're in compliance? If you look carefully, you'll see that it's tremendous. Oversight is not just how senior leaders of an organization "look over" the progress of an investment, but is also how mechanisms are built into everyday activities to "ensure" that they stay on track. Organizations pay a high price for the risk reduction that their oversight provides.

For a given dollar of productive spending, how much is it worth spending to mitigate the risks of that dollar? Or to make sure that that dollar is spent wisely? I don't know the answer, but I'm fairly certain that many organizations are spending considerably more than a dollar to make sure each dollar is spent wisely.

Let's divide the activities of the firm, or of a unit of the firm like an IT department, into activities that are *doing* and activities that are *watching*. Doing, in IT, generally means that fingers are striking keyboards to develop software, deploy it, or test it, or plugging cables together, or calming down frustrated users (yes, I'll classify that as productive *doing*), or trying to operate Kubernetes.* Pretty

---

* Kubernetes is a piece of software that is notoriously difficult to operate. -ed.

much everything else is watching—attempting to make sure that each doing dollar is spent wisely.

Almost all the activity of managers and leaders is watching, right? We CIOs might be pounding keys on keyboards, but it's mostly for writing overcomplicated business cases and making imprecise financial projections—both of which are *watching* to make sure dollars are spent wisely. Project management is watching, as is Agile coaching and much of QA, aside from testing, which is mostly done by software developers today. Pretty much any time spent in meetings is watching. Committees, tiger teams, task forces. Enterprise architecture, defining and enforcing standards. Consultants. CMMI specialists. Time spent negotiating contracts with suppliers is watching (intended to make sure each dollar is well spent), much of Legal, all of Finance. Everything in MD-102 is watching.

Much of this watching doesn't show up in the IT budget, because "the business" is also spending a lot of time watching—sitting in status meetings, building business cases, participating in steering committees and governance processes, writing requirements documents, debating what to do about schedule slippages.* And don't forget that much of the watching is done by high-paid managers and senior executives.

I'm certainly not saying that watching is bad. I'm saying that there's a reasonable ratio between watching and doing. And if the budget needs to be cut by a marginal dollar, will it be cut from doing or watching? (Hint: an organization will need to be more "careful" with its spending if it has a dollar less, so it will probably cut two dollars from doing and add another dollar to watching).

The federal government conducts phenomenal amounts of watching. When I first joined USCIS, I met with each of my teams to learn what they did. I was introduced to about twenty-five people on the security team who, I was told, managed compliance. As mystified as I was by this, they were even more mystified by my mystification. They explained that FISMA, the Federal Information Security Management Act—obviously, you clueless new CIO—required whaleboats-worth of reporting and documentation to prove compliance. They were not security engineers—that is, they didn't devise new ways to make

---

* Schedule slippages are interesting—if schedules get behind, typically IT folks spend a lot of time in meetings to explain why and what they're going to do about it, thereby further increasing the ratio of watching to doing and slowing the project even more. -au.

systems more secure—they managed the paperwork that showed that the systems met security requirements. I'm emphatically not saying anything negative about them—I admired their skill, their expertise, and their hard work. In any case, they're watchers, and go into that category.

What if you added up watching and found that it amounted to ten dollars on every one dollar of doing? I wouldn't be surprised if that was the total in the government, where employees must also respond to frequent "data calls," undergo audits by the Inspector General and GAO, reassure the White House that they will accomplish their priorities, and read the six thousand pages of the behemothic FAR.

Controls are great. Watching is necessary. But how often do we consider their cost against their benefits? Or work to reduce the cost of the watching? That's precisely the activity of a lean bureaucracy.

Automation Again

One way to make bureaucratic controls leaner is to automate them. As rules become automated, they become fast and waste-free. They can be changed, like any code, as the organization learns. And they enable the IT delivery teams to proceed with their work rather than waiting for bureaucratic trolls to look up from their policy-writing and conduct a review. An automated bureaucracy reduces the need for red tape intended to "prove" compliance, because when compliance is enforced automatically, we can be sure it's occurred.

An example comes from the rules to ensure that procurements are conducted fairly. When a contract for IT development services ends and a new one is to replace it, the government must ensure that the incumbent vendor doesn't have unfair advantages over other bidders. There must, therefore, be a way for new vendors to become productive as quickly as the incumbent if they're selected.

In the past this need was satisfied by having the software developers write piles of documentation that could later be excavated by any incoming vendors. Among the required documents was a Version Description Document (VDD)—a list of the files that would need to be deployed each time a change was made to an IT system. With the magic of DevOps, we replaced the VDD with a deployment script, a set of automated instructions for deploying the system. The script included—as the VDD did—all the necessary information about what files had to be deployed. But it was even better at meeting the procurement objective, since both the incumbent contractor and an incoming contractor could simply push a button to run the script, rather than reading a set of instructions. This script was simply an artifact of the DevOps process; it didn't add any extra work or cost.

In fact, we can reduce our cost of watching in general by automating any parts of it that are best done without human intervention. In addition to security enforcement, we can automate status reporting, many financial controls, and even the production of many MD-102 artifacts. Some federal agencies have even begun producing automated reports that demonstrate FISMA compliance, so that the twenty-five compliance experts can focus more on ensuring security rather than documenting controls.

Kicking MD-102

Time for a few more kicks at MD-102, my bureaucratic strawman. Among its eighty-seven documents are many that are designed more for building Coast Guard cutters or helicopters used at the Mexican border than for overseeing IT system delivery. Other documents just repeat information from earlier ones. The cost of complying with MD-102 is even higher than it might seem, because whenever plans change, text might need to be updated in a number of documents, which then must be put through the approval workflow again. There are some documents that might—in some bureaucrat's fantasies—be imagined to help control the project, but the cost to prepare them is far greater than the anticipated benefit, especially since every project must use the same template, whether its sections are relevant or not. Remember the sign-out sheet from the corkboard example, which applies to forgetful and nonforgetful people alike.

The piles of paperwork make the oversight even *less* effective, because important points are lost in the information glut and because the overseers don't really have time to read it all. Their reviews wind up focused on whether there's anything missing, rather than on the content itself. For example, in one of the document templates, we were asked to propose a goal for the uptime of one of our IT systems. We naturally chose a goal that would be easy to hit, something like 94%. That's absurd—mission-critical systems need something more on the order of 99.9% uptime. But no one questioned it, presumably because we'd filled something into the blank space in the template.

The difficulty with a process like MD-102's is its emphasis on completeness. That makes sense; its assumption, probably valid, is that project teams often forget to plan for things that turn out to be important later. Writing the document forces the project teams to think ahead. But how valuable is that, really? Events they don't plan for will still turn up by surprise; it's impossible to foresee everything in such complex undertakings. On the other hand, the detailed planning effort is often wasted, because not all of the "expected surprises" will occur. MD-102's documents turn what should be a checklist (Q: Did you consider logistical support? A: Yes) into a game of devising something clever and wordy to write in a template section (Q: Describe your Integrated Logistical Support Plan. A: Objective consideration of contemporary phenomena compels the conclusion that logistical support necessitates integrated planning wherewith . . .).

For example, take the requirement that project teams write a CONOPS (Concept of Operations):

> The content of the CONOPS includes a description of the operations processes and associated roles and responsibilities of operators. It addresses the full Doctrine, Organization, Training, Materiel, Leadership, Personnel and Facilities (DOTMLPF) and Regulations/Grants (RG) spectrum.[3]

Now imagine writing that for a simple software delivery project, and the creativity it takes to come up with something relevant about your facilities, materiel, doctrine, and regulations/grants. Worse than that, writing something that addresses your *full* doctrine or organization. Is your "full" doctrine really important to this particular project? When MD-102 tries valiantly to capture everything that might turn out to be important, it places a burden on *every* project, whether facilities and materiel are relevant or not.

Often, in fighting requirements like this, I'd be asked something along the lines of: "Okay, it might not be especially important for an IT project, but how can it hurt? It just might turn up something useful." Yes, it hurts. It hurts a lot. It's waste. In this case, waste of taxpayer money, but it could be waste of a business's resources, a reduction of the net return on an investment—and always, a waste of that critical resource, time.

Ideas like requiring teams to address their "full" doctrine could only survive in an environment that does not consider the cost of its bureaucracy. MD-102 seems to assume that no price is too high to pay for mitigating risk. Even if we accept that principle, paying $2 to mitigate a risk where $1 would do makes Khepri mad.

Analysis of Alternatives

The best way for me to show how bureaucracy can be made leaner is to take a close look at the MD-102 Analysis of Alternatives document. Here's its description:

> An Analysis of Alternatives (AoA) is an analytical comparison of the operational effectiveness and other benefits, suitability, and risk of alternatives that satisfy established capability needs. Initially, the AoA process typically explores numerous conceptual solutions across DOT-MLPF/RG with the goal of identifying the most promising options to achieve the desired capabilities, thereby guiding the Concept Refinement Phase.[4]

In other words, the AoA must describe a broad range of options that were considered for meeting the mission need, and then explain why one of them was chosen over the others. Now, it is certainly important that the project team consider a range of possible solutions across DOTMLPF/RG (which is one of the few acronyms I've ever encountered that cannot possibly have a pronunciation). But much of what gets written in an AoA is a detailed description of possible solutions that obviously will not work, only to arrive at the conclusion that they will obviously not work. Here's the template we were to use in writing an AoA:

Executive Summary
Provide a brief (one to two page) summary of the Analysis of Alternatives/ Alternatives Analysis. Highlight the salient points of each section in the document.

Revision Summary (if applicable)
The Revision Summary should provide a bulleted high-level description of major changes.

Section 1: Introduction
1.1 Background
Summarize the relevant studies/analyses that were accomplished prior to initiating the AoA/AA process. Reference the ADE-1 Acquisition

Decision Memorandum, Mission Need Statement, CONOPS and any approved Exit Criteria. Identify (if applicable) any related science and technology research projects or activities.

1.2 Purpose
The purpose of this document is to record the results of the Analysis of Alternatives/Alternatives Analysis and identify the optimal method of satisfying an identified mission capability gap.

1.3 Scope
Describe, in broad terms, the nature of the possible alternative solutions to be considered. Identify any constraints on alternatives identified by the Mission Need Statement (MNS), Capability Development Plan (CDP), and/or Concept of Operations document (CONOPS).

1.4 Study Team/Organization
Outline the AoA/AA study organization and management approach. Provide short summaries (one paragraph apiece) on the qualifications and experience of the study director and key personnel. The program office may provide support to the study team, but the responsibility for the performance of the AoA must not be assigned to the program manager, and the study team members should not reside in the program office, with the exception of Subject Matter Experts which can be consulted on an "as needed" basis.

1.5 AoA/AA Review Process
This section describes the planned oversight and review process for the AoA/AA. The review process should comply with the review and approval section of this guide as well as Component requirements.

Section 2: Ground rules and assumptions
2.1 Scenarios
Describe the scenarios for employment of the alternatives. The scenarios should be derived from the CONOPS and augmented by more detailed and intelligence products as appropriate.

2.2 Threats

Identify the threats to which the alternative will be exposed and/or be required to counter as per the CONOPS.

2.3 Environment

Describe any environmental factors that may impact operations (e.g., climate, weather, or terrain) based on the CONOPS.

2.4 Assumptions

Identify the most significant (i.e. fundamental) assumptions made in the course of the analysis and any potential impact on the results. The description of these assumptions should be at a very high level for the items with the most influence on the Analysis.

2.5 Constraints

Identify any constraints or limitations of the analysis and identify any potential impact on the results.

Section 3: Alternatives

3.1 Description of Alternatives

Identify and provide a detailed description of each possible alternative that was analyzed. Provide a table with a side-by-side comparison of the alternatives, if possible. Identify the legacy baseline (current system and its funded improvements) that is being replaced, if applicable. Include a discussion of the role Doctrine, Organization, Training, Leadership, Materiel, Personnel, Facilities (DOTLMPF) and Statutes, Regulations and Grants (SRG) played in the selection of alternatives, if significantly different/changed from the MNS discussion.

3.2 Non-viable Alternatives

Identify any initially-identified alternatives that were not included in this analysis and describe the rationale for non-selection.

3.3 Operational Concepts (CONOPS)

Describe the details of the peacetime, contingency, and emergency employment of the alternative. They should include basing and deployment concepts including the numbers of systems required for each alternative.

3.4 Support Concepts

Describe the support concepts relevant to the analysis to include plans for training, maintenance, supply support, use of Performance Based Logistics, etc.

3.5 Interoperability Concepts.

Describe interoperability issues, if applicable.

Section 4: Determination of effectiveness measures

This section describes the hierarchy of metrics selected to assess the relative effectiveness of the alternatives.

4.1 Mission Tasks

Mission tasks are usually expressed in terms of the general tasks needing to be performed to correct the identified gaps, or to obtain the needed capability.

4.2 Measures of Effectiveness

Measures of Effectiveness (MOEs) are the first step in the AoA metrics process. They describe the mission utility of the capability in operationally meaningful terms. They typically derive from detailed operational analyses and are qualitative in nature.

4.3 Measures of Performance

A Measure of Performance (MOP) is a quantitative measure of a system characteristic (e.g. range, speed, logistics footprint, etc.) chosen to support one or more MOEs. Measures of Performance may, in turn, be linked to Key Performance Parameters (KPPs), Critical Operational Issues (COIs), or other parameters in the MNS, ORD, TEMP, and contract system specification.

Section 5: Methodology
5.1 Models, Simulations and Source Data

Describe any models, simulations, or other analytical tools used during the course of the analysis. Describe each tool's capabilities, limitations, and sources of input data.

5.2 Operational Effectiveness Analysis

Fully describe the methodology to be used to determine the relative operational effectiveness of each of the alternatives.

5.3 Cost Analysis

Briefly summarize the techniques and data sources used in development of the LCCE, e.g., indexes, parametrics, cost estimating relationships and models, learning curves, etc. The LCCE should be attached to the AoA/AA as an appendix. If a Cost-Benefit Analysis (CBA) is required (e.g., for Capital Planning and Investment Control), briefly summarize the techniques and data sources for this information.

5.4 Cost-Effectiveness Analysis Approach

This section is the heart of the AoA/AA. It should include a complete description of the approach to relate cost and effectiveness in order to determine the best alternative.

5.5 Sensitivity Analysis

Describe how sensitivity analysis on both cost and effectiveness measures will be performed to determine which measures have the greatest effect on a given alternative.

5.6 Schedule

Include a study schedule showing the major milestones planned for the effort.

Section 6: Analysis Results

Provide an objective presentation of the results of the analysis. Results should be shown in tabular or graphical form to clearly show differences in the results for each analyzed alternative.

Section 7: Recommended Alternative and Rationale

Provide the recommended alternative and provide the detailed rationale for this recommendation, based on analytic results. Identify key parameters and conditions that drove the selection and may impact the acquisition.

Appendices:

(A) LCCE

(B) References

Knights of Occam—prepare your weapons! We'll take our razors to the AoA template.

It starts with an executive summary, which is necessary only because the rest of the document is so long. Slash! There follows a background section, which requires repeating information that was in previous documents like the CONOPS. Slash! Then comes a particularly delightful section explaining the purpose of the AoA, which presumably is the same for every AoA. It even says right there in the template what the purpose is, yet it must be written into every AoA document. Slash! A scope section then repeats what was written in previous documents. Slash! Next, sections on the team that wrote the AoA and the team that reviewed it. Relevant for anything but finger pointing?

Now it asks us to document our assumptions, including the impact of the weather and the terrain on our software system. Yes, really. A good opportunity for creative writing—that's rare in federal bureaucracy. Khepri, keep the rain from us!

To the meat of it. We'll document the alternatives we considered, including the ones that were not viable. So, for our payroll software system, we'll write about how we considered having a team of monkeys in a cage calculate payroll figures, but decided it wasn't viable because of our lack of bananas. This section includes yet another recapitulation of the CONOPS (Section 3.3). We'll also describe our concepts for support and interoperability. ("We will support the software by fixing the bugs. The system will interoperate with our other systems." And then shovel in the stuff about objective considerations compelling various conclusions.)

Next we're asked the legitimate question of how we'll know which alternative is best, and to formulate MOPs and MOEs (Measure of Performance and Measure of Effectivness, respectively) that by coincidence prove that the alternative we selected is better than the others. I believe that Section 4.1 is a repeat of Section 2.1 because I'm not sure how to distinguish between the "tasks" and the usage "scenarios" for my proposed banana-tracking software system.

Now we describe our analysis methodology. Interestingly, to do so we include Section 5.2, a description of a completely separate document (the LCCE), and in 5.5 a description of the schedule for the project, which does not seem especially relevant to our analysis methodology and anyway is covered in other documents. Section 5.3's template content seems to give away the whole point: our methodology was to weigh the costs versus the benefits of each solution.

Finally, we write the results of our analysis, and then, in the next section, which alternative we chose and our rationale for it. I think in most cases we choose based on the results of the analysis, and the rationale for it is the analysis. So, Section 7 probably says exactly that.

Sarcasm and joking aside—there's very little wrong with the template. It makes sense. It's a very complete list of the things one should think about in analyzing alternatives. But it cost us about $3 million to prepare one each time we did it, contracting it out to a specialist firm, and it took at least as long as gestating two human babies in sequence. Here's a new version of the template I've concocted:

1.1 Name of Program
State the name of the program.

1.2 Analysis of Alternatives
Describe the alternatives you considered, the choice you made, and your rationale. Make sure you have considered any of the following that are relevant: the terrain, the facilities, the inventory of bananas, etc. Please be brief.

I think that more or less covers the AoA's intent, and it would encourage the program team to write only what pertains to their decision. It would be considerably leaner. When we tailored MD-102 down to fifteen documents and two (online) gate reviews rather than eleven, I don't believe that we sacrificed any control. Our tailoring plan showed why we thought our simplified version fully met the intent of MD-102, and in fact met the intent better than MD-102 itself.

Centralizing Subtleties

Within our component agency of DHS, we were all more or less familiar with everything our documents talked about. But we weren't the intended audience for the documents: the DHS oversight body (the ARB) was, and they were much further removed from the day-to-day activities and trade-offs our mission involved. The documents, therefore, had to lay out in detail many things that could have been communicated much more succinctly if the readers had been more familiar with the context.

That is to say, the documents were bloated partly because oversight was centralized. Centralization and bureaucratic waste are related. A new principle akin to Occam's Razor might be Occam's Centrifugal Whirl, a principle of spinning decisions out to the periphery.

The Analysis of Alternatives conceals another trade-off: that between governance and management. MD-102 is governance: it enforces rules on project teams. An alternative is to *manage* the project teams—that is, to charge managers with making sure that employees consider all of the DOTMPLF/RG/Bs* and any other necessary alphabet letters rather than making the document template do all the work. Implicit in the AoA template is an unwillingness to trust managers to manage their employees.

The more that trust is devolved, the leaner the document can be, because there's less to "enforce" from the center. In fact, it seems like the AoA template takes a hesitant step in that direction, because it asks who was involved in approving the plan. If it followed through on that idea—validated that trusted managers had done the approving and that therefore the template didn't need to include the team's entire thought process—then it could be made leaner.

Verdict: Blubber, Away

I see no reason we can't make bureaucracy lean. We just need to agree on its control objectives and then find the leanest way to meet those objectives. Automation is a great help, but the entire Lean playbook is available to us.

In my experience it is this lack of leanness that is one of the greatest frustrations in a bureaucracy. When we have to fill out pointless forms, lose ourselves in piles of red tape, answer the irrelevant questions of customer service reps on

---

* I believe Schwartz has added the "B" at the end to represent "bananas." -ed.

the phone who have to follow their scripts, get sign-offs from people who don't know anything about what they are signing off on . . . these are the things about bureaucracy that send us reeling around the Palace of Dreams,*† crying out to Khepri for a paper shredder.

---

* Ismail Kadare's novel about bureaucracy, mentioned in Chapter 4. -ed.

† Yes, the reader can remember back to Chapter 4. -au.

BUREAUCRACIES OF METRICS

The falseness of a judgment is for us not necessarily an objection to a judgment. . . . The question is to what extent it is life-promoting, life-preserving, species-preserving, perhaps even species-cultivating.
—Friedrich Nietzsche, *On the Prejudices of Philosophers*

Never look for your work in one place, then, and your progress in another.
—Epictetus, *Discourses*

A Chapter of Warning and Whining*†‡§

Weber assumed that organizing scientifically meant taking a legal-rational approach, with well-thought-out, impersonal rules and specialized, hierarchical roles. But today's management books advise leaders to control their organizations, at least in part, through metrics—to select performance indicators for employees to focus on, set targets, and then give employees freedom to improvise ways to achieve them. The metrics-based approach has become more

---

* This chapter is a digression on how metrics, as well as rules, can be bureaucratic. It can safely be skipped if that is not a topic of interest. -ed.

† No it cannot. This chapter is essential. It makes the crucial point that even when we try to avoid bureaucracy, we wind up creating a control mechanism that is more or less equivalent to it. -au.

‡ It is Exothermic Press's policy to inform busy readers of what sections they may safely skip. -ed.

§ Please read the chapter. -au.

popular as companies strive to be more "data-driven," as software tools make it easier to harvest insights from data, and as so-called unicorn technology companies, largely metric-driven, succeed spectacularly.

In *Measure What Matters: How Google, Bono, and the Gates Foundation Rock the World with OKRs,* venture capitalist John Doerr recommends that companies organize their activities around *objectives and key results* (OKRs). Objectives are set by senior leaders and cascaded through the organizational chart; key results are chosen by employees in collaboration with their managers to support those objectives. OKRs, in Doerr's view, give clarity and focus to everyone's efforts, provide an objective and meaningful way to gauge progress, and rock the world.[1]

Even companies and public sector organizations that don't specifically use OKRs increasingly insist that their employees deliver measurable results and use quantitative indicators to report on their success. Management theorist Peter Drucker's claim that what gets measured gets managed[2] has become a leadership cliché, and Douglas Hubbard's book *How to Measure Anything,* as its title suggests, brings the happy news that measurement is always possible.*

The metrical approach at first appears to be an alternative to bureaucracy, since it frees employees to use their creativity in finding ways to meet their targets. But in fact, as I'll show, the culture of metrics and the deep faith it inspires merely qualify as a new kind of hyperbureaucracy,[3] *rational-metrical* rather than *rational-legal,* if you will, where control by rules is replaced with control by metrics. As such, it shares many of traditional bureaucracy's advantages and disadvantages. Again, that is not to say that it is bad, simply that it is—like traditional bureaucracy—a control paradigm based on rationalizing employees' activities.

Rational-Metrical Bureaucracy

In our new world of rational-metrical bureaucracy, employees who want to justify their performance cite metrics. Resumes are virtually required to include quantitative indicators of success. It's not enough to raise employee morale; that morale increase must be measured in an employee net promoter score or

---

* Fortunately, business strategy rarely requires that we simultaneously measure the position and momentum of a subatomic particle. -au.

some other happiness indicator. Customers can't just be elated, they must be measurably elated.

Any cascade of measures and targets requires a hierarchy and division of labor just as a traditional bureaucracy does. Targets are broken into subtargets that apply to each employee's area of accountability, based on the location of their little circle on the organizational chart. The logic with which responsibilities are distributed might be different from that in traditional bureaucracy—the structuring principle is often nonfunctional and more product oriented—but nevertheless the delineation of responsibilities must be clear if each manager is to have ownership over accomplishing their own metrical objectives.

Willmot takes Google, Doerr's case study for the use of OKRs, as an example. The CEO of Google, he tells us, "is reported to have said that the goal of the company is to 'use "metrics of performance" to "systematize" every aspect of its operations.'"[4] "Systematizing every aspect" certainly sounds Weberian. Although Google became famous for its "20% time," by which employees were encouraged to spend one day a week working on new ideas outside their normal tasks, that time is now increasingly subject to audit and performance measurement, and their ideas must be entered into a shared database.[5] "Google's operation," Willmot adds, "is accompanied by a specialized division of labor and many recognizable features of bureaucratic governance."[6] Many of us are familiar with Google's innovations in the division of labor, such as their Site Reliability (SRE) role, which has become common across the IT world.

Graeber sees the metrical trend as an increasing pivot toward pleasing shareholders.[7] As a result of it, entire organizations become focused on "producing" numbers. But the focus on metrics has now spread to everything we do:

> It set the stage for the process whereby the bureaucratic techniques (performance reviews, focus groups, time allocation surveys . . .) developed in financial and corporate circles came to invade the rest of society— education, science, government—and eventually, to pervade almost every aspect of everyday life.[8]

Impressive Numbers

Just as Weberian bureaucracy was considered the underpinning of the modern age, metrical bureaucracy is coming to be seen as the underpinning of the digital age. But a machine driven by numbers can come to seem as faceless and mindless as a traditional bureaucracy.

I've just come from a presentation by a management consulting firm. It was marvelous how many measurements appeared on each of their slides: percentages, dollars and euros, ratios, net promoter scores—the numbers shown in bold text spattered over the PowerPoint presentation. Measured in terms of efficiency (numbers per slide, I guess) or productivity (total number of characters in bolded text) the presentation seemed to rate well, though I couldn't help feeling that its rigor was more the rigor of an Integrated Logistical Support Plan.

The metric has become the message, and the medium.*† It's not hard to find metrics; they're on a dashboard. But it's become hard to find the dashboard, we have so many of them. And it's hard to sort through the noise of so many metrics and compare them pineapples-to-pineapples—the noise is overwhelming, the units noncomparable. Who wins when a four-hundred-pound sumo wrestler goes up against Tolstoy's twelve-hundred-page book?‡ Fine to say you don't know, but pity the sumo wrestler, trying to meet his annual goal for pages-per-bout, cascaded from a sumo league goal of increasing literacy among lemmings.

Let's compare metrical-rational bureaucracy item by item to the disadvantages of bureaucracy from Chapter 4: "Why Bureaucracy Is Bad."

1: Surprise!—It's Inefficient

The trouble with metrical bureaucracy is that chaos monkeys find themselves pinned beneath mountains of data.§ While we've been having nightmares about piles of paperwork, the trolls have been stealthily replacing them with piles of measurement data.

As with classical bureaucracy, metrical bureaucracy can inadvertently work against efficiency. To begin with, there's the cost of the metrics them-

---

* A reference to Marshall McLuhan's famous statement about the media: "The medium is the message." -ed.

† Dear -ed.: If it's a famous statement, why do you need to footnote it? -au.

‡ The answer's probably "whale brain," their least common denominator. -au.

§ Another foreshadowing reference to the Monkey King in Chapter 12 pinned under a mountain by the angry gods. -ed.

selves: gathering them, organizing them, reviewing them, and formulating action plans to address them. "Metric fixation leads to a diversion of resources away from frontline producers toward managers, administrators, and those who gather and manipulate data," Muller says.[9] It diverts effort from doing to watching—reporting, meetings, documentation, and dissemination of data take time from actually giving customers what they need.[10] Spreadsheets and fancy graphs may just be creating an illusion of rigor and depth.

Metrics can be effective for diagnosing problems and finding improvement opportunities. The problem is that they're often collected across the board, even in places where they won't lead to actionable insights. Again, the parallel with classic bureaucracy is noteworthy: in my corkboard example, the sign-out process was wasteful because it applied to all employees, not just the forgetful ones. There are diminishing returns to metric collection; sooner or later the marginal cost of recording and analyzing a datum exceeds its benefit.[11] Unfortunately, as employees find ways to game their metrics, new metrics must be added to control for that gaming, adding to the cost and flood of data.[12]

Budgets are a traditional way for organizations to manage to metrics. Subbudgets are passed down through the hierarchy, and each manager is held to keeping their unit's spending below the amount they are given. But controlling performance through budgets poses some difficulties. First of all, budgeting is enormously expensive—companies spend an average of twenty-five thousand person-days per billion dollars of revenue on it.[13] Second, spending caps can leave business value on the table, for example if incremental spending in IT could have increased revenue or reduced costs in other parts of the enterprise. Third, it leads to a sense of entitlement—if you have the budget, no one can stop you from spending it. Fourth, it leads to wild spending sprees at the end of the fiscal year so that the budget will not be reduced in the next year. Fifth, there's the inefficient and demoralizing gaming that takes place in the budgeting process, where managers ask for more money than they need, knowing that it will later be reduced.

When metrics assume an outsized importance to a company, the special skills and knowledge of line employees can be underused, since objectives are set by managers who are at some distance from the action:

> Front-line service providers—often, relatively high status, professionals or "knowledge workers"—end up regulating and disciplining themselves in line with centrally determined performance metrics and targets that

are designed and monitored by technical specialists who are relatively detached from the formal authority hierarchy insofar as they are located within specialist units directly responsible to governing elites.[14]

2: Its Goals Are Displaced

Just as classic bureaucracy leads employees to focus on the rules rather than their intentions, metrical bureaucracy can result in *surrogation*, the tendency to focus on the metrics rather than their ultimate objectives.[15] In practice, metrics result in gaming, perhaps through a hyperfocus on what is being measured to the exclusion of all else, or perhaps through *creaming*—the practice of only accepting tasks that will improve the metric. Studies of pay-for-performance medical programs, for example, note that they "can reward only what can be measured and attributed, a limitation that can lead to less holistic care and inappropriate concentration of the doctor's gaze on what can be measured rather than what is important."[16]

In "Don't Let Metrics Undermine Your Business," Harris and Tayler cite Wells Fargo's debacle in which 3.5 million accounts were opened without the customers' authorization. Wells was using a cross-selling metric to track its progress against a strategic objective of deepening relationships with customers. Unfortunately, the metric itself became the objective, and the company wound up accomplishing the opposite of the strategic goal that inspired it.[17]

When a window tax was instituted in England in 1696 and later in France during the revolution, the result was unfortunately predictable. The tax was intended to be progressive, based on an expectation that houses with more windows would be larger and would belong to richer folks. Unfortunately, the revenue brought in by the tax decreased from year to year as property owners bricked over their windows and new houses were constructed with fewer openings. The airless homes inevitably led to both health problems . . . and tax rate increases, as the tax failed to raise the expected revenue.[18]

3: It Stifles Innovation

While metrical bureaucracies appear to leave employees free to innovate, it's not clear that they do so in practice. For one thing, the uncertainty surrounding innovation makes it risky for those who are determined to hit their predetermined goals. For another, targets are not likely to require innovation, since it would be unfair to the employee to set a goal that stretched far enough to include anything radically new. Employees are also less likely to innovate in any way that is outside the scope of their critical metrics, since that would divert their attention from what they're held responsible for.

Metrics also tend to be oriented toward the short term, while innovation's results usually appear only in the long term.[19] A metric must be accompanied by a way to continually track progress—that's their point—so a metric that is primarily affected by the periodic breakthroughs typical in innovation is largely useless when used for day-to-day control. In fact, trying to "control" innovation through metrics or any other tactic is likely to be ineffective; innovation targets are tantamount to requiring employees to have creative ideas at a particular pace.

4: It Fosters Blind Spots

Just as rule-based bureaucracy causes "professional deformities" that lead employees to resist adapting or reinterpreting rules when necessary, metrical bureaucracy creates blind spots by avoiding goals that are important but difficult to measure. The result is that we find ourselves controlling employee behavior to accomplish the wrong things.

Choosing only easy-to-measure goals is understandable given that there's a cost to measure results, in time if not directly in dollars. Most of us intend to do a good job, regardless of what our measures say, so when it's in our power we'll opt for goals that take less fuss to measure—we're mostly going to ignore them and do what's right anyway. It's more of a problem when the easier-to-measure goals we select divert our efforts from a real goal whose success is too much trouble to evaluate.

These blind spots of metrical bureaucracy have already been thoroughly satirized, so I'll just point to some of the "laws" that others have formulated:

> The **McNamara Fallacy** is the mistake of making decisions based only
> on quantitative factors and ignoring all others. It was identified by Rob-
> ert McNamara, the US Secretary of Defense, during the Kennedy and
> Johnson administrations, and refers to mistakes he and his fellow "best
> and brightest"* advisors made during the war in Vietnam, particularly

---

* McNamara and other policy makers during the Vietnam war are the subject of David Halberstam's book *The Best and the Brightest*. -ed.

declaring that the war was going well based on the count of dead bodies ("body bags") rather than considering less tangible factors like strategy, leadership, group cohesion, morale, and motivation.[20]

Goodhart's Law, named for economist Charles Goodhart, tells us that when a measure becomes a target it stops being a good measure. His original framing was that "any observed statistical regularity will tend to collapse once pressure is placed upon it for control purposes."[21] It doesn't quite say that observing a metric changes it, though the analogy to quantum mechanics is tempting, but that turning it into a goal rather than using it for diagnosis causes it to lose its meaning.

Newton's Flaming Laser Sword, also known as **Alder's Razor**, is the principle that what cannot be settled by experiment is not worth debating. It's a principle of parsimony, like Occam's Razor, but it shears away any ideas whose effects are not observable and measurable. It's a broader philosophical version of "what gets measured can be managed"; in the world of management science, nonmeasurables are nonrelevant. But is that nonreasonable?

The **Streetlight Effect** is the well-known absurdity illustrated in many stories, including this one about Hoja Nasruddin, a Turkish satirist, Sufi wise man, subject of thousands of stories, and one of my favorite trickster characters:

> Mulla had lost his ring in the living room. He searched for it for a while, but since he could not find it, he went out into the yard and began to look there. His wife, who saw what he was doing, asked: "Mulla, you lost your ring in the room, why are you looking for it in the yard?" Mulla stroked his beard and said: "The room is too dark and I can't see very well. I came out to the courtyard to look for my ring because there is much more light out here."[22]

The point is that we're tempted to choose metrics that we can measure rather than the things we really care about, which might be more difficult to measure.

What we can call **Scott's Law**, introduced in *Seeing Like a State*, is a variant on the streetlight effect: it's his observation that there is a "strong incentive to prefer precise and standardizable measures to highly accurate ones."[23]

Gresham's Law, named for Sir Thomas Gresham, a sixteenth-century financier, is an economic principle that bad money tends to drive out good money. James Q. Wilson gives us a variant that he says applies to many government bureaus: "Work that produces measurable outcomes tends to drive out work that produces unmeasurable outcomes."[24]

5: It Dehumanizes

An obsession with metrics can lead us to simplify human behavior into numbers. Bogsnes observes that "most merit or performance-based pay plans share two attributes: they absorb vast amounts of management time and resources, and they make everybody unhappy."[25] Human beings and their actions are nuanced. But just as classical bureaucracy tries to turn humans into executors of algorithms, metrical bureaucracies may try to represent human behavior in numbers. Either way, bureaucracy can be dehumanizing.

Promoters of performance measurement argue that they aren't judging employees personally, but merely judging their performance. This is deliberately and insultingly naive. Chances are good employees are doing their best to be successful. So, if you say their "performance" is not adequate, you're saying that they are not adequate. And if they're not trying hard, then you as a manager should reflect on why.

I'm going to whine a bit now. I entered the government with enthusiasm and energy. In my first year I accomplished what many considered to be startlingly impressive. At the end of the year, I was assessed according to the government's official performance management system for senior executives. It's a pretty good one—I mean, I can't really quarrel with the categories of the assessment. Here they are: Principled, Effective Communicator, Performance Centered, Diversity Advocate, Highly Collaborative, Nimble and Innovative, Steward of Public Resources, and People Centered. Not bad, right? My manager rated me on a scale of 1–100 in each of these areas and then combined those into a single number by some weighting algorithm.

I scored quite well, a 96, which meant that I'd "achieved excellence." But why not 100? I told you, I'm an overachiever, and arrogant to boot. I couldn't figure out where I'd gone wrong.

The next year I thought I'd done even better. Unfortunately, that year I had a different manager and when she ran her calculation and totaled up my results, they came to only 92. I was told that it didn't matter, since I'd still "achieved excellence." But I wanted to understand what I'd done that wasn't as good as in my first year.

When I looked at the evaluations my middle managers were giving their employees (these were done on a different scale), I saw something amazing: about 85% of their employees were getting the highest rating possible. I questioned a few of them. "Last year I gave them a lower rating and the union protested" or "Last year I gave them a lower rating and they escalated it to my manager, who overrode my decision."

Some organizations solve this rating inflation problem by enforcing a bell curve, insisting that a certain percentage of each manager's employees fall into each rating category. Does that really solve the problem? Is there truly a bell curve in performance? How do you know? And with a small sample size (the manager's direct reports) why would you think that a bell curve would be represented? It seems like shaky math.

Yes, yes, I know that in some cases managers need to prepare a case to fire a Royal Fool, and it will have to be an objective case, so they need to have a formal performance management system. And yes, you can argue that the problem in the cases above is that the rating was not objective—that my managers were making up numbers that weren't tied to a concrete objective I could have achieved. Maybe. But those precise-sounding ratings of 92 and 96 made me feel a bit of metaphysical pathos, to be honest.

6: It Oversimplifies

Science understands the world by simplifying and abstracting away details, at least temporarily. As Scott says, "the assumption is that there are a small number of principles that you can discern by looking at things in their pure state," and then trying to put those principles together in more complex ways if possible.[26] This has led to scientist jokes that "assume a spherical cow".

It is told in many variants, including a joke about a physicist who said he could predict the winner of any race provided it involved spherical horses moving through a vacuum or a physicist whose solution to a poultry farm's egg-production problems began, "Postulate a spherical chicken . . ."[27]

There's also that chemical substance, in high demand by physicists, called unobtanium (also known as *handwavium* and *hardtofindium*).

Just as legal-bureaucratic rules have triggers based on membership in simplified categories, metrics simplify complex and nuanced business results so that senior leaders can process them. A bureaucratic rule might simplify the world into "applicants" who will all be treated alike, even though their circumstances differ in many other ways. A business metric might be a simplified "summary" of a measure, like "average processing time" for immigration applications. But such a simplification neglects the distribution and variance of processing times, and of course leaves out quality, customer service, cost, and all sorts of other factors that are usually relevant. In any case, the idea that an average is always a good measure of the central tendency of a variable is widespread and misleading.

Such simplification may be necessary, though, for as Muller says,

> those at the top face to a greater degree than most of us a cognitive constraint that confronts all of us: making decisions despite having limited time and ability to deal with information overload. Metrics are a tempting means of dealing with this "bounded rationality," and engaging with matters beyond one's comprehension.[28]

But even if simplification is necessary for understanding the state of the enterprise at a given moment, it might not be effective when it's used for everyday decisions. Graeber's point applies to both legal and metrical bureaucracies:

> Bureaucratic knowledge is all about schematization. In practice, bureaucratic procedure invariably means ignoring all the subtleties of real social existence and reducing everything to preconceived mechanical or statistical formulae. . . . It is a matter of applying very simple pre-existing templates to complex and often ambiguous situations.[29]

As an example, I was in a meeting today to plan a small conference. We were holding a retrospective to see what had worked last year and what we could improve, and the primary data we had before us was the attendees' ratings on each of the last conference's sessions. They were on a scale from one to five; now we were looking at the average rating for each session.

The meeting organizer told us that the target for the conference was a rating of 4.25, and since our average was 4.27, we were above target. My thought: How was that target chosen and how had it driven any behaviors? We probably always strive for a 5.0, right? Since we aren't deliberately trying to find sessions that would score 4.25, the target was irrelevant.

One planner noted something strange about the numbers: he had spoken to a number of people who'd complained about one of the sessions, yet its score was high. Another session had blown us all away, but its score was lower. Did the ratings really depend on the quality of the sessions? The poor but higher-rated session was early in the morning, and the excellent but lower-rated session was in the late afternoon. Could tiredness have affected the audience's ratings? Or were results biased because participants rated the morning session before they had anything to compare it to, while the afternoon session followed other very good content?

The precision of answers when scoring on this 1–5 scale is necessarily low. It's probably misleading to think of 4.27 as a higher score than 4.25. Yeah, we were approximately on goal. Were the numbers a good representation of what the attendees really thought? Well, they were limited to integer scores between 1 and 5, so it's possible that a very good session and a stellar session were both rated 5, because that was the highest choice.

The use of averages here is also tricky. Averages are meaningful when data is normally distributed (a bell curve), and when they are reported along with a standard deviation. In this case, we clearly didn't have a bell curve, because of the cutoffs at 1 and 5. But perhaps more important was that the variances in the data showed interesting patterns. Some sessions, for example, got a large number of 5s and a number of very low ratings, with almost nothing in the middle. That important fact, obscured when we looked only at the average, might suggest that the session was perfect for some attendees and not for others—perhaps we should figure out how to distinguish the two types and next year we divide the conference into two tracks.

What should we change for next year, given these results? Our company loves to make data-driven decisions and especially prizes feedback from customers, so this was an important and reasonable discussion to have. Some data is better than no data, we believe. But there's a risk that oversimplified data will lead to the wrong follow-up actions.

Another example came up recently with regard to our blog, which is intended to be a thought leadership blog for senior enterprise executives. A report had indicated that it was (only) the eighteenth most trafficked blog on our company's site, in terms of the number of visitors. Someone asked what we intended to do about it.

Good question? The questioner implied that we needed to improve the quality of the blog. But our blog targets a very small audience—senior executives—while the other blogs target a much larger one (generally all customers of our services). It's also meant to focus on cutting-edge thought leadership—new ways of thinking about the cloud. We could increase readership by writing about topics that have broader appeal—but why? Is there anything wrong with being number eighteen, which puts our blog toward the middle of the pack? Some blog has to be in the middle, and these blogs are all for the benefit of our customers, so it wasn't a competition.

My point: the simplifications that are required to use a single metric leave out a great deal of information. And using a metric like unique visitors that is easy to measure can lead to problems in interpretation, and as a consequence drive the wrong behavior. But for bureaucracies of metrics, it's tempting to pounce on every scrap of data and try to wring meanings from it.

6: Oversimplification (Continued)—Targets

Organizations that control employee activity through metrics do so by setting targets to represent success—that is the "key results" part of Doerr's OKRs. But how do you decide what targets to set for a metric? One way is to start from its current value, add a percentage for desired growth, and then add some "stretch." Or to set it based on wishful thinking, or on working backward from a hope ("we want to break even, so our goal is to sell 100,000 units of this product"). It's rare to set a target that is lower (worse) than the current value, even in a declining market.

In Chapter 7 we talked about the assumption of recalcitrance in coercive bureaucracies. I think there's a similar assumption here. Perhaps employees are already trying their best to improve the metric—in which case, how does setting a target help? In the absence of a target, they might surprise us by doing orders of magnitude better than we expect. On the other hand, the target might demotivate them and give them an excuse to "coast" once they've hit the goal. Or if the target is too high, it gives them an incentive to game the system.

When we set the target hoping to get them to perform better than they otherwise would . . . we're assuming that they're putting in less than their full effort.

Setting a target turns the metric into a judgment, not just a way to communicate objectives and focus. You either hit your target or do not, and the trolls will get you if you don't. This is true whether it's an individual's target or a group's. The target sets up a binary orientation—yes or no—in an area where you really want the metric to be *as high* (or *as low*) as possible.

If you accept that we're in an environment of uncertainty and rapid change, then you're mistaken in setting a metric's target at the beginning of the year, at a moment when you have the least information about what results are possible. As the year progresses, you'll learn more about what you can achieve, say, on revenue per customer. Your industry will change, your customers will change, trade wars will break out, someone will tweet an unfortunate meme.

I accept that targets play an essential role in communicating what's important. Leaders can use an aggressive target to focus their employees to say, "This is more important than other things." Perhaps it's the number of new customers we want to focus on this year. Perhaps it's revenue per customer. An aggressive target can tell employees which it is. But there are other ways to communicate the same thing, and the message is often watered down by using multiple measures, as with a balanced scorecard.

Jerry Z. Muller, a history professor at the Catholic University of America and author of *The Tyranny of Metrics*, has this interesting take on target setting:

> The fixation on quantifiable goals so central to metric fixation—though often implemented by politicians and policymakers who proclaim their devotion to capitalism—replicates many of the intrinsic faults of the Soviet system. Just as Soviet bloc planners set output targets for each factory to produce, so do bureaucrats set measurable performance targets for schools, hospitals, police forces, and corporations.[30]

This gets at my discomfort with targets. They're irrelevant to the real dynamics of a changing environment, and if they're used, they arbitrarily direct activity before any market feedback is available.

I admit that I do sometimes set targets as a manager. For example, our procurements at USCIS sometimes took as long as three years, and almost never less than six months. I set a goal for my team of finding a way to do some of them in less than thirty days. I used a precise target because I felt a need to communicate that I was talking about *radical* change to our procurement process, not just incremental change. Implicitly, I was saying that I'd help by removing impediments, because I wanted *serious* change. I also wanted to emphasize that we wouldn't rest—even if we reduced procurements from three to two years, we'd keep working at it. My target of thirty days was carefully chosen: I could communicate why thirty days mattered from a business perspective. As I explained to them, if we could do procurements that quickly our vendors would know that we could take the risk of replacing them. The target, essentially, was a communication strategy.

Another case where I set a target was when we moved to DevOps. Our average release cycle time was about 180 days at that time. I set a goal of doing multiple releases every day and doing all of our deployments during normal business hours (in other words, to do them without disrupting business operations). I knew that if we could hit those targets it would mean that we'd succeeded in moving to a best-practices DevOps approach. It was a shortcut to making sure we were adopting the right practices.

A notable example where I chose *not* to set targets was one I've described in previous books—our E-Verify modernization effort. We knew that we wanted to increase the number of cases that a status verifier could process, which was, on average, seventy per day at the time. While that would be our most important metric, I declined to set a target for it, reasoning that any number I chose would be arbitrary—we had no data that would tell us how high we could raise the number, or more precisely, no data that would tell us how much each incremental case per day would cost us on a marginal basis. Instead, I figured, by experimenting and trying ideas, we would discover the right target.

That meant that my business case for the initiative was weaker (some would say). It proposed that we spend $X to get the number "somewhat higher." I argued that imprecision didn't matter, because we weren't committing to spending the $X, but could stop funding the initiative at any moment, and could begin delivering and affecting the metric immediately, and three times a day after that. A vague business case fits the need when the risk is low, the results are immediate, and the funding is incremental.

Incidentally, it wasn't really a weaker business case than usual. A traditional business case might have set a target but would have had no real justification for it. We could have said that the goal was to get to a hundred cases per day, and that would justify the $X. But we had no real data that indicated we *could* get to a hundred cases per day, and who's to say that getting to ninety cases per day wasn't a success if we wound up spending only a small portion of the $X on it? Traditional business cases are built on the fiction that we know what business results we'll get, despite all the uncertainty we face.

An aside for the IT folks: Agile techniques like Scrum insist on setting targets for each sprint, based on story points. Why?

7: It's Not Enough

With or without setting a target, a metric doesn't really tell us whether we're doing well, except in the most superficial sense. Let's say that we're focused on revenue per customer, and we find that we've raised it by 15%. We can certainly say that that is better than 0%. But is it good? Could we easily have raised revenue by more than 15%, but didn't? Or is it amazing that we were able to raise it more than a couple of percentage points given the state of the market? If the PRA's annual reports had shown a 2% reduction each year in burden (they didn't), would that have been good? To know if the metric is good or bad, we would have to know how much it could have reduced burden, given all the helpful improvements in digital technology. Metrics are not really a way to judge success.

We think we know success. Apple is successful, right? Yes, they've made a lot of money. Could they have made more? Is it possible that they were just in the right place at the right time? People writing about Steve Jobs often imply that his genius was somehow related to his nasty management style, and they point to Apple's success as if his nastiness was a necessary part of it. I don't know—if he'd been less nasty, perhaps Apple would have done better. For most businesses, there is no data from controlled experiments to make decisions from.

Comparison

In summary, Table 2 compares the negatives of rational-metrical bureaucracy to those of rational-legal bureaucracy from the earlier chapter. It also addresses a few of the disadvantages I haven't explicitly mentioned yet.

Table 2: Rational-Legal versus Rational-Metrical Bureaucracy

	Rational-Legal	Rational-Metrical
1: Surprise—It's Inefficient!	Inefficiency due to siloing and slow-changing rules	Inefficiency due to side effects and effort required to manage metrics
2: Its Goals Are Displaced	Goals are displaced to rules	Goals are displaced to metrics
3: It Stifles Innovation	Innovation reduced by rules that emphasize stability	Innovation reduced because it doesn't yield progress on metrics
4: It Fosters Blind Spots	Rules cannot completely determine activities; Professional Deformation	Easy-to-measure metrics drive out harder-to-measure metrics
5: It Dehumanizes	Rules are dehumanizing and take away individual decision-making power	Metrics used to measure performance are judgmental, insulting, and easily gamed
6: It Oversimplifies	Rules require simplification and generalization and therefore overlook exception cases	Metrics are simplifications that lose important details

7: It's Not Enough	Misses key point: the inspiration that allows the company to grow and succeed. Vulnerable to work-to-rule strikes	Metrics do not really measure success
8: It's Coercive	Assumes recalcitrance or untrustworthiness	Sets up a way to judge employee, sometimes to make case for dismissal
9: It Petrifies	Rules change very slowly	Locks in goals, usually for a year
10: It's Risk Averse	Employees can hide behind rules to avoid taking responsibility	Employees are disincentivized to do anything that won't improve their metrics

PART III

THE PLAYBOOK

THE PLAYBOOK: HOW TO BUST BUREAUCRACY

He would not go into the Central Registry, not even if someone were to promise him the extraordinary good fortune of discovering the document everyone has been looking for since the world began, nothing more nor less than the birth certificate of God.

—José Saramago, *All the Names*

Well, well; I heard Ahab mutter, "Here some one thrusts these cards into these old hands of mine; swears that I must play them, and no others." And damn me, Ahab, but thou actest right; live in the game, and die in it!

—Herman Melville, *Moby Dick*

Absolute Certainties

So, you're in an organization, running up against bureaucratic impediments when you try to do what you're pretty sure is the right thing. Perhaps you're leading a digital transformation and your company's bureaucracy is resisting change, fighting to lock in ways of doing things that belong to the days before the Paleolithic era. You're up against a vast leviathan of a bureaucracy, like that of MD-102. What should you do?

Like many business and technology authors, I'm going to tell you a bunch of stuff based on my limited research—stuff that seemed more or less to work with a sample size of one—and try to write it in a way that sounds compelling. I already know that putting it into a book is going to give it more authority, plus you'll have cognitive dissonance if you paid to read it, so you'll tend to believe what I say. Since I want to help you succeed, I'm going to let you in on my secrets and idiosyncratic behaviors that were probably effective. I think, maybe.

There, that's my disclaimer, in case your bureaucracy fails to bust. I think the plays in this playbook are sensible and will make a good starting point for your own experiments. If you're sitting with your head in your hands, overwhelmed by metaphysical pathos, and can't figure out what to do next, try some of these tricks. But if, say, play *B13: Hunt Monkeys* doesn't solve your problems, don't think you're some exception to a technique that's been working for every master bureaucracy buster in the world.

The most important thing I have to teach you is the importance of banging your head against the wall, repeatedly, until the wall starts to move. It worked for me. Next, I suggest keeping a sense of humor, even when the stakes are high. Even *Moby Dick* has some funny chapters. Can you think of a single comedian who has had their digital transformation derailed by stubborn bureaucrats? No, you can't.

My suggestion throughout this book has been that you stop doing the metaphysical pathos thing. The bureaucrats in your way are probably trying earnestly to do their jobs. The crazy stuff that's blocking you was put there for very good reasons. You have to show that (1) those reasons are no longer important, or (2) that there are better ways to satisfy those reasons, or (3) that while those reasons are good, there are more important considerations that override them. Ultimately, fixing bureaucracy has to come down to those three things.

Yes, you can make a little progress riding in with noisy urgency around "bureaucracy busting." You can also get some things done with just your charisma and some impressive-sounding certifications after your name. But in an organization where people really do care about results, about mission accomplishment, you'll eventually stumble if you aren't replacing the bureaucracy with something even better.

Everyone knows it's important to surround yourself with good people. So, I'll introduce you to three of my assistants who can help with your bureaucracy-surmounting efforts: the Monkey, the Razor, and the Sumo Wrestler. Please take them as seriously as they merit. For an encore, I'm going to show you how to forge your own bureaucracy, making good use of spherical cows and unobtanium, minus the metaphysical pathos.

Have fun.

THE WAY OF THE MONKEY

I tell you, one must have chaos in one, to give birth to a dancing star.
—Nietzsche, *Thus Spoke Zarathustra*

I am the golden dog-headed ape, three palms and two fingers [high],
which hath neither arms nor legs, and which dwelleth in Het-ka-Ptah.
I go forth as goeth forth the dog-headed ape who dwelleth in Het-ka-Ptah.
—*The Egyptian Book of the Dead*

Meet the Monkey

Monkeys are mischievous and curious—everyone knows that. They appear widely in the world's stories, legends, myths, and religions. A favorite of mine is the Monkey King of Chinese legend, who features in the traditional Buddhist story of *The Journey to the West*. In it, a monk makes his way to the lands of "the west" to retrieve sacred scriptures from the Buddha and bring them back east. He faces a perilous journey (especially perilous because it's meant to be a metaphor for reaching enlightenment) and can only accomplish it with the help of Monkey, a powerful but mischievous trickster who's been pinned under a mountain by the gods for causing too much trouble up in heaven.

A few facts about Monkey will make it clear why he's your ally in clearing away bureaucracy to make way for digital transformation. First of all, Monkey's magical superpower—I couldn't make this up—is his ability to transform. Good start. When he developed his magical powers, he changed his name to Great Sage, Equal of Heaven, a name that Heaven didn't like much. He quickly got himself into even more trouble by crashing a gods-only party, stealing and drinking a magic beverage prepared by Lao-tzu, and causing chaos and destruction throughout the heavens. A change agent, right?

When he starts his religious journey, Monkey is given a new, religious name: he becomes known as "Aware of Vacuity." We'll just translate that as "Aware of Bureaucracy," since he does all of his trickery within a supremely bureaucratic heavenly environment—you know, the Star Lords of the Five Constellations, the Four Emperors, and the Heavenly Immortal of the Great Nomad from the Eight High Caves.

When the monk and monkey and their companions finally make it to the west, the bodhisattva Kuan Yin points out that it's taken them 5,040 days but that they are receiving 5,048 scrolls. Therefore, she concludes, the gods should make sure their return journey takes eight more days. Also, she notes that the monk has survived eighty ordeals, but his enlightenment is supposed to require eighty-one, so his adventure is out of compliance. If that's not formidable bureaucracy, I don't know what is. "Make it so," says the Jade Emperor, and the gods pursue the adventurers to arrange one more disaster.*

The Monkey King's not the only important monkey to bring chaos to management strategy. There's the Chaos Monkey, of course, and the Signifying Monkey of African-American tradition. And then there are the many non-monkey tricksters of other cultures . . . let's see, the Raven of Native American cultures, religious troublemakers like Hoja Nasruddin, disruptive innocents like Gimpel the Fool,† and the good soldier Svejk. . . . Well, you should have no trouble hiring change agents.

The Way of the Monkey

All transformation starts with the Monkey. Something has to cause a disruption, because people need to understand that the status quo is no longer okay. The Monkey probes and provokes, learns how the organization really works—its politics, dynamics, people's hidden motivations—then uses those learnings as a lever to move the unmovable. The Monkey does so with good humor and a light touch (the Sumo Wrestler weighs in later), along with an annoying persistence and lack of fear. He's the iconoclast who questions what's obviously true, just because it is obviously true. He's not bothered

---

*Wanna bet that -ed. is going to add a note about Gimpel to my next paragraph? -au.

† No need. -ed.

when he's pinned under a mountain of bureaucracy, because sooner or later he'll move the mountain. He winks as he disrupts and smiles—because after all, this is kind of fun.

Here are some techniques you'll want to borrow from the Monkey.

M1: Provoke and Observe

This vast judicial organism remains, so to speak, in a state of eternal equilibrium, and that if you change something on your own where you are, you can cut the ground out from under your own feet and fall, while the vast organism easily compensates for the minor disturbance at some other spot—after all, everything is interconnected—and remains unchanged, if not, which is likely, even more resolute, more vigilant, more severe, more malicious.[1]

As Kafka implies, bureaucracy in a large enterprise is complex, nuanced, and self-healing. If you change something, it adjusts and restabilizes in a new obstructionist way. As in any complex system, it's difficult or impossible to know in advance, through pure analysis and planning, how to drive change successfully. Instead, the monkey proceeds empirically, trying out ideas, learning from their impact, and readjusting. That's the principle behind Agile software delivery and behind most Lean-influenced process improvement methodologies.

Provoke and observe is the ultimate monkey technique. It's the tactic of testing the bureaucracy by provoking it and seeing what happens. I use the term provoke to mean test, discomfort, or the like—I'm not saying that you have to be obnoxious, which is how you wind up pinned beneath a mountain. The goal is to learn whether there's resistance, and if so, what it looks like. "We can't direct change, but we can provoke the system and observe the response and then provoke again," Chris Avery says.[2]

A fine example of provocation was releasing MI-CIS-OIT-001. I wasn't really sure what would happen, to be honest. I waited for a reaction and was astonished to see none, at least until GAO finally surprised me by saying that it wasn't agile enough. Another provocation was a new contracting structure we devised, something we called FADS, which set up a competition framework for the four contractors we awarded the contract to. We designed FADS using the rules of the mammoth six-thousand-page FAR in ways no one had tried before, without fully knowing how it would affect our contractors and how they'd respond. By repeatedly soliciting feedback from them, we were able to mold the idea to make it work better for everyone.

Our provocations generally took the form of choosing a direction for improvement and then cautiously stepping a toe in that direction, watching for the consequences. When I asked my team to find a way to do procurements in thirty days instead of three years, I knew they wouldn't be able to do it easily. But the procurement process was so complex, beginning with the colossal FAR, that I didn't know exactly what obstacles we'd discover.

The most immediate obstacle turned out not to be in the blubberous six-thousand-page FAR at all, but something more lumpish called the Balanced Workforce Assessment. DHS's procurement rules, to make sure that we always had the right balance of contractors and government staff to oversee them, required us to prepare an analysis that justified the ratio we planned to apply. That document had to be approved by seven (!) relatively senior managers, each of whom was given one week to review and sign it. Since their reviews were conducted sequentially—not in parallel, as any spherical cow would suggest—the Balanced Workforce process itself took longer than the thirty days I'd allotted for the entire procurement.

Useful information. The next steps were to annoy people with questions about how many signatures were really needed, how long each signatory was given to review the document, and whether they could do their reviews in parallel. In the end, we created a "template" procurement package and a templated Balanced Workforce Assessment to accompany it, and we got all the signatories to agree that if we used them in the future, we wouldn't need to go through the approval process again. Score one for the monkey.

We also targeted the thousands of pages we were writing and managing for each project under MD-102. MD-102 demanded that we write Integrated Logistical Support Plans and Section 508 EIT Accessibility Plans and Security Requirements Traceability Matrices and Technology Insertion Decision Requests—but didn't say how long each document had to be. Our teams typically filled each templated section of each document with words, words, words,* out of a fear that Polonius and his trolls would reject it if they didn't see a big block of text.†

---

* A quote from Hamlet. -ed.

† -ed.: Let's see you find a citation for "text." -au.

That's a banana for the monkey, a temptation right up his tree.*† Provocation one: we started preparing our documents with much less text, and asked our QA staff to review each one to make sure it was as brief as possible while still conveying the relevant information. Provocation two: we started leaving out entire sections of the templates that we didn't think were useful for the project at hand. These provocations taught us where there was pushback, which began a conversation with the overseers. They surprised us by agreeing with many of our provocations—they wanted shorter documents, since they took less time to review.‡

M2: Be Curious

There's a reason for each bit of bureaucracy. It's not always a good reason, but the Monkey can sniff it out. Sometimes it's there to solve a problem that no longer exists. Sometimes it encapsulates the best way that was known to solve a problem . . . in the days of Genghis Khan. Sometimes it's a plausible-sounding control that just doesn't happen to work. Or a two-year process like the PRA's that does the opposite of what was intended.

But there's a reason it's there. The PRA's purpose is easy to ascertain: reduce the public burden. Sometimes it's a lot harder to figure out why the bureaucracy is forcing you to waste your time—like a pointless sign-out sheet for documents that are pinned to a corkboard that's been in use since the twentieth century. In the case of an audit control, you might have to ask the auditors what its *control objective* is.

Once you know why a bureaucratic rule is in place, then you can be creative in finding better ways to satisfy its intent. Perhaps instead of the sign-out sheet, you can install a video camera near the corkboard. The separation of duties that the auditor demands might turn out to be the wrong separation of duties, or perhaps there's a different set of controls that will satisfy its objective even better. That was actually the case for an early objection to DevOps, which removed the separation of duties between developers (who worked in

---

* Probably a reference to *Moby Dick* and its ship, the Pequod. -ed.

† -ed.: Prove it. -au.

‡ It's been a pleasure working with you all, but my duties at Strozzapreti U. require my full-time attention now, so this will be my final note. Stay in touch! -ed.

test environments) and operators (who deployed the developers' code and managed it in production environments). The traditional separation of duties wasn't actually a very effective control; in its place DevOps puts controls that include peer code reviews, automated testing and assurance, automated deployments, and an audit history of every change that's made to production code.

Sometimes understanding a control's intent helps you argue that it isn't necessary, though that's a harder case to make. It's most effective in cases where the control no longer makes sense due to business or technology changes, or in cases where you can show that the control has never actually prevented a risk from materializing. In any case, the Monkey's job is to open up options that others haven't been considering.

M3: Ban Learned Helplessness

Often, when we figured out the right way to do our work, some annoying colleague would point out that we'd never be allowed to do it that way. The walls that box employees in are hammered in place by security and procurement organizations, by policy and law, by no-sayers in all the dark dusty corridors of the bureaucracy. But if the box is too small for them to do what's right, they just have to find ways to make their box bigger. I think of this as an ethical responsibility: just as bureaucrats leave their biases at home, monkeys fight against inappropriate constraints.

That's the opposite of how people beaten down by bureaucracy tend to act. They've learned helplessness; they accept the constraints they're given. It's easy for me to say, I know, since I came into the government at a high rank and always felt comfortable fighting against constraints. But that's also a clue you can use to move immovable walls: get the support of someone high up who is comfortable pounding on them till they budge.

Consider our approach to MD-102. True: our new best practices were not allowed under MD-102. True: as DHS employees we had to follow MD-102. False: MD-102 (or its interpretation) couldn't be changed. It couldn't be changed *easily*, that's all.

Imagine that you're a medical doctor in the 1940s and the hospital you work for has bureaucracy that makes it impossible for you to treat patients with those newfangled antibiotic things. Are you going to continue applying leeches? Of course not—you're going to do what it takes to get the hospital to change its policy. You're a professional.

Here are some techniques we used for executing Monkey Play M3:

First, we made sure that employees saw themselves as professionals, with a responsibility to their craft. We maintained a library of technical books in the office, brought guest speakers, conducted "safaris" where we'd visit companies to learn from their IT people, sent employees to training, and, probably most impactful, sent them out to speak at events about the innovative things we were doing. As they became more sophisticated in their knowledge of cutting-edge techniques, it was natural for them to resist the stale bureaucratic rules that had been carved in silicon in the days when it was a good practice to keep hitting the reset button on your computer and stacking your punch cards neatly.

Second, we coached employees on how to reconcile our new techniques with the rules, or in finding ways to get the rules changed. They were often already in the best position to know how to do it. It was my bureaucracy-savant employees who found the right medium in which to cast our own bureaucratic artworks—I would never have thought of declaring a Management Instruction without their help. It was our project managers, well experienced in doing ineffective procurements, who could teach us what we had to change in the procurement rules.

Many of the techniques in this playbook were hashed out in brainstorming with formerly helpless employees. We as a management team helped them construct the arguments they'd use when talking to the authorities, find alternative controls that were leaner, and apply for exceptions—with our signatures—when appropriate. Everyone had permission to "use my name" when dealing with those outside IT.

And third, we promoted our successes far and wide. By showing employees that we were actually getting somewhere in bringing new ideas into the bureaucracy, we reduced their feeling of helplessness, one shoulder-shrug at a time.

M4: Repersonalize

Bureaucracies may try to be faceless, but they unavoidably still have faces. Even when the bureaucracy is automated, there's someone who created the automated scripts and periodically updates them. Weber, as we know, filled his ideal bureaucracy with competent officials: he understood that rules themselves were not sufficient, but had to be supplemented with expertise.

Our bureaucrats were working in the agency because they were passionate about its mission. By building trust with them, showing that we understood their controls' intentions, and making clear that our goal was to promote mission success while still ensuring their control objectives, we could sometimes engage them in helping us overcome impediments.

Often, we'd sit down with them, explain what we were trying to do, and ask for their suggestions. They'd tell us that the rule blocking our way was actually meant to be blocking someone else's way, and they'd either change how it was applied or find us an exception to it. When we told them that others on their staff had been forcing us to shovel ever more text into our documents, they became our allies in retraining their teams and clarifying what they were looking for.

Oversight bodies often don't have enough "skin in the game." They face too little downside to saying no; the area they're directly responsible for will not benefit if an initiative moves forward even if it's completed successfully. The decision-makers for MD-102 were the Acquisition Review Board (ARB), a group of leaders at DHS who didn't have to run the immigration system day to day. While they were nominally responsible for the success of the entire DHS enterprise, they'd be assessed mostly on avoiding large failures, so even when they said yes, they'd happily add red tape and extra work—for the project teams, that is, not themselves. By engaging them more in our change initiatives through pilots, by framing our presentations around mission needs, and through storytelling (see next section), we motivated them to help us succeed.

In a business context, I frequently encounter companies that are trying to be more innovative in meeting customer expectations. But their initiatives are stopped by financial gatekeepers whose concerns are risk, cost, and investment governance. The underlying problem is that those no-sayers don't have enough accountability for growing revenues. They must be engaged in innovating and growing the company, or they'll always pose a bureaucratic obstacle.

M5: Motivate through Stories

The Monkey's job is made easier through storytelling. Stories work at an emotional and even physical level. They make abstract points more concrete and show the human consequences of moving forward with or delaying an initiative. They connect the eighty-seven documents to the immigrants starting new lives or the refugees escaping from persecution.

We learned that the amount of paper we received every day at USCIS, if stacked up, would be 1.8 times the height of the Statue of Liberty. What a great story element to help convince everyone of the importance of going digital! So much paper had to move between our offices that some of the offices had their own zip codes. All that paper eventually had to wind up in our storage cave, since immigration applications are historical records and can't be destroyed. In that cave, they occupied six football fields worth of several stories-high shelves until they were moved to National Archives and Records Administration's larger cave when we no longer needed them.

That's the story we wanted to tell—not one about our Integrated Logistical Support Plan or Analysis of Alternatives. Immigration is filled with moving stories. We unfortunately allowed ourselves to get sucked into discussions about paperwork and signatories when we should have been talking about the difficulties Albert Einstein would face today if he tried to immigrate. Storytelling would have helped us build trust and urgency, because in the end, the overseers care about mission accomplishment as well.

Every business has stories to tell. There's power in any change agent's stories about how unexamined bureaucratic bric-a-brac is cluttering the way of accomplishing the company's mission and frustrating customers. It's a mistake to think that only the CEO tells stories. It's true that in Weberian bureaucracy the emotional, human element doesn't enter into how the rules are applied. But it can enter into the form the rules take or the changes that are made to the rules over time to better accomplish business objectives.

And when it comes to those gaps in the rules—like whether the text in template sections is wordy or brief—stories can help align everyone behind "brief."

M6: Accept Personal Risk

Bureaucrats are not big fans of personal risk. After all, it's fundamental to bureaucracy that individuals don't make decisions on their own behalf but on the company's, and that their actions are determined by someone else's rules. Legitimately or not, a bureaucratic official has a simple route for avoiding risk: follow the rules as exactly as possible, relying on precedent whenever there's a doubt.

Anyone willing to accept personal risk therefore has an advantage in wrestling with a faceless bureaucracy. When metrics assume an outsized importance to a company, the special skills and knowledge of line employees can be underused, since objectives are set by managers who are at some distance from the action:

> Front-line service providers—often, relatively high status, professionals or "knowledge workers"—end up regulating and disciplining themselves in line with centrally determined performance metrics and targets that are designed and monitored by technical specialists who are relatively detached from the formal authority hierarchy insofar as they are located within specialist units directly responsible to governing elites.[3]

The Monkey is a risk-taker; he's willing to face off against a gang of semi-deities all by himself, or to shrink himself, pop into a goddess's party as it's being set up, resume his normal size, and empty the punch bowl into his mouth.

DHS's security compliance rules, having been written for earlier times, seemed to hold us back from achieving the best possible security posture. We were determined to do *better* than the rules required. And we were in a good position to do so, because I was officially the Authorizing Official for our IT systems, the person who had to decide if a system was secure enough to grant it an ATO (Authority to Operate). My standards were high. My security experts assessed each system and assembled a group to advise me; I asked probing questions, and only then made my decision. Sometimes my decision was to waive controls because I thought they didn't give us the best security, or because there were compensating controls that did better.

I could personally assume all the risk on behalf of my security team, because I knew that my decisions were based on their good advice, a sincere orientation toward raising the bar on security and a thoughtful assessment of risk. That's the intent of the bureaucratic ATO process—that a human being will make the final decision, weighing all the relevant factors. It's why someone is designated as the authorizing official. But it's too easy for authorizing officials to hide behind the formal requirements and only approve systems that technically meet all the conditions.

The key to taking risks is to not really take them. It's to assess risk better than the official process does. I was confident that our security posture would be better than if we strictly followed the requirements, otherwise I wouldn't have signed the ATOs. While it might have seemed to be riskier for me, it was less for the agency. And, come to think of it, less for me.

M7: Create Urgency

Bureaucracy resists change because it's oriented toward stability. Its goal is to find a process that works well and make it law. Though the law can be changed when someone finds improvements, doing so is not a bureaucratic priority, so change cycles are slow. Instead, bureaucracy begins from the assumption that the current state is okay as a baseline, and any change needs to be justified. In the absence of urgency such as that provided by a disaster like Healthcare.gov or the OPM breach, and when there's no chaos monkey available, predictability—calculability—win out over change and better results.

Digital transformation proceeds from the opposite set of assumptions: that change is constant and essential; that process improvement must be continuous; and that predictability should come more from removing the sources of variability (large batch sizes, for example), which are also sources of waste. It works toward leanness—that is, producing value as soon as possible, in a continuous, repeatable way. It's not change that needs to be justified, but the status quo—which should be challenged every day.

To get bureaucratic change to happen, you need to inject urgency by showing that today's practices is unacceptable. Continuous improvement requires the continuous application of a force to fight inertia. The question should never be whether changes are justified and riskless, but whether they will improve on the status quo.

The Monkey finds ways to shake the bureaucracy out of its comfort. When there is no convenient crisis to create urgency, one technique for doing so is BHAGs—big hairy audacious goals. A BHAG is deliberately calibrated so that it can't possibly be accomplished given "the way things are"; it requires disruption and ingenuity, a questioning of deep assumptions or routines. A properly set BHAG is a force to disturb the status quo.

An example from my time at USCIS:

The traditional way for software engineers to deploy new code was to come in late at night or on weekends with pizza and Red Bull and make their changes when they wouldn't disrupt company operations. Inevitably they did—when the other employees came in on Monday there was surprise, confusion, software bugs, and a mad scramble to fix unexpected problems.

As we were moving to DevOps, I set the goal of doing all deployments during normal working hours. To do that without destroying the agency, the engineers had to make a number of deep changes. They had to make sure they could roll back a software change instantly if any problems were discovered. They had to have good monitoring so that they could see immediately if the new code was causing any problems. They had to have a suite of automated tests they could trust and that they used before each deployment. They had to make sure each code deployment was small and therefore less likely to introduce errors and to make it easier to find and fix the errors quickly if something went wrong. That, in turn, meant they'd have to deploy changes more often. And to do that, they'd have to change the rules around approvals for deployment, the bureaucracy of change management.

This BHAG worked well. Everyone could see how being able to deploy during business hours without causing disruption would be a good thing. It was impossible given the status quo, so everyone's creativity was engaged in change, and bureaucracy provocation flowed naturally.

M8: Advertise the Cost of Delay

Let's say that there's a *mission need* for a project. Or that there's a large positive return expected from it. Or perhaps that the company is in mortal danger from an industry-disrupting competitor. In any of these cases, there's clearly a cost for every day it takes until the project is finished. If bureaucracy is slowing it down, then that cost of delay should be charged against the Department of Obstructive Bureaucracy's budget. You're tracking that category, right? There's a cost to bureaucracy that should be weighed against the benefits of the controls it provides.

MD-102's workflow begins with a project team establishing that there's a mission need for their project's objective. That word "need" is a strong word to me. If there is a real need—if that word is to be taken seriously—then the agency is necessarily suffering until the need can be met. That means that every day matters—and every day that the administrative overhead of MD-102 adds is a day that's like passing kidney stones. Even assuming that each element of MD-102 was put there for a good purpose, its pain (cost) should be balanced against mission *needs*, and the lead time burden of MD-102 should be minimized.

For any business, if a project will result in a positive return, then every day the project is not complete has an opportunity cost. Each passing day destroys business value, as capital is not being put to use to earn that return. Any bureaucratic overhead that draws out the project's lead time should be permitted only if the value of the bureaucratic control is higher than the value being left on the table. For example, every day spent building and evaluating a business case has a cost. Every form that must be filled out and every signature that must be affixed to the bottom of a document is not only a direct cost (the salary of the people involved) but also a much larger opportunity cost of delay.

In my experience, these tradeoffs are rarely considered—having more controls is assumed to be better. But aren't there diminishing returns to incremental bureaucratic controls? If so, when does their value drop below the cost of delay? A monkey tactic is to make the cost of delay visible by estimating and exposing it.

Here's an advanced version of the monkey tactic: Personally assign the cost of delay, if it's excessive, to the official who causes it. It's harsh, but they're wasting the company's money or preventing the agency from accomplishing its mission. For example, if we need a change to one of our IT systems because of a terrorist incident and that change is being held up by minimal-value signature hunting, let's frankly confront an official and say, "Are you comfortable that you're risking having more people die because you're making this take longer?" (See also M4: Repersonalize.) Or, once having agreed with enterprise leaders that their security posture will be improved by moving to the cloud, I've asked pointedly, "Don't you think you're taking an excessive risk for your company by moving so slowly into the cloud?"

M9: Apply Servant Leadership

Red tape is an impediment. Whose job is it to remove the impediment? Yours and mine.

Employees believed that DHS would object to any changes. The Brobding-nagian six-thousand-page FAR wouldn't allow it. The CFO wouldn't let us spend money on it. Our people didn't have the right skills. The PRA process would take years. Given that there would always be impediments, it was important not to let the team get stopped or slowed by them.

I solved these problems by assigning the impediments to myself, not because I've read management books that recommend doing so or because I love stress, but because I was in the best position to handle blockers—as CIO I had the necessary organizational power. From my position in the hierarchy, and with my ownership of the vision, I could negotiate on behalf of the team or press for change. By making my bureaucratic powers available to the team, I was helping to make our bureaucracy *enabling*. Although Agile IT discourages the use of command-and-control authority in favor of collaborative networks and empowered teams, I found that using it to *remove impediments* for a team was another matter. They usually didn't object to it.

But, to be honest, sometimes they did. They referred to me as the "nuclear option" and sometimes hesitated to escalate impediments, out of sensitivity to folks outside the team. At Amazon, on the other hand, we use a principle of "escalate quickly." It reinforces the culture of leanness and urgency. I wanted my teams to believe that passively accepting an impediment and allowing it to cause delays was not okay. But, of course, their sensitivity to using the nuclear option quickly is understandable. So, I leave it up to you how best to negotiate that trade-off.

An interesting application of servant leadership appears in John Shook's description of the NUMMI plant. Shook writes that if a worker pulled the *andon* cord to stop the production line when they noticed a problem, it was the *obligation* of the team lead to come and help fix the impediment immediately (actually within one job cycle, which was often just one minute).[4]

M10: Conduct Pilots, Get Exceptions

When the rules can't be changed directly, these two other approaches are often effective, because they're risk reducing for officials in the bureaucracy. The first is to take advantage of any exception process allowed in the rules themselves. There often is one, like the Project Tailoring Plan that we exploited in Chapter 2. Exceptions usually require justifications and sign-offs, but obtaining those can even be useful as a way to bring issues to light or to open discussion on new ideas.

Pilots saved us from MD-102. When we'd reached the bedrock objections using our provoke and observe technique, instead of trying to force immediate change, we suggested piloting a new oversight approach. We argued that it would be advantageous for the overseers themselves and asked for permission to show them how. By requesting permission for a pilot rather than a change to the rules, we reduced risk for the overseers—they didn't have to let anyone else in on it until we proved it would work—and also guaranteed that their feedback would be incorporated. We told them we'd treat them as our "customers" and make sure our approach met their needs, which we understood were considerable—they had to satisfy Congress that they had control over DHS investments.

We could then wield the fact that it was officially a pilot as a weapon in provoking others: "Don't worry, we're just piloting this for the oversight folks." We were confident that if we piloted the approach everyone would come to love it.

The Monkey: A User's Guide

The monkey wants to find out "How can I?" never assuming that he can't. The answer is different in each organization and with each piece of bureaucratic apparatus. He asks questions like these:

- What can I do that will help me learn how to get things done?
- How can I get the overseers to have skin in the game?
- How can I use my personal relationships?
- What's the critical impediment right now? What can I do to overcome it?
- How can I make people understand the cost of delay?

A monkey "uses wile and cleverness to accomplish what he cannot accomplish with brawn; his mode is a verbal judo, for he uses his enemy's own excessive ego against him, and he does it all with words."[5]

THE WAY OF THE RAZOR

Give me a condor's quill! Give me Vesuvius' crater for an inkstand! Friends, hold my arms! For in the mere act of penning my thoughts of this Leviathan, they weary me, and make me faint with their outreaching comprehensiveness of sweep.

—Herman Melville, *Moby Dick*

Drawing on my fine command of the English language, I said nothing.

—Robert Benchley

Meet the Razor

Whales, my friends, have a lot of blubber. If you're going to do battle with a leviathan, you'll have to trim some whale fat. Law of nature, sorry.

The Razor is the enforcer of bureaucratic parsimony. It's wielded by us, Knights of Occam, the bureaucratic equivalent to Six Sigma Black Belts. Bureaucracy is a factory whose output is compliance. A good bureaucracy—like a good factory—is one that uses the least effort and lowest cost to produce its product and can produce it fastest. The Razor strives for minimal viable compliance—meaning the fewest number of constraints consistent with the company's situation and risk posture—and strives to achieve its desired controls with as little whale bulk as possible. The Razor trims bloated bureaucracy into lean bureaucracy; ponderous whales into sleek and speedy marlin; trolls into trainers. A visit to the Razor provides a shave and a haircut that costs less than two bits and makes a whale spiffy and fun to swim with.

This next set of tactics is from the playbook of the Razor.

R1: Step Out of the Circle

The less risk, the less oversight that's needed. We faced a vicious circle in the government: our programs were large and therefore risky; because they were risky, they needed more oversight; because they needed so much oversight, the oversight process was burdensome; because it was so burdensome, no one wanted to do it too often; because no one wanted to do it often, they loaded all their work into a single, monolith of a project, which made it riskier; because the project was risky . . .

Here's another vicious circle: a project that seems to be running behind schedule attracts more "help" from overseers; the help requires burdensome meetings and additional work to report on the project's status and the planned remediation; that additional work takes time away from project activities; the project goes further behind schedule . . .

One more: projects sometimes fail spectacularly; when they do there's a call for additional oversight; the additional oversight mechanisms constrain future projects in ways that make them likelier to fail—or, if nothing else, add lots of costly overhead that reduces the return on each dollar invested; the poor return causes calls for additional oversight . . .

Perhaps you have a friend who has experienced one or more of these scenarios. There's a way to break out of these vicious circles, and it's simple: Only do small projects.

R2: Shrink Everything to Skunk Size

A smaller project is a less risky project, and therefore requires less governance ceremony. We surely understand that a multibillion-dollar, five-year government IT project will require very formal and extensive oversight. But a single DevOps team working for a month?

What could a single DevOps team accomplish in a month? A lot, if they can focus on producing results rather than writing eighty-seven documents and enduring eleven gate reviews. DevOps and the cloud provide leverage for a small team: they amplify its efforts and magnify its returns. Small government IT investments sounded crazy when we started down the path at USCIS. Of course, the point was rarely to end the work after a month but to reevaluate the investment and make incremental decisions to continue funding it. So, while the risk was only for one month, the *vision* was much larger.

In the government at least, differentiated controls based on spending levels are common. If we could hold our spending to less than $10 million and use our standard DHS contract vehicles, for example, then we wouldn't have to do extra work to protect ourselves from vendor protests and would face a less burdensome set of procurement controls. If we kept our contracts to less than about $4 million, we could award them directly to disadvantaged small businesses without the overhead of the usual competitive process. At under $150,000 there was a simplified acquisition process available under the prodigious six-thousand-page FAR.

Businesses too are used to applying simpler controls to less risky spending. For example, for expenses less than a certain amount employees might be able to use a purchasing card rather than a formal purchase order. Even if the bureaucracy is not yet set up that way, tailoring administrative burden to the level of risk might be palatable to the enforcers of the spending controls.

To be clear: I'm not suggesting that you get around regulations by chopping a large project into projects that are just barely small enough to avoid oversight. I *am* suggesting that you minimize the scope of an investment, following the Agile law "Maximize the Amount of Work Not Done," and that you break large projects into staged incremental deliveries, each of which stands alone as a valuable product. In other words, don't just make projects smaller— make them smaller in a way that truly reduces risk, because that's what justifies a simpler oversight process.

The cloud, DevOps, and other contemporary IT delivery approaches make it possible to work iteratively and incrementally. You can produce valuable business results in just days, and then build on them in small increments. We even broke down our largest initiatives—let's say, modernizing the E-Verify system*—into small, specific, and concrete business goals (five in all), which we then assigned to small teams and invested in individually.

The ultimate of smallness is the skunkworks. A skunkworks is a below-the-radar team that gets stuff done fast with minimal administrative ceremony. A skunkworks should not be sneaky, though sometimes it works stealthily. Rather, it should be small enough—and therefore low-risk enough—that it appears so much like a rounding error that it escapes attention. It should require a smaller

---

* E-Verify is a USCIS system that companies use to verify that their employees are eligible to work in the United States. -au.

commitment of resources than the finest-grained decision-making threshold. You can "just do it" because it uses odds and ends of resourcing.

Ideally, the result of a skunkworks project is that you can now ask permission to conduct a project, using the argument that its risk is low because it's already finished. Or at least you can show a prototype or proof of concept that is vastly risk lowering for a decision-maker.

For example, one of my employees at USCIS told me of an idea he called Network in a Backpack. He stopped by my office one day with a small daypack and dumped out its contents on a table. His team had stuffed this backpack full of hardware to solve a business challenge that I was already familiar with: our refugee officers travelled to refugee camps around the world to interview refugees for admission to the US. These refugee camps were often in difficult locations—sometimes desert shantytowns where power and internet connectivity were inconsistent and where dryness and dust, bouncing on desert roads, and other physical hazards led to damaged equipment that we couldn't replace quickly in time.

Network in a Backpack contained ruggedized equipment that would allow our officers, with no technical skills, to quickly build a network in a refugee camp to connect their laptops and printers together. They could then connect it to our fingerprint databases and other information back in the States. We'd be able to control and monitor it from Washington, DC. And it would meet our security needs, even assuming a hostile local government and terrorist recruiters in the refugee camp.

There was very little risk for me as a manager in supporting Network in a Backpack—because, well, it was already done. It solved a problem that I wanted solved but hadn't yet dedicated any effort to. I'd had no idea that his team was working on it. They'd done it on their own initiative, knowing the business challenge and hoping to solve it creatively. It cost so little that I hadn't noticed. It was a perfect skunkworks project.

R3: Shift Left

Bureaucratic workflows often require employees to stop and seek approval to continue to the next phases of a project, and very often require approval of the finished work product before it is used. In old-school IT, a formal SDLC (software development lifecycle) governs the stages and reviews of an IT delivery project. MD-102's eleven mandated reviews were used to verify, among other things, that the project's requirements had been fully documented before design work could begin, that design had been fully completed before building could begin, and, at the end, the big one—that the system had been fully tested and secured and that users were ready for it before it could be deployed.

DevOps brought us the concept of "shifting left"—moving these validation activities earlier in the delivery process (to the left on a Gantt chart) or, ideally, just absorbing the validation activities into the everyday flow of work. For example, instead of checking a system's design in a design review to make sure it follows enterprise architecture standards, the architecture team now gets involved before and during software development. They might write their own reusable code that implements their preferred architectural patterns for the development teams to use. They might make their preferred open-source products easily available and coordinate different teams to make sure their code interoperates smoothly. The overall impact is that the system doesn't need to be reviewed later for compliance, because it's been observed to be compliant all along.

Shifting left doesn't remove bureaucratic controls—on the contrary, it increases their effectiveness. It makes the bureaucracy lean and enabling. It's leaner because shifting left removes sources of waste like rework and waiting time (waiting for the gate review). It's enabling because the approved architectural building blocks become tools in the developers' hands: they help them do their jobs better and help the enterprise architects stop being no-saying trolls. And those subject to the standards can question and participate in formulating them.

At USCIS, we also shifted left through training. In the gate-rich process we'd started with, QA testers reviewed each system before release to make sure it was fully accessible to people with disabilities, and rejected the code when they invariably found that it wasn't. Instead, we trained the development teams on accessibility and how to test for it themselves. We certified "Trusted Testers" who could demonstrate their skills in accessibility testing, then required each development team to have at least one Trusted Tester. The effect was to make each team responsible for its code's accessibility.

We discovered that the majority of accessibility flaws came from one or two programming mistakes (forgetting to include alternate text for images, for example). We gave the programmers automated test tools that would help them find those sorts of mistakes and quickly eliminate them.

The "shift left" strategy is broadly applicable. For example, it can be used to encourage the organization to agree in advance what conditions need to be satisfied for compliance (thereby increasing the rigor of the bureaucracy!). In the security example I gave earlier, by definition, if the code passes the tests, it is compliant. The tests could be updated any time security learned something new. They served, therefore, to memorialize best practices and all the organizational learnings around security.

We used a similar tactic to implement financial controls. Under MD-102, the overseers became involved only after a project "failed" by "breaching" its agreement to reach certain cost and schedule milestones. But in our revised oversight process, we gave the overseers a monthly analysis based on hard data and *invited* them to interfere. We shifted their oversight to the left and made it participative instead of punitive.

Shift left uses guardrails to create a framework within which delivery teams can be creative. As long as their code passed its security tests, software developers could move as quickly as they liked and try out any new ideas they came up with. And the automated policy enforcement tools in production provided an extra safety net to encourage developers to make changes, knowing that their risks were mitigated.

R4: Respect Diminishing Returns

IT is filled with situations where there are diminishing returns to incremental effort. The bureaucratic overhead of IT projects is also often subject to diminishing returns.

For example, one of our MD-102 documents, the System Design Document, was considered important because it helped when a contract ended and one contractor was replaced by another. In the interests of fairness and agility, we wanted to make sure a new contractor could pick up the work and quickly continue with it. So, the design document's purpose was to teach the new contractor everything they would need to know to do so.

The problem is that there is more or less an infinite amount you can write about the workings of a system, and no matter how much you write, the new contractor will still not be fully up to speed. And they probably won't bother reading all of it anyway, especially if it's too long. Ultimately, they'll need to look at the code itself to fully understand it. There are diminishing returns to documentation, in other words.

So, the standard of trying to bring the new contractor 100% up to speed through a design document didn't seem right. We realized that the automated test scripts we were now writing would do some of the work, since the new contractor could learn what a given piece of code was supposed to do by looking at its tests. As for the design document, we decided that its goal would be to get the new contractor something like 60% of the way toward understanding the system. Because of diminishing returns, that decision vastly reduced the amount of documentation teams created. We also asked the software developers themselves to write the documentation, since they'd know best what information would be most useful to incoming developers. And to make it easier and faster for them, we let them write the documentation on a wiki that they could easily change.

The goal of getting a new contractor 100% oriented through a design document was causing waste and bloat in our practices; a simple acknowledgement of diminishing returns was the key to trimming it.

R5: Address Costs of Compliance

Bureaucracy, as we know, can be wasteful—it leads to delays and hidden costs. Those costs fall through cracks unobserved or unacknowledged because (1) people assume that no cost is too high when trying to avoid "failure," (2) they are hidden in different budgets, and (3) they are largely personnel costs, and no one tracks exactly how knowledge workers spend their time. Because bureaucratic costs are hidden, they're not well controlled; often they're thought of as nondiscretionary spending. But that's wrong—except when they're absolutely required by compliance frameworks like SOX and HIPAA, they are, actually, discretionary.

Add up the costs of red tape. First look at lead times, then actual costs. The cost of writing all the documents for MD-102 was tremendous. Add the cost to get them all signed—feedback, rewrites, and approvals. The meetings required for assembling the documents, reviewing their status, and discussing them. The document reviews, the people attending, the time it took to get them all in the same room. The status meetings to check on the progress of each large project in progress. (As opposed to incremental delivery, where status is conveyed simply by what has been delivered.) The Gantt chart for one of our projects became so large and cumbersome that it required twenty full-time people just to update it.

There is some cost at which incremental controls become value destroying. What's the *right* level of spending?

Advanced razor tip: Add up the time spent *doing* versus time spent *watching* as I discussed in Chapter 9. This is an advanced tip because it can make people feel threatened. Don't cheat by only including the IT department. *Doing* includes things like writing code, testing, deploying, and engineering infrastructure. *Watching* includes things like project management, status meetings, management, writing (certain) documents, getting sign-offs, governance processes, compliance specialists, CMMI experts . . . probably most of your costs.

Once you know your cost of watching, you can make decisions about whether you're doing the right amount of it. It will probably cause a monkey-shock and generate urgency. What's the right ratio of compliance to productive activity? What's the company's actual ratio? Is it possible to reduce that cost of compliance without changing the amount of risk mitigation?

This ratio should matter a lot to us if we're trying to cut costs. Sometimes, the cost of controls is the best place to begin trimming.

R6: Promote Transparency

Disasters are often public; the costs of guarding against them are not. This difference allows blubbery bureaucracy to flourish, perhaps even incentivizes it. But what if those risk-mitigation costs were public, or at least publicized within the organization, even if just at senior leadership levels? The fact that it took seven weeks to complete a balanced workforce assessment was a dramatic statistic that stimulated action.

What if everyone knew that it can take two years to complete the PRA process? Now that I've told you about it, aren't you outraged? The ratio of watching to doing is another area for generating shock and awe. Do you feel good that your tax dollars are paying for watchers, not doers? That they're writing about their "full doctrines" for facilities and materiel when they should be building software? Or that seven people must sign off on a document that says the workforce is balanced? Boards of directors and company shareholders might feel the same way.

These details lie buried in our processes. But between the Monkey and the Razor there's plenty to surface that would outrage shareholders. Would they really be happy with the time it takes to make decisions? The amount of time spent in meetings?

R7: Apply Lean Techniques

We don't often look at bureaucracy as a problem of leanness. But that's precisely what it is, once you've divorced yourself from metaphysical pathos. Fortunately, the entire toolkit of Lean techniques is available to those who wield the razor. Here are a few types of waste that tend to accompany bureaucracy.

1. **Waiting time:** Some causes: Waiting for people who have to sign off on documents. SLAs within parts of the value stream, which cap the maximum amount of time the process can take, but also tend to determine the minimum time, as people work backward from their deadlines. Waiting until meetings take place (coordinating everyone's schedules!). Waiting for security reviews.

2. **Handoffs:** Because bureaucracies tend to have a functional division of labor, work must pass between different teams, with each hand-off adding overhead. For example, the handoff of requirements from the non-IT part of the business to IT adds tons of overhead—the requirements must be fully documented and signed off on, and additional requirements tend to be added because later scope creep will not be allowed.* The handoff to oversight bodies and steering committees for review tends to add plenty of waste, because those bodies are less familiar with details and day-to-day activities and have to be educated.

3. **Rework:** Because no-sayers and reviewers arrive late in a process and their job is not to improve the work but to return it for changes, rework tends to be maximized. If the pharaoh reviews the pyramid after it's built and decides that he doesn't like the view from his tomb—or wants more room for his harem in the next life—then the slaves will have a lot of rework ahead of them.

4. **Overspecification:** You know the story of the $3,000 military coffee pot from Chapter 1. If you write specifications for a product before you know how much each requirement will add to the cost, then you're making decisions with incomplete information, and it will cost you. This often happens with requirements given to an IT organization—

---

* I've discussed these topics in detail in my previous books *War and Peace and IT* and *A Seat at the Table*. -au.

somewhere embedded in those requirements is a feature that is enormously but not obviously expensive—only IT will know it, upon deeper analysis, but not the requestor. In a one-way, bureaucratic process, where someone issues orders and someone else follows them, there are bound to be requirements that are costly but don't really mean that much to the requestor.

5. **Learning the rules:** Ever add up the cost of training people on the rules, correcting them when they get them wrong, or interpreting the rules when their application isn't clear? If the policy is that employees should only fly economy class, what happens when business class turns out to be cheaper? One employee after another will ask questions, and the guardian of the rules will spend time interpreting the rule. The *War-and-Peace*-times-five-length FAR takes time to read and understand, and the chance of making a mistake and needing correction is high. There are many training classes offered inside and outside the government on how to understand the FAR. The more bureaucracy, the more waste there is in learning the bureaucracy.

Those are just some examples—a bureaucracy that has not previously been subject to Lean treatment will undoubtedly be holding in plenty more waste. Although bureaucracy tends toward bloating (a law of bureaucratic entropy?), it doesn't need to. Even within a bureaucratic structure, we can enforce lean practices.

User's Guide to the Razor

By all means, look at your value streams and see where bureaucracy is adding to your lead times! Calculate its cost, in lead time and dollars, then find ways to reduce it while still mitigating the same risks and achieving the same results. Keep in mind:

- The Razor reduces your costs, sometimes significantly, as a byproduct of reducing your lead times.
- If you have a choice between reducing productive activities and reducing watching or wasteful (in other words nonlean) compliance efforts, think carefully . . .

- You can't just shave once and be done with it. You gotta do it every day. Under the blubber there may be more blubber.
- Razoring is the easiest aspect of digital transformation to sell to others. Who doesn't want to eliminate waste? The CEO and CFO, in particular, are likely to be supportive if you show them data.

THE WAY OF THE SUMO WRESTLER

Oh, thou clear spirit, of thy fire thou madest me, and like a true child of fire, I breathe it back to thee.

—Herman Melville, *Moby Dick*

The commentators tell us: the correct understanding of a matter and misunderstanding the matter are not mutually exclusive.

—Franz Kafka, *The Trial*

Meet the Sumo Wrestler

The application of just the right amount of force in just the right place to throw a four-hundred–pound wrestler to the ground. The slow wearing away at a fault line between two geological plates that suddenly results in a vigorous shaking of the earth. The one or two harpoons that tire out a sixty-foot, forty-ton whale so that it can be killed by a precisely directed lance thrust. These are the ways of the Sumo Wrestler.

Sumo is a traditional Japanese martial art that really does resemble an earthquake. Two inconceivably massive tectonic plates in loincloths and strange hair-knobs push up against each other, the tension building until it is suddenly released and one of the wrestlers shakes the stadium by falling to the ground. (Actually, a wrestler can win either by pushing his opponent out of the ring or by making his opponent hit the ground with anything but his feet.) Here's the subtlety: if you push too hard, your opponent might simply yield, and you'll go flying. If you don't push hard enough, then your opponent will push *you* and you'll go flying.

A sumo match can be a delicate balancing of forces, where each wrestler is trying to find exactly the right moment to apply exactly the right amount of force to exactly the right place to get the opponent off balance.

Our ally the Sumo Wrestler meets bureaucracy head-on and pushes with the just the right strength at just the right point to win the match.

S1: Refocus on Objectives

We've already noted the bureaucratic dysfunction of goal displacement: focusing on the rules rather than their ends. The Sumo Wrestler remedies this by realigning bureaucratic rules and bureaucratic roles to support the real objectives. Whenever an employee is working toward the enterprise's goals, the bureaucracy should be facilitating rather than hindering their efforts. Sometimes it's not.

The Sumo Wrestler starts by examining a bureaucratic impediment. If the control purpose behind the impediment is valid and reasonable—for example, it will help the company comply with HIPAA—then the Sumo Wrestler tries to find an equivalent control that will accomplish the same objective but not get in the way. If he finds that the bureaucratic impediment does not serve a useful purpose, he pushes it out of the ring. He conserves his strength for stomping out the useless bureaucracy and uses leverage and balance adjustments to deal with the right-meaning bureaucracy.

A sumo wrestler doesn't get overly attached to a single plan, but keeps his objective in mind, sometimes pulling, sometimes pushing. When we hit a bureaucratic impediment, it may be possible to take a different approach that skirts it. Since there may be many routes to accomplishing an objective, we find the one that gets us there, despite roadblocks.

For example, at USCIS we were often told that we should not use time and materials contracts because they were too risky for the government, which might have to keep spending at hourly rates until the work was finished. Instead, we were "strongly encouraged" to use firm fixed price agreements, where the vendor would agree to complete the entire scope of a project for a fixed fee, because those contracts were believed to transfer risk to the vendor. Agile IT, however, has found that by far the biggest risk in an IT project is in the requirements themselves, and the firm fixed price arrangement effectively puts all that risk on the government.

It seemed like we were stuck because we needed time and materials contracts for our Agile software practices, but the procurement authorities were adamantly opposed. In the end, though, we found that we could work within a firm fixed price structure while still leaving system requirements open, thereby mitigating the most important risks *and* satisfying the bureaucracy. The technique we evolved was to distinguish between contractual requirements and system requirements—holding the vendor to the former while leaving the latter flexible. In any case, the Sumo Wrestler had pulled rather than pushed—and won the match.

S2: Never Waste an Emergency

When President Obama announced that we would launch DACA in sixty days, our agency recognized that it faced an emergency. We knew that we'd find some way to get it done, and of course we did. Mission-driven people in organizations are pretty good at dealing with emergencies. The difference between what you can do in a crisis and what you can do on normal days is, more or less, your bureaucratic waste. It becomes easy to identify.

As I explained in Chapter 2, emergencies can also help you sell ideas and convince others of the need for change. When the president's signature healthcare initiative was derailed by the failure of the Healthcare.gov site, our case suddenly became stronger: "Do you really want a repeat of Healthcare.gov?" Or, "Haven't we learned anything from Healthcare.gov?"

Another productive disaster for us was the theft of personnel records from OPM's databases. While its immediate impact was to tighten controls around security, it also became useful support for our argument that we needed to rethink our security approach altogether. It opened up the possibility of change.

As I write this, COVID-19 is the emergency of the day. I'm certain that many companies will be using the crisis to advocate for loosening restrictions around telework. The need for sudden change to respond to Brexit, for many firms and government agencies, will be a good argument for increasing IT agility and disposing of old IT systems. Who knows what we'll be able to do when comes the zombie apocalypse . . .

Sometimes you can create urgency through BHAGs (big hairy audacious goals). To maximize their impact, though, you need to connect them to mission outcomes. Employees will internalize the goals much better if they are not just aggressive targets someone has set to drive them to higher efforts.

S3: Call and Raise the Bureaucracy

Fight bureaucracy with bureaucracy. As Provoke and Observe is to the Monkey and Lean Technique is to the Razor, Call and Raise is the core principle of the Sumo Wrestler. If your opponent is large, be larger.

You saw this technique at work in Chapter 2, "Chaos Monkey in the Bureaucracy," where we fought MD-102 by introducing MI-CIS-OIT-003 and 004. To prevent backsliding into MD-102, we set up a magnificent bureaucratic IV&V process that would make doubly sure that Agile practices were being followed. It even helped the auditors do their jobs, as there was now a paper trail showing that we had done exactly what we said we would—that is, be agile.

A wonderful thing about bureaucracy is that it can be turned upon itself very productively. By writing a Project Tailoring Plan that said we'd do the opposite of what MD-102 required, we made our process compliant with MD-102. It was like matter and antimatter annihilating one another in a burst of energy. What was left was a clear field where we could build freely.

In a variation on this strategy, we learned to check all the compliance boxes even before anyone told us to. We tried to be even more bureaucratic than the bureaucracy. Where there were FISMA controls that had to be implemented, we found ways to implement them so quickly and effectively that we could immediately claim to be compliant. That earned us trust from the bureaucracy and also advanced our efforts to be lean.

S4: Read the Fine Print

Myth grows up quickly around rules. People don't like to fight, so they "play it safe" by conservatively interpreting the rules or setting even stricter rules for themselves . . . just to be sure. That's why we were told that we weren't allowed to sign time and materials contracts because "they were frowned upon," and that there had to be parity between paper and electronic forms. Contracting authorities told us we couldn't require bidders to submit to an in-person test of their abilities. Security people told us that we couldn't have a datacenter that allowed non-US citizens inside. None of these was actually in the original rules, even if they later became codified in policies and memos and imagination.

We learned to ask, first, where a rule came from—"Is that *your* rule or is it required by some law or policy?" The answer was almost always "No, it's not my rule, it's the law." The second question was: "Can you point me to exactly where it says that in the law or policy?" In many cases, we found, the law said something different, if it existed at all.

Asking "Where exactly does it say that?" graciously can help convince bureaucrats that you're in earnest—that you respect the humongous FAR or the PRA and are eager to abide by their precise terms. If you become an expert in the rules, you'll find ways to be creative within their constraints, and you can bond with the enforcers over a discussion of the finer points of the law.

So, the "don't do time and materials contracts" thing was not a rule, it was just "frowned upon," whatever that means. And actually, there was nothing in the whalelike FAR that said or even implied that we couldn't test the contractor's skills. The PRA doesn't literally say that there has to be parity between electronic and written forms. And the rule around non-US-citizens in the datacenters, I think, turned out to say something more like "Each agency needs to decide whether it will allow non-US-citizens into its datacenter." Some did, and some didn't, have a rule that applied.

Our QA organization had encouraged project teams to write those really long answers in each section of MD-102 documents because they were afraid that the overseers would otherwise reject them. And they *occasionally* did. But there was nothing in the rules that said we had to—and it turned out that we didn't.

And I'll say it again—those conservative interpretations have a cost. The way of the Monkey is to expose the waste. The way of the Razor is to cut it away. And the way of the Sumo Wrestler is to gain and use leverage by questioning the enforcers and examining the rules more closely.

Pseudo-rules proliferate when there's gatekeeping late in a workflow. Because everyone is afraid that the overseers might reject something at the last minute, they're more conservative early on. It's a little like superstition—you don't really know what the bureaucrat's going to do, so you think "Once we tried this and the overseers rejected it, so we won't do it again." I remember a psychology professor telling our class of an experiment where researchers gave lab rats food pellets at random times. The rats developed strange, quirky behaviors—running in circles, dancing the Macarena, rebooting their computers—believing that doing so might trigger the reward.

The Sumo Wrestler wisely refuses to dance the Macarena and suggests that bureaucrats stop as well—the costs of watching are just too high.

S5: Redefine Quality

What you're allowed to do is often determined by whether or not what you do is challenged. When you understand auditors' objectives, you can work backward to what you can do without their objecting. A Sumo Wrestler technique is to create your own definition of quality that you can map to any framework you must comply with—then enforce your definition rather than theirs.

It's useful to think of quality as encompassing a broad range of attributes. In IT, for example, quality might include not just passing tests, but also accomplishing business objectives, being usable and accessible, and being secure. High-quality code is readable and maintainable, scalable and reliable. It is simple and straightforward. And it complies with any frameworks the company is subject to.

When an organization defines these attributes precisely, it can automate the process of testing for them. The definition of secure code (more or less)* is code that passes the automated security tests. Accessibility, scalability, and framework compliance may also be defined by the set of tests the code must pass. These objective ways of judging quality can replace quality assurance by trolls and arbitrary "conservatism" applied "just to be sure."

If you're making your bureaucratic controls lean and enabling, then you have as much interest as the auditors in making sure they're enforced—your incentives are aligned. You don't want to wait until an annual audit finds problems. Instead, you can define quality in a way that will satisfy auditors, then "shift left" and enforce it throughout the delivery process, avoiding the waste that would otherwise come with bad audit findings and rework. Yet you don't add superstitious effort based on fear of the bad audit.

Another place where you fight bureaucracy by creating more of it!

S6: Show Success

When things are going poorly, the bureaucratic trolls come out of their caves and compete with each other to demonstrate their commitment to fixing your problems. When things are going well, they just stay home and barbecue spherical cows. A good way to escape costly scrutiny is to be successful.

---

* I say "more or less" because we also do manual penetration testing and put guardrails in production environments. -au.

Since the purpose of much oversight is to mitigate risk, it often has triggers that force attention on something that is not going well. A typical scenario we faced was that a project would be ignored by the overseers until it suddenly found itself "in breach" of a schedule or cost milestone. Then the bureaucracy would come crashing down hard on it.

Fortunately, today's techniques are troll repellent—they make it easier to stay in success mode. With DevOps and the cloud, we can release IT capabilities quickly and begin to accomplish business objectives, then build on them incrementally. That means we can demonstrate success consistently throughout a project. Agile techniques are designed to show business outcomes (rather than to hit cost and schedule milestones), really, so we should have confidence that that's exactly what we'll do. And if you demonstrate success quickly, before you're tied up in red tape, then no one will remember which form you "forgot" to fill out. It's rare for bureaucracy to descend on a project that's popular and successful, especially one that returns money it was budgeted.

Agile projects are designed to correct their own course, quickly, and without the interference of authorities. They're constantly and rapidly knocked back on track before administrative interference is launched. In the new oversight process that we piloted, the overseers were involved every step of the way, so a "breach" was no longer a breach of an implicit contract—it was simply a measurement of how far away from hoped-for results a project was. It was not a question of blame or poor execution, just a reason to reevaluate and redirect the investment.

S7: Listen to the Bureaucracy

We asked our bureaucratic overseers: What would make your job easier? We treated them as the customer of our new and improved oversight process. We took in their feedback frequently and adjusted our process. They hadn't fully realized how much of a burden the old oversight process was on them, with its long and wordy documents and its drawn-out review meetings. Since our MD-102 documents were so long-winded, they didn't actually have time to read them—so they delegated the review to others. But that meant that they didn't really have a handle on important information and sometimes missed problems that were brewing. If we could reduce the noise and the blubber, then they could focus on the important stuff and oversee better.

We showed them that some of the information they were collecting was just a proxy for information they really wanted—and that we could cut right to what was important. For example, instead of telling them that a particular piece of work was 42% done (but hadn't produced results yet), we could show them that we had finished and deployed about 42% of the functionality they expected, that employees or customers were using it, and that it was accomplishing the business results we wanted. That was much more valuable information for them.

We arranged frequent meetings with the overseers. Instead of giving them a stack of paper that didn't have any actionable information, we agreed that there were really only two important questions they had, and that there were four key pieces of information that would answer those two questions: (1) Is the project healthy? and (2) What is the project planning to spend money on next?

To answer question (1), the two key pieces of information were: (a) how much we had spent so far, and (b) what business results we had accomplished so far? Comparing those two, the overseers would know whether the project was healthy. To answer question (2), the key pieces of information were (a) what we were planning to do next, and (b) how much we were planning to spend. We did this at a relatively fine-grained level for the upcoming month and at a coarse-grained level for the next few years. Comparing the plan and the cost, the overseers would have a sense of the business case for the future work—very approximate, but they would be revisiting the investment decision every month, so they were risking only one month of investment.

We were pretty sure that when the oversight group got used to this, they would find that it gave them exactly the information they needed in the most concise way. We were available to answer any remaining questions and we proposed a formal one-hour presentation and discussion every quarter. This pilot approach would be extremely lean but give the overseers more real control than they had had before.

But that was only a hypothesis on our part. Just as with any new product design, we needed to get feedback from our "customers" on how well it was working for them, and adjust based on what they told us. We set up a feedback loop with the bureaucracy and listened as the oversight committee reviewed our presentation and discussed it among themselves. We evolved the new technique over the course of several months based on what we learned.

S8: Reduce Risk and Increase Controls!

Like a bureaucracy, I'm pretty risk averse. That's why I think we should make bureaucracy lean, learning, and enabling: doing so greatly reduces risk. The Sumo Wrestler outbids the bureaucracy by substituting lean controls that are *even more* risk mitigating than the old ones. We loved to take a "more risk-averse than thou" posture when needling the bureaucracy.

With the cloud and DevOps, we mitigate risk with speed. For example, DevOps automates testing and deployment so that completely regression-testing an IT system can take minutes to hours, where traditional manual testing took weeks to months. As a result, we can run our tests, including security tests, every time any change is made to the code or the infrastructure. That's every time. Imagine how much more risk that mitigates. Our mean time to repair (MTTR) is also vastly shortened through automation, which means that when we discover a security vulnerability (which happens as hackers learn new tricks), we can fix it much faster, again lowering risk. Though new techniques can appear risky just because they are new, digital transformation in fact reduces risk.

It follows that the traditional bureaucratic controls, though put in place to reduce risk, actually increase it when compared to new alternatives. The Sumo Wrestler is not shy about pointing this out. "*J'accuse!* You, you supposedly risk averse fiduciary, you are holding onto old bureaucratic constraints that prevent us from responding to competitors and adapting to changes in the market. You are risking the entire company! That's risk aversion?" My monkey side always wants to jump in and say "How can you keep those wasteful bureaucratic processes in place when they make it harder for us to respond to competitors and changes in the markets, and therefore threaten our entire company?" But this chapter is about the Sumo Wrestler, who turns any questions about the risk of the new around, using the force of the bureaucracy against itself. How can you, of all risk-hating bureaucracies, not change to a safer way?

A bureaucracy that fails to learn despite living in a fast-changing environment—one that petrifies—adds risk to its organization. That risk might be an "opportunity risk" (a parallel to "opportunity cost") where new, risk-reducing practices have been invented but the organization is not taking advantage of them, or a more direct risk, where slowness to act threatens revenue streams. The Sumo Wrestler takes the power of risk aversion and turns it back on the bureaucracy to cause change.

User's Guide to the Sumo Wrestler

A bureaucracy is a huge immovable object—a leviathan, a tectonic plate, a four-hundred-pound guy in a loincloth. The Sumo Wrestler uses bureaucracy's force against it; he finds a small leverage point and applies force right there. Where does the bureaucracy have weaknesses?

- It's risk averse, but is maximizing its risk.
- It loves formal ceremony, so it may be amenable to new formal ceremony.
- It can panic when something bad occurs and open itself up to new ideas that let it declare that it has addressed the problem.
- It is probably not serving its own guardians well; that is, its rules and processes may be inconsistent with what the people in authority actually want or are tasked with.
- It has little to say about success, since it's oriented toward avoiding failure, so success can allow one to move more freely.
- Because of its commitment to the rules, someone with expertise in the rules can often take advantage of overlooked or reinterpretable rules to cause change.

THE BLACK BELT BUREAUCRAT

There are certain queer times and occasions in this strange mixed affair we call life when a man takes this whole universe for a vast practical joke, though the wit thereof he but dimly discerns, and more than suspects that the joke is at nobody's expense but his own.

—Herman Melville, *Moby Dick*

What I had intended to ask of you as a favour you have generously made a duty, leaving me the appearance of merit when I am merely following my own inclination.

—Friedrich Schiller, *On the Aesthetic Education of Man*

Black Belt Bureaucracy

There are times when bureaucracy is the best available solution. You reach into your tool bag as a leader and what comes out is a sticky, gooey gob of rules that you have to enforce, maybe to ensure your company stays compliant with GDPR or your expense and HR policies are applied fairly. Or, if you're an IT leader, perhaps you need to brew up some rules around security, enterprise architecture standards, or shared services with chargebacks to business units.

What's the recipe for a bureaucracy that doesn't stir up metaphysical pathos among those subject to it? How can you use a bureaucracy the way Weber intended—to promote efficiency, fairness, and merit-based organization? To make it "domination through knowledge" rather than through petty authority and arbitrariness? How do you make sure it doesn't pettifog?

Of course: you need to make it lean, learning, and enabling.

B1: Move Incrementally

Why exactly are you manufacturing bureaucracy? I don't mean at a superficial level, like "we need to have control." I mean, really, why? Is it to make sure you comply with GDPR? Is it to reduce travel expenses? To make sure workers show up to work on time? If you're introducing IT standards, you might not have asked yourself why exactly—IT standards are as much a habit as a meaningful tactic.

You can't skip this step, because the next step is to figure out the minimum bureaucratic constraints that will accomplish your objective. It's an application of the Agile principle of "Maximize the amount of work not done"; in this case, it's "Maximize the amount of bureaucracy not imposed." Or you can think of it as an MVB—minimum viable bureaucracy—to which you will add more bureaucracy only if it becomes necessary. Start small, add incrementally, like everything else in the Agile world.

To build your bureaucracy empirically, you need to ascertain the results of each incremental piece of bureaucracy. That's your feedback loop. If you add a bureaucratic mechanism and it doesn't help accomplish your objective, roll it back!

Clarity on your objective is also important because you'll need to compare the benefits to the costs you're adding through your bureaucratic controls. Why not subtract your bureaucratic costs from your bureaucratic benefits and call it your profit from bureaucracy? If the profit isn't looking too impressive, roll back, roll back!

You can give people transparency into the purpose of the rules, at least for those who are interested in questioning them. You *want* the rules to be questioned (see Hunt Monkeys, below). The critical point is to be clear on the purpose—because that leaves open the possibility of satisfying the purpose in better ways.

You must do an honest job of calculating the costs of your bureaucracy, not necessarily in dollars but in additional lead time for getting things done. Doing so is hard because your costs are scattered all over the enterprise. How many hours do people spend in meetings? Who has to review, edit, and sign off on documents? If you have an enterprise architecture standard, what does it cost you when employees forego using a tool or technique that more exactly fits the situation? Do you have an Enterprise Architecture Review Board, or a governance board? Do people have to prepare packages for that board, endure uncomfortable reviews, gather information to complete the packages?

B2: Do Marginal Doing

When you add bureaucracy, you will be adding *watching* to your *doing*. Your ultimate goal, though, is to maximize the amount of successful doing per dollar invested. So, a marginal dollar of watching had better increase the productivity or success of each of your doing dollars. You spend each watching dollar with the hypothesis that it will do so. Perhaps making this hypothesis explicit will bring clarity to your bureaucracy-making effort.

For example, you might be introducing a control that will help you comply with GDPR. In that case, it will probably make a lot of your doing more successful, because you'll be allowed to do your doing in Europe or with Europeans as customers. Let's say instead that you'll require all software development projects to write an Integrated Logistical Support Plan. Your implicit hypothesis is that doing so will make the dollars you spend on each project more effective. This is a hypothesis that you really should test, because its truth isn't all that obvious.

When it's time to cut costs and take a marginal dollar out of your budget, seriously consider taking it from watching, not doing. You might be tempted to do the opposite, since with a lower budget, you feel you need better control over spending. But over what spending? If you're not spending on doing, you're done.

But the best way to frame this decision is to consider the goal: maximizing the amount of successful doing per dollar invested. You should take the dollar from whichever bucket will lead to that outcome.

B3: Substitute Values and Principles

As I noted in Chapter 7, it's sometimes possible to replace bureaucratic controls with strong cultural norms and agreed-upon values and principles. Amazon is a good example, with its fourteen leadership principles that guide day-to-day decisions and reduce the number and extent of rules necessary. They don't exactly replace bureaucracy, but they do fill in gaps between the rules, even if you make those gaps satisfyingly wide.

We're trying to avoid this kind of thinking (in Muller's words):

"Voiding human choice in public decisions is not just a theory . . . but a kind of theology. . . . Human choice is considered too dangerous." As a consequence, "Officials no longer are allowed to act on their best judgment" or to exercise discretion, which is judgment about what the particular situation requires.[1]

Instead, we want to use our bureaucracy to provide minimal guardrails and then ask employees to use their judgment—guided by the organization's values and principles. That doesn't mean that management loses its control (in the broadest sense of the word), because employees are expected to use good judgment and will have to answer for their actions. At Amazon, each of us is free—encouraged, I should say—to make our own decisions on how to use the principles "Customer Obsession" and "Bias for Action," but we have to use them and our decisions may be scrutinized.

When setting up your bureaucracy, there are many areas where you'll do better to establish principles rather than rules, particularly in situations where cases are so varied that rules are necessarily incomplete, in areas of high ambiguity where you want employees to exercise judgment, and in areas where creative interpretation is necessary. On the other hand, values and principles will probably not help you prove your compliance with formal compliance regimes.

B4: Work inside the Frame

Continuing that train of thought—bureaucratic rules are just one way of many to steer employee behavior. It's not necessary to use governance rules to control every aspect of their behavior because principles, management, and norms among their peers also contribute to guiding them. In particular, each employee has a manager who—get ready for this—manages them. Not necessarily in a command-and-control way, but in a way that influences their behavior. The bureaucratic rules are a "frame," you might say, within which employee behavior is both free and managed.

An example that often comes up in our IT discussions is the use of standardized development and deployment platforms. In many DevOps organizations, a central group makes a set of tools available—a build pipeline—for all the developers to use. Leaders sometimes ask whether they should *require* all the teams to use it.

Not necessarily. Some enterprises have decided to leave the choice up to each team, with the provision that if the team uses the standard toolset, it will be managed and maintained by the central platform team, thereby freeing them of the burden. Since that's a compelling proposition, most teams will choose to use the standard platform. A few teams might decide that the standard toolset isn't right for what they're doing and will choose a nonstandard one.

The next question we hear from leaders is "But what if they don't use the standard when they should? What if they just prefer a different tool and decide to use it even though it adds cost and effort? Don't we need a governance control to make sure they don't?"

No. The people on these teams have managers who should question their decision to use a nonstandard toolset. The manager should ask "Why did you decide to do something that cost the company extra money? Was that a wise decision? Why are you going to waste your time managing the alternate tool instead of doing other, more productive work?"

This is how most knowledge-work employees are managed. Their actions aren't fully governed by bureaucratic rules, but they are expected to make responsible decisions, and their managers are responsible for making sure that they do.

Even self-organizing teams in the Agile world are not free from control by managers.[2] One Agile thought leader, Mike Cohn, says that "a Scrum team's job is to self-organize around the challenges, and *within the boundaries and constraints put in place by management.*"[3] That's the key: freedom is the freedom to accomplish objectives that matter to the business.

As you build your black belt bureaucracy, you want to use it as a tool to constrain only what must be constrained. It's tempting to make the frame of governance small out of a fear that employees will make bad decisions and managers will fail to correct them. But you're hiring those employees to make good decisions. What you don't want to do is make it harder for them to do what they were hired to do, which is to use their brains, skills, and professional knowledge to further the goals of the enterprise.

B5: Make It Easy to Do the Right Thing

When we at USCIS realized that employees were almost always going to fall for social engineering scams, no matter what our rules said and how much we trained them, we backed off from bureaucracy and tried a different approach.

We introduced multifactor authentication, where employees had to use their badges to log in along with a simple PIN they'd memorized and did not need to change often. They no longer had a password for an attacker to steal.

Instead of frustrating employees with complicated password rules, we'd made it easy—once they got used to the new process, at least—for them to do the right thing to maintain the agency's security. The principle works for many bureaucratic rules. How easily can employees file their expense reports? Has marketing made it easier to follow brand guidelines, maybe by providing corporate logos in different image formats?

If you do require management's signatures on documents, make it easy to get them. Is there at least a cultural norm that managers will quickly make room on their schedules or even drop whatever else they're doing to review and sign the document?

B6: Build for Self-Service

In the chapter on *enabling bureaucracies*, I presented the idea of self-service bureaucracy. For example, software development teams often need to use third-party software such as open-source components. A coercive model would force them to get permission from the security department each time they wanted to use such a product. With a self-service model, the security team makes available to the developers a vending machine full of software that's been pre-vetted and secured. The developers can serve themselves without asking permission.

The self-service model works in many situations that previously required bureaucratic red tape and sometimes long lead times. One of the biggest drains on IT's time used to be password resets. It was frustrating for everyone else around the company as well. But today most organizations have automated this process. Any user can click the "forget password" link and obtain a reset code. Security controls are automated and built in.

At Amazon, we have a strong culture of self-service. In fact, a new employee's first few days of work resemble a scavenger hunt: they must figure out what they need, search for instructions on how to get it, and make their way through portals and installation scripts. I remember ordering my own business cards, joining email groups, requesting a company credit card, getting administrator access to my own laptop, and probably thirty or forty other self-serve tasks during my first day or two. Yet all of the bureaucratic and security controls are still applied—they're just built into the self-provisioning process.

Ask yourself: If employees were given the choice, would they use your bureaucratic mechanisms? If they simplify or speed up a repetitious task, probably yes. If they needlessly constrain the employee, the initial answer is probably no. Of course, if you can show them why the mechanism is needed, it might change their minds. For an employee who is truly motivated to help the company succeed, a mildly annoying control that is clearly necessary to keep the company in compliance with GDPR might be easy to accept. You want to make sure that the employee willingly goes to your vending machine and gets the healthy noodles rather than ordering in from the ice cream shop, as I do.

B7: Automate Compliance

Automating bureaucratic controls makes them lean and removes the annoying toil associated with them. It's a standard DevOps technique. Wherever you need to enforce a control, either set up an automated process that enforces compliance or automate a test that checks to see if compliance is occurring. It's fast, easy, and doesn't involve personal impositions of authority or troll-keeping.

For example, say that you want to deploy the financial controls I talked about in Chapter 7, requiring employees to tag (or label) infrastructure that they spin up in the cloud with a cost center code so that you can allocate costs. Old school bureaucracy: tell everyone they have to label their infrastructure, and have Finance periodically check to see that they did. New bureaucracy technique #1: set up an automated control in the cloud that continuously checks to make sure all infrastructure is tagged and if not, either shuts it off or reports that it is noncompliant. New bureaucracy technique #2: create a template script that employees will use to stand up their infrastructure and have it automatically look up and insert the right cost center code based on which employee or project is using it. That way the employee doesn't even have to do anything to remain compliant.

Old-school bureaucracy required that employees use the right red tape to prove that they had followed the required processes. This created a paper trail so that auditors could later verify compliance. But all that paper adds costs and slows work down. Instead, with well-implemented automation, you should be able to give the auditors as much red tape as they can consume, with no added effort and no slaughtering of trees. Electronic audit trails are even better than paper ones, because they can record more detail and, in many cases, can't be altered. Leaner bureaucracy and even better compliance.

I mentioned earlier that much of the documentation required by MD-102 is really a disguised checklist: an inefficient way to have someone sign off on the assertion that they did what was required. After each gate review meeting, we were required to write a memo saying that we'd reviewed the project and approved it to proceed into the next phase. The words in the memo weren't important—it was just a wordy checkbox.

Fortunately, we can now automate many of the tasks whose only purpose was to show that rules had been followed. For example, one of our gatekeeping reviews checked to make sure that a new system had been fully tested before releasing it to production. But today we can write our automated deployment scripts to make sure that all of the code's tests have been passed. We not only know the code works but also have an electronic audit trail showing exactly when the tests were run and what their results were. Since we can also electronically track any changes to the tests and the deployment script, we know exactly what tests were used and can confirm that nothing was deployed without adequate testing. The trolls rest contentedly in their caves.

B8: Get Skin in the Game

Our initiatives were overseen by disinterested parties who had little incentive to see the project completed successfully, only an incentive to stop it from proceeding if they discovered any risk. And, of course, there's always risk. MD-102 was burdensome because those who imposed it had no incentive to make it less burdensome. Quite the opposite: the thicker MD-102 became, the easier it was to show Congress that they had DHS's investments under control.

What if the burden were reversed: If the overseers had to justify every document and gate review they demanded? If they had to prove that the expense of an Integrated Logistical Support Plan was justified by the value it created for every software development project required to produce it? (It isn't.) This exercise isn't likely to happen because oversight is usually imposed by managers high in the hierarchy on employees who are low in the hierarchy, who have no right to demand justification. But you're building your bureaucracy from scratch, so make those overseers work for their piles of red tape!

We had a similar problem with IV&V (independent verification and validation). It was performed by a contractor or a team that was not directly involved in the project—that's what made it "independent." That independence was valued by the devisers of MD-102, since their process was based on distrusting the project executors. That same independence, though, was also a problem—their incentive was only to find problems, not to support well-reasoned trade-offs.

Since they were never part of the decision-making and learning that went on every day during a project, they could only compare the result to the original plan. If a manager had decided that one of the requirements no longer made sense because of changing circumstances, and therefore was not worth its cost to implement, IV&V would flag it as a deficiency, in effect insisting that the money should have been wasted. When you're setting up your bureaucracy, make sure that it supports the behaviors you want to encourage.

B9: Redraw Organizational Charts

Sometimes, changing the organizational chart can reduce the need for bureaucratic ceremony. You'll often find wasteful formality at those seams where one silo meets another. In my previous books I tried to show how the traditional separation between IT and something called "the business" led to waste as requirements were tossed over the wall to IT and results tossed back over the wall to the business. Much of IT bureaucracy follows this separation: for example, the overhead of requirements documents, the sign-offs required to approve them, and the Gantt charting and status reporting that uphold the arms-length, contractor-like relationship that such a structure requires. There are a number of ways to solve this; one is to simply move the technologists onto product teams within the "business" part of the organization.

The problem is more general, though. In earlier chapters I showed that bureaucracy arises as interactions between silos are formalized, in a sort of Conway's Law of Bureaucracy. This can often be remedied by some simple pencil strokes on the organizational chart.

Weber's division of labor was along functional lines. His assumption—typical of the twentieth century—was that the increasing sophistication of different technical areas would require increasing specialization on the part of employees. DevOps and other cross-functional team-based approaches have called this into question. Generalist skills are more highly valued today, and we like to work backwards from the customer, organizing around product areas that directly deliver customer value rather than around technical skills.

Generalist skills, in fact, may help soften the rigid formalism that one functional group must impose on others. A security geek who understands the operations of the business might be able to develop better, or at least more informed, security policy that is easier to stomach. On the other hand, a business operator who has some understanding of security might have a bigger stomach for policy. Rigid siloing into functional groups exacerbates the pain of bureaucratic paraphernalia: policies that are forced on someone by security technocrats they don't understand and whose measures of success are different and harder to accept.

When crafting bureaucracy today, you'll want to make sure there are clear—but not necessarily technical or functional—accountabilities. Cross-functional teams can sit comfortably in a Weberian hierarchy, happily occupying a bubble on the org chart, sometimes within the product part of the organization. Generalists, exiled from Weberian bureaucracy, can have specific accountabilities, but they also play a helpful role in making coercive-sounding bureaucracy more enabling.

B10: Formalize Agility in Policy

Despite the constraints you're imposing, you still want speed and agility. Since what is set in policy will tend to win out against what is not, consider writing speed and agility into formal policy. For example, it would have been helpful if the Analysis of Alternatives template had mandated that each of its sections be filled out as briefly as possible. Perhaps MD-102 could have required a QA analyst to sign off on each document as being the briefest possible document that answered the questions in the template. That would be fine agile bureaucracy.

I've given you a head start with MI-CIS-OIT-003 and 4 in Appendix A to this book. You can also require that continuous improvement be applied to your own policy, as we did with the addendum to MI-003, which you'll also find in this book's Appendix. As I mentioned earlier, we erred in not formalizing a process for regularly updating the addendum—you might want to try doing so in your own policy and let me know how it goes.

B11: Practice Occam's Centrifugal Whirl

In Chapter 9, I introduced Occam's Centrifugal Whirl, a tactic of spinning authorities out to the periphery, or decentralizing controls when possible. In the tension between centralization and decentralization, centralization has a bureaucratic cost. It's sometimes the right answer; the benefits outweigh the costs. But the default should be decentralization; it's centralization that must be justified.

In DHS, where our investments were overseen centrally, the overseers were not familiar with our day-to-day needs and constraints, so there was additional cost to us in documenting and explaining things that were obvious to everyone in our component agency. The central overseers didn't have to make the difficult trade-offs that we made every day; they didn't feel the pain of delays to our initiatives that jumping through their bureaucratic hoops caused. Centrally based decision-makers are forced to see everything through the lens of simplified metrics and simplified categories. MD-102, as a central oversight framework, had to be general enough to apply to missions as distinct as vetting immigration applications, operating Coast Guard carriers, protecting the president, and responding to natural disasters. It could do none of these well. And centralized service provision ("shared services") can add overhead and checkpoints to operations that could otherwise be self-service.

There are alternatives to centralized activity that can be effective and still allow for a degree of centralized management. Information security policies, to the extent that they need to be shared across the enterprise, can be delivered to the periphery in the form of automated test suites, which can then be applied by the decentralized teams. At AWS, the teams that create our products and services are highly decentralized and autonomous, but still implement guidance they are given by centrally based leaders; for example, continually working to reduce their costs and pass the savings on to customers.

Centralizing is sometimes necessary and sometimes productive, but it should not be a given.

B12: Dashboard Your Successes

In the first play, B1, you made sure you understood your objectives. Why not measure against those objectives and expose your results on a dashboard? The enforcers of MD-102 could have created a dashboard to show whether projects overseen by MD-102 were delivered on time and within budget. The results would not have been impressive. Even better, it could have reported on the cost of complying with MD-102 versus the benefits in on-time performance.

If you're going to continuously improve your bureaucratic controls, then the improvements you make can be represented on the dashboard as well. Doing so will help motivate those on your continuous improvement team and those on whom the bureaucracy is enforced. As I've said, the PRA had many good aspects, one of which was that it tracked a specific metric—the number of burden-hours reduced. Let's do the same with all of our bureaucracy shrinking.

You can treat the oversight process—the bureaucratic symphony you're composing—as an investment and, just like any other investment, see what value you're getting from it. The result should be a fine-tuning of your bureaucracy to get the best results.

B13: Hunt Monkeys

The best way to make sure your bureaucracy evolves is to find monkeys within your organization who'll keep pushing to make it better. Hunt for monkeys and support them. At Amazon, we have the concept of a "bar raiser," particularly in our hiring process. The bar raiser's job is to make sure that we keep getting better and better—they're a force or an energy that keeps the process of continuous improvement running. Old-school bureaucracies hate monkeys; new bureaucracies promote them, in both senses of the word.

In our hiring process, a bar raiser oversees the debrief after interviews, when the interviewers discuss their results and make their hiring decision. The bar raiser's job is to make sure that the candidate is only hired if they'll be better at doing their job than 50% of the people who are currently doing it. We also have bar raisers for our AWS blog who make sure that the quality of our content keeps going up. As a master bureaucrat, you can't just subscribe to the principle of continuous improvement; you must also set up a process where it will necessarily happen.

A monkey should constantly question bureaucratic controls to make sure they're still justified and suggest alternatives that might accomplish the same objectives better. Where bureaucracy tends to accumulate more and more controls, the monkey is a force for divesting controls that are no longer necessary and eliminating duplicative controls. A master bureaucrat makes sure there's always a monkey handy.

B14: Bureaucrats Must Work Too

The overseers work for the executors, not the other way around. Making this clear is one way to give them skin in the game. It's also a way to increase doing and reduce watching. Just as automating security controls turns them into tools that developers can use to make sure their code is secure, your oversight process should be a tool that project teams can use to make sure their efforts deliver business value and are aligned with strategy. Which is something they actually want.

In my IT organization, we pushed this principle even further by mandating that overseers such as QA, Enterprise Architecture, and Security do hands-on technology work: they became doers rather than watchers. Instead of issuing and documenting standards, Enterprise Architecture began creating reusable software components that implemented their standards. Security created or assembled automated security tests and placed automated guardrails in production. QA set up automated quality monitoring tools ("static code analysis") and trained other technologists on how to improve quality. In all of these cases, the overseers were doing work that helped the people they oversaw.

The ARB, which consisted of officials rather high in the bureaucratic hierarchy, could also have worked for the projects they oversaw. They could, for example, have asked us an additional question in each meeting: What impediments are you facing and what can we do to help remove them? In other words, the overseers could have acted as servant leaders. From their positions in the hierarchy they would have had a lot of organizational power to apply. They could have seen across the many investments DHS was making and found ways to coordinate them for mutual advantage. They could have financed subsidiary activities that would help the project.

If the overseers were truly invested in the success of a project, they would be contributing however they can. The fact that we rarely saw that behavior from DHS overseers is a clue that their focus was on application of the rules rather than outcomes—that is, that there was a displacement of goals. But there's no reason why they can't bring a supportive attitude to oversight, even in a compliance-oriented bureaucracy. Ideally, they would have been dedicated to helping us comply with their rules rather than acting as judges of whether we were complying or not.

B15: ASAP Is Good

Perhaps you're familiar with some pointy-haired boss* who wants everything ASAP. Well, he's right. Everything should be done ASAP. This sounds strange

---

*A reference to the cartoon strip Dilbert. -au, standing in for -ed.

because the pointy-haired boss is a jerk and when he says ASAP he means that his employees should work nights and weekends to finish the work. He means that he doesn't want to make decisions about priorities, he just wants everything right away.

The sense in which he's right is that a lean organization always tries to reduce lead times as much as possible (without demanding unsustainable effort from employees). When managers want something as soon as possible, they're then committed to removing any waste or impediments that will slow their employees down. A typical impediment is that the manager does not prioritize the work—Lean theory teaches us that limiting work in process will reduce lead times. A good manager shouldn't settle for having work delivered "on time," but should insist on having it delivered with the shortest possible lead time—and be committed to making it possible.

This is important because bureaucracy is comfortable dealing with pre-dictability (calculability)—focused on outcomes like delivering "on time." But that's not really what we want in a modern organization—we want short lead times (work completed ASAP). A culture of ASAP provides the urgency and the impetus for improving bureaucracy. You can help the Monkey in his task of showing that the status quo is not okay by making it clear that speed is valued. Bad bureaucracies bloat, which means they have waste, which means they are not lean, which means they lead to long lead times. ASAP is what's missing.

Let's say that you're setting up a governance process for IT projects—a process for deciding whether to fund proposed IT investments. You should have two lean goals: make sure your process makes its decisions as soon as pos-sible (no sooner than possible, though), and make sure that the investments you fund will deliver their results as soon as possible.

An example where ASAP urgency was lacking was our delightful Balanced Workforce Assessment approval process.* Each official was given one week to review and sign the assessment document. But since it only took fifteen minutes to do so, and since desk aging does not improve the quality of a spread-sheet, the rest of the week was waste. Each official should sign the document as soon as they can, and that's that. If they sign it in barely less than the week they are given, that's not bureaucratic success.

---

* This was the process that prevented us from achieving thirty-day procurements that I mentioned in Chapters 2 and 10. -au, standing in for -ed.

B16: Everyone Owns the Rules

Rules should almost never be enforced, in the coercive sense. If every rule is there for a good reason, and if employees are motivated toward the success of the enterprise, then they should want to follow the rules.

For example, the only way that a company can be successful at securing its information assets is if it builds a culture where security is valued. Everyone, regardless of their role in the hierarchy, should care about their company's security posture and consider security to be part of their job.

An employee in Marketing or Sales, for example, should care about the privacy of their customers' information—they're implicitly promising it when they promote the company's products. A COO should care that the company's operations can continue running rather than being halted by a hacker who compromises an important IT system. The CEO and CFO have a fiduciary duty to the shareholders to prevent security breaches. Complying with the security rules is not a matter of obedience—it is a matter of doing what's necessary to accomplish your own goals, which should include keeping your company secure. No one can really be doing their job right if they don't participate in securing the organization.

Bureaucratic hierarchies with their strict divisions of labor can have this danger: that because security is specifically the goal of a security team, everyone else believes that it's not their own job. As a result, they comply minimally and grudgingly with security policies, and make no attempt to fill in the gaps between the official rules. It's like a work-to-rule strike, a way of taking policy literally and thereby subverting it.

Instead, all employees need to take ownership of securing the company, and use the security folks as enabling experts, the geeks who can help because they understand security deeply. To move from a coercive security bureaucracy to an enabling one everyone else has to want help from the security experts. The fact that they often don't is largely a leadership and management challenge. Employees who are truly motivated to see the company succeed should also be motivated to see the company secured.

Yes, there's some bureaucracy that must be enforced because it does not serve employees' objectives. I'd like to fly first class, but my company's rules say I must fly coach. But to a large extent, bureaucracy can serve the goals of employees as well as management—as long as management and leadership do what it takes to motivate the employees. Making bureaucracy pleasant turns out to be no more and no less than good organizational leadership.

To join an organization is to agree that you'll be committed to serving its goals. A well-designed bureaucracy harnesses that commitment, joins it to the commitment of others, and directs it toward the organization's mission. *Homo bureaucraticus* is born with an understanding of how to do that.

And that's my final word on metaphysical pathos.

AFTERWORD

God keep me from ever completing anything. This whole book is but a draught—nay, but the draught of a draught. Oh, Time, Strength, Cash, and Patience!

—Herman Melville, *Moby Dick*

The court wants nothing from you. It receives you when you come and dismisses you when you go.

—Franz Kafka, *The Trial*

Well, now you've done it. You've become a Kafka villain. I've taught you how to spin webs of bureaucracy and showed you that it's a natural thing for a *Homo bureaucraticus* like you to do. You'll thank me some day.

I've also shown you how to bust through someone else's bureaucracy when it's in your way. You're now a certified Monkey, an intrepid Knight of Occam, and an imposing Sumo Wrestler. You'll thank me some day.

For a next step, I suggest that you read some of the fine books and articles I've referred to. I only did as much justice to them as my sense of humor would allow; there's lots more to be learned. And read some of the fiction I mentioned—especially "Bartleby"—it will help you regain your metaphysical pathos so you can be like everyone else. You'll thank me some day.

Appendix A: MI-CIS-OIT-003

MEMO

Office of Information Technology
Management Instruction for Applying Lean- Agile-DevOps Principles at USCIS
Effective Date: 1 April 2017 Management Instruction: CIS-OIT-003

I. Purpose
This Management Instruction (MI) establishes the United States Citizenship and Immigration Services (USCIS) policies, procedures, requirements, and responsibilities for the use of Lean Thinking, Agile Development, and DevOps capability. It supersedes MI CIS-OIT-001 (Agile Development) and MI CIS- OIT-002 (Team-Managed Deployment Onboarding) and should be considered the current guidance for delivering Information Technology (IT) solutions within USCIS.

Lean, Agile, and DevOps methods enable the delivery of fit-for-purpose IT solutions with very short lead times, as measured from identification of a mission need to the delivery of IT capabilities meeting that need. These methods have been shown to produce IT solutions that:
- Satisfy customers
- Maintain ongoing operational capabilities
- Are high quality, thoroughly tested, and technically excellent
- Rapidly adapt even in an uncertain operating environment
- Continuously improve time-to-mission-value

This MI increases emphasis on DevOps thinking to improve USCIS IT service delivery agility and increase the business value of IT projects. DevOps strategies should be used to deploy software more frequently and reliably, act faster on feedback from system operations, and establish a culture of continuous experimentation and learning. These methods have been shown to:
- Enhance quality, reliability, and security of products and services over the long term
- Decrease business risk by lowering change failure rates and system downtime
- Improve outcomes and experiences for system stakeholders, developers, operations engineers, and end users
- Reduce total investment costs

Lean, Agile, and DevOps methods are consistent with the Department of Homeland Security (DHS) Acquisition Management Directive (MD) 102 and the DHS Systems System Engineering Lifecycle (SELC), the Digital Services Playbook, "Modular First" guidance from the DHS Chief Information Officer (CIO), the Federal Chief Information Officer's 25 Point Implementation Plan, and the Office of Management and Budget (OMB) Modular Contracting Guidance. The "modular and incremental" approach encouraged in these documents mandates that the government continuously learn and improve at delivering low cost, low risk IT solutions. In order to monitor these outcomes, this MI includes governance designed to provide rich, ongoing visibility into USCIS system development, delivery, and operations.

II. Scope
This MI applies to all employee and contractor teams involved in the planning, development, and deployment of software and systems throughout USCIS.

III. Authorities
The following laws, regulations, orders, policies, directives, and guidance authorize and govern this Management Instruction:
1. DHS MD 102-01 Acquisition Management Directive, and associated Instructions and Guidebooks
2. Section 5202 of the Clinger-Cohen Act of 1996

3. OMB Circulars A-130 and A-11
4. 25 Point Implementation Plan to Reform Federal Information Technology Management (U.S. Chief Information Officer, December 9, 2010)
5. Contracting Guidance to Support Modular Development (OMB, June 14, 2012)
6. Memorandum on Agile Development Framework for DHS, by DHS CIO, Richard A. Spires, issued June 1, 2012
7. Digital Services Playbook (https://playbook.cio.gov)

IV. Policy, Procedures, and Requirements

Except in cases where a waiver is granted by the USCIS CIO, all systems development and maintenance projects at USCIS will follow this Lean-Agile-DevOps MI. Such projects include custom software development, Commercial Off-The-Shelf-Software (COTS) integration and configuration, business intelligence, and reporting capabilities. Where appropriate, Lean-Agile-DevOps approaches may be used for other IT and non-IT projects. For the purposes of this MI, projects will be considered in compliance if they achieve the outcomes specified in Sections A and B. To achieve these outcomes, teams and programs may elect to use practices from the set of Generally Accepted Agile Practices listed in the Appendix and work with Independent Validation & Verification (IV&V) teams to ensure that they fulfill the MI CIS-OIT-004 (Agile Independent Verification and Validation).

USCIS Office of Information Technology (OIT) management will ensure that appropriate training, coaching, and tools are available to facilitate the success of all projects. Teams are encouraged to work with OIT support groups to implement this MI in a manner appropriate for their particular context.

A. Lean-Agile and DevOps Approaches Defined

Lean can be characterized as "the art of maximizing work not done" by increasing flow and reducing waste. Leanness is measured for IT projects by the lead time from identification of a need to the time a corresponding capability is delivered. Waste is defined as work that does not add enough value to justify itself, such as handoffs, delays, and unnecessary intermediate work products. Lean IT projects at USCIS continuously improve efficiency and responsiveness to mission needs on behalf of the public.

Agile approaches use an iterative, incremental, and collaborative process to deliver small, frequent software releases. Effective agile methods yield rich information from tight feedback loops, providing customers and delivery team's frequent opportunities to adapt based on changing project conditions. A number of agile methods are in common use at USCIS, including Kanban, Scrum, and Extreme Programming (XP). The values common to agile practices are articulated in the Agile Manifesto, which elevates interaction, working software, customer collaboration, and responding to change. The intent of the agile values is not to prescribe a set of mechanical steps or ceremonies but to guide an empirical, feedback-oriented agile mindset. Teams that follow agile values are likely to benefit from the "guardrails" inherent in the agile approach. Teams are encouraged to use practices from one or more agile methods as appropriate and to incorporate innovations from the agile community.

DevOps approaches subscribe to a seamless collaboration of operations and development engineers to fulfill business needs through delivery of stable, secure, and reliable services to customers. DevOps methods yield timely feedback at all points in the service lifecycle, improving the ability to reliably deploy software, respond to feedback from production operations, and continuously improve quality. A number of DevOps strategies are commonly used at USCIS, including Continuous Integration, Continuous Deployment and Continuous Operations.

B. Required Outcomes

USCIS develops IT solutions to support the mission of the agency. In order to achieve the desired impact, we require certain outcomes from software development, deployment, and operations processes. Where required outcomes are difficult to measure directly, measurement and observation can be used to infer them. These observations are guided by asking key questions to assess whether the desired outcome is being achieved.

The key questions presented for each outcome in this MI are not a definitive list. Programs should determine effective outcome measurements in their own context and track the trends of those measurements. Programs are also expected to change the questions and measurements over time to ensure they are checking the most important concerns. In addition to self-assessment, programs should coordinate with USCIS Independent Verification and Validation (IV&V) to assess effectiveness, facilitate transparency and accountability, and provide feedback to teams and management from an independent viewpoint.

Outcome #1: Programs and projects frequently deliver valuable product

Earlier delivery allows earlier accrual of value. Earlier use provides feedback on suitability.

Key Questions

- How frequently is the working system delivered to stakeholders for review?
- How frequently is the working functionality delivered to end users for use?
- What is the cycle time (mean, distribution) from start of work on a feature to delivery?
- What is the lead time from ideation/approval to use?
- How do you verify that the systems you're developing are solving the intended problem?
- How quickly do you know?

Outcome #2: Value is continuously discovered and aligned to mission

Teams and their business partners continuously discover emerging needs for their products. Delivered capability can and should trigger new discoveries.

Key Questions

- What business outcomes or strategic objectives are supported by the work being done?
- How do you know that you're working on today's highest priority items?
- What is the customer (stakeholders, users) satisfaction with delivered functionality?
- What actionable insights from end users are addressed over time?
- What is the team satisfaction with business engagement and direction?
- How can the value delivered be measured (understanding that sometimes a quantitative measure is not appropriate or feasible)?

Outcome #3: Work flows in small batches and is validated

Batch deployments significantly reduce risks associated with deployment. Low risk deployments promote flow of new capabilities to production.

Key Questions

- How is daily progress toward goals made visible? Is it a reliable progress indicator or does it hide surprises?
- Is work in progress finished before new work is started?
- How completely is incremental work validated before it is considered done?

Outcome #4: Quality is built in

Work processes address quality as a matter of course rather than as remediation. Avoiding problems provides more benefit than solving problems.

Key Questions

- What is the demand for remedial work?
- What is the incident rate of escaped defects?
- Are your tests automated and structured to provide the quickest feedback (unit tests)?
- Are you testing at all layers of the application with appropriate investment (test pyramid)?
- How easily does the system architecture and design allow for modification and extension?
- What precautions have been taken to reduce consequences when there is a system failure?
- What measures are in place to monitor the intrinsic quality of the code?
- How frequently do commits fail in the build/test/deploy pipeline?
- Does the system meet appropriate performance thresholds? As the system is modified, what are the trends in performance measurements?

Outcome #5: The organization continuously learns and improves

Improvements come from increased knowledge and skill. Performing the work provides deeper insights into improved methods.

Key Questions

- How freely can teams innovate and improve daily work?
- How inclusive is the collection of improvement ideas?
- How safe is it to try experiments that may not lead to expected results?

Outcome #6: Teams collaborate across groups and roles to improve flow and remove delays

The desired result is more than the sum of individual roles. Overlap is needed to prevent gaps between business and technical roles. Handoffs result in lost information and delays. Much important knowledge is tacit, and can best be shared by working together.

Key Questions

- How much code is reused across teams?
- What diverse roles explore the details of the requirements and what are the indicators of satisfaction of the requirements?
- What indications are there of responsibilities being shared across groups? How much time is spent waiting for another team's work?

Outcome #7: Security, accessibility and other compliance constraints are embedded and verifiable

Systems must not only have to work correctly for intended use, but also resist unintended abuse. In addition, there are mandates in law and executive direction that must be followed. Notable among these are disability accessibility and privacy protection. There are also constraints about the language used to communicate with the public.

Key Questions

- How are security, accessibility, and organizational constraints communicated throughout the project community? What indications are there that these constraints are well understood?
- Are security, accessibility and privacy requirements treated the same as functional requirements? How are they addressed in the requirements process? Are they prioritized as highly?
- How are security, accessibility and privacy addressed in system design and code structure?
- To what extent are security testing and controls integrated into daily work? How much is automated? How early does it detect issues?
- How is compliance with all security requirements verified in an ongoing manner and documented with auditable evidence?
- How is Section 508 Compliance verified as the system is developed and documented with auditable evidence? What controls are in place to notice undesirable changes or other actions made by an individual? How do we confirm and provide evidence that controls are operating effectively?

Outcome #8: Consistent and repeatable processes are used across build, deploy, and test

Consistency is required to maintain quality across delivery. Teams who have an understood and repeatable process can gauge the efficacy of the improvements made.

Key Questions

- How many manual steps are there in the current build, deploy, and test process, and what is the team doing to reduce that number?
- Is there a common code repository/branch that is built, tested, and deployed on every commit?
- How long does code exist on other branches or the developer's machine before merging to the common code?
- What degree of confidence does the suite of automated tests provide? o How quickly and easily can build failures be resolved?

Outcome #9: The entire system is deployable at any time to any environment

Unfinished work in progress provides no benefit and may block the efforts of others. The system should be maintained in a working state even as modifications are being made.

Key Questions

- Can the same automated script deploy to every environment?
- Are database changes and rollbacks automated with version-controlled scripts?
- To what extent is the setup and configuration of environments automated with version-controlled scripts?
- To what extent is the build/deployment pipeline automated with version-controlled scripts?
- How long does it take to stand up a complete test environment with production or production-like data?

Outcome #10: The system has high reliability, availability, and serviceability

Attention must be focused on the robustness of the system in the face of errors, the ability to be used as development proceeds, and the ability to quickly detect and correct latent problems.

Key Questions

- Can various parts of the system be built and deployed independently?
- To what degree is the system meeting the reliability, availability, and serviceability needs of the mission?
- How long does it take to detect, ameliorate, and correct operational problems?
- Are the operational characteristics of the system being validated in production through monitoring, reporting, and alerting? How?
- Is the system designed in such a way as to be cost-effective in operation?

V. Generally Accepted Agency Practices

Each program or project chooses a baseline set of practices that support the Lean-Agile-DevOps outcomes listed in this document. The chosen practices should be documented in the Team Process Agreement (TPA) and improved over time. The program or project may solicit an independent assessment of its practices following the USCIS IV&V Policy and will be expected to justify its practices to the RPR Authority (USCIS CIO or designee). Improvements that are material should be documented by updating the Team Process Agreement (TPA) before the next RPR and the program or project should be able to justify its TPA practices if questioned about them in the RPR.

MI CIS-OIT-003 Appendix A lists typical agency practices, derived from Agile and DevOps methods commonly followed in the software development industry. Nothing in this document should be construed as prohibiting even better practice, but is intended to guard against insufficient discipline or governance. Practices may be reviewed by the CIO or designee at any time, particularly in the RPR, or on the advice of Quality Assurance, and the program or project should be able to justify the chosen practices.

VI. Governance

The purpose of this governance is to ensure the government's interest in delivering appropriate IT solutions on behalf of the public. Governance responsibilities include:

- Ensuring changes to IT systems pose appropriately low risk to mission fulfillment
- Portfolio management and alignment with the overall strategic direction of mission
- Providing transparency to project stakeholders and opportunities for involvement by those impacted by system changes, including end users
- Verifying projects are carried out with appropriate procurement, contracting, and hiring practices in order to meet fiduciary constraints
- Continuously improving governance and oversight mechanisms to ensure that they accomplish project goals in a lean manner

This MI represents a tailoring of the SELC included in the annexes to DHS acquisition guidance presented in DHS D-102. Appendix B provides the tailoring plan that demonstrates this alignment with D-102. By following this MI, USCIS Lean-Agile-DevOps projects will maintain compliance with D-102. Programs on the DHS Major Acquisitions Oversight List will, in addition, need to fulfill the requirements of the D-102 Acquisition Lifecycle Framework (ALF).

A separate MI, CIS-OIT-004, describes the USCIS Agile Independent Verification and Validation USCIS Independent Verification and Validation (IV&V) approach that will be used to evaluate adherence to this MI and will inform governance activities.

During the "Obtain" phase of the program acquisition lifecycle, system development activities will proceed through a number of increments, or release cycles. For each increment, the following gate reviews will be held:

Lean Release Planning Review (Lean RPR)

Lean Release Planning is the means by which USCIS agile projects establish time, cost, and a notional plan for delivering new capabilities. Lean Release Planning artifacts should include minimum documentation necessary to effectively communicate release plans and should be published in a location accessible to all stakeholders. Once a minimum set of artifacts is established at the outset of a project, artifacts should be updated incrementally throughout the release cycle to reflect current reality.

The RPR Meeting is a gathering of stakeholders to review release plans and align resources to support them. The RPR Authority (USCIS CIO or designee) will assess a project's readiness to proceed with a time boxed release cycle of no more than six months. A business decision will be made as to whether the investment in the release cycle is justified by the expected results (capabilities to be produced). The project may not proceed to release activities (development, testing, etc.) until it has secured RPR approval.

The RPR Authority will assess the project's likelihood of achieving the outcomes required by this MI (sections A and B). The RPR Authority will review appropriateness of resourcing and skill levels, agile team processes, technical practices, the team's understanding of capabilities to be developed, oversight and transparency mechanisms, and dependencies on other projects and infrastructure. The project will demonstrate its readiness through thoughtful discussion with the RPR Authority, by providing evidence that stakeholders and delivery team members concur with release plans, and by producing a set of Lean RPR artifacts.

Core RPR Artifacts:

- Capabilities and Constraints (CAC)
- Project Oversight Plan (POP)
- Test Plan

- Team Process Agreement (TPA)
- Release Characteristics List

Other artifacts, such as Section 508 Compliance Determination Forms (CDF), may be required depending on the specific project, which will be established by agreement with the RPR Authority.

Team-Managed Deployment (TMD) Onboarding

TMD Onboarding is an IV&V process to validate a system's capability to operate with high reliability, availability, and serviceability using robust automated build, test, and deployment practices. Systems should be on boarded to TMD when they fully satisfy outcomes 7, 8, 9, and 10 in this MI. Following TMD onboarding, RPR approval constitutes authorization for teams to deploy directly to production for up to six months. To minimize risk, teams are encouraged to deploy as often as multiple times per day, and must deploy to production at least every two weeks.

TMD requires ongoing communication and collaboration of development engineers, operations engineers, and business stakeholders. The following team agreements are required to facilitate effective teaming across the project community.

1. *Product Owner Acceptance* – The Product Owner retains full authority and responsibility for approving features deployed both through feature toggles and by direct code push to production. Teams are strongly encouraged to make this Product Owner approval a step in the continuous delivery pipeline.
2. *Communications Agreements* – Teams make agreements with key stakeholders regarding notifications before, during, and after deployment. Stakeholders include the user community, operations support engineers; help desk personnel, the Information System Security Officer (ISSO), Quality Assurance, and other impacted groups. Teams are encouraged to provide notifications via an Operations Monitoring Dashboard.
3. *Monitoring* – Teams prepare an Operations Monitoring Plan or Dashboard showing the practices, tools, and measures that will monitor applications in production. The plan will include an operations review schedule and escalation procedure when monitoring thresholds are breached. In lieu of a document, an Operations Monitoring Dashboard is the preferred long-term approach.
4. *Documentation* – Teams regularly and appropriately update the document set in accordance with their Program Oversight Plan (POP). Artifacts requiring regular updates may include a Pipeline Design Document, System Design Document or Wiki (SDD/W), Interface Control Agreements (ICAs), and Section 508 and Security Documentation. Teams are encouraged to use agile documentation approaches such as self-documenting code and tests expressed in a business-friendly language. Agreements regarding such approaches should be noted in the POP.
5. *Periodic Audits* – Teams make agreements for periodic audits of 508 compliance, security compliance, and other auditing oversight deemed necessary during the RPR.

USCIS OIT Applied Technology Division (ATD) will support the team in this effort by providing an independent assessment on pipeline suitability for TMD Onboarding. TMD is encouraged for all USCIS teams but granted on a contingent basis-provided the system remains in compliance.

Release Readiness Review for TMD Systems (TMD-RRR)

RRRs for TMD systems will be held periodically to approve the release of major new functionality to users through a deployment or feature toggle. The criteria and/or schedule for holding TMD-RRRs for a particular system will be determined according to risk, using the risk model described in the USCIS IV&V Policy, and will be documented in the system's TPA. RRRs may also be held on demand by the CIO and on the advice of Quality Assurance, based on risk.

Legacy Release Readiness Review (RRR) and Electronic Release Readiness Review (eRRR)

Systems without TMD approval must hold a Release Readiness Review prior to each production deployment unless a waiver is granted by the Delivery Assurance Branch. An RRR may be conducted as a meeting or, per agreement with the RRR Authority, as a sequence of electronic approvals. In order to assess whether the current increment is ready to be deployed, the RRR Authority will assess whether the deployment was adequately tested, reviewed by the product owner and users, and is compliant with enterprise architecture, coding standards, Section 508, and security requirements. The RRR Authority also verifies that release activities were coordinated with business stakeholders and that the business is prepared for the impact of the release. Finally, the RRR Authority assesses the deployment and rollback plans and ensures the deployment package is ready to be submitted to applicable change control boards (CCBs). If the RRR Authority approves the release, it is then submitted to Change Control and deployed.

Core Deployment Artifacts (TMD-RRR, RRR, and eRRR):
- System Design Document or Wiki (SDD/W)
- Automated and Manual Build and Installation Scripts

- Automated and Manual Test Scripts
- Automated and Manual Deployment Scripts
- ICCB or Change Control Board Package
- Security Plan (SP)
- Security Assessment Report (SAR)

Other artifacts, such as Section 508 Compliance Determination Forms (CDF), may be required depending on the specific project, to be established by agreement with the RRR Authority.

Post Implementation Review (PIR) / Release Cycle End

During the PIR, the PIR Authority (USCIS CIO or designee) and the team will analyze the project's successes and failures during the release cycle to identify improvements to the next release cycle. The review will include the Product Owner's assessment of the business value generated during the release cycle, software quality measurements, Section 508 compliance, security compliance, and POAM resolution. The PIR also constitutes the formal end of a release for IUS purposes. The primary focus of the PIR, though, is to celebrate value that was delivered and identify continuous improvement opportunities. Teams should work with USCIS IV&V teams to provide an independent assessment of key measurements and outcomes of the release. Teams are encouraged to hold the PIR in conjunction with the RPR meeting for the next release cycle.

Additional Procedures

Lean-Agile-DevOps projects must conform to the USCIS policy IV&V in order to:
- Provide transparency and accountability to the public
- Inform management and oversight bodies with an independent view of what is working or not working in program execution, based on data and analysis
- Provide feedback to program executors to help them improve their processes

VII. Questions, Comments, and Suggestions

Please address any questions, comments, or suggestions to: USCIS-QA-TEAM@uscis.dhs.gov

VIII. Approval

Signed:_____ Date:_____

OFFICE OF INFORMATION TECHNOLOGY

Addendum to MI CIS-OIT-003 Management Instructions for Applying Lean-Agile-DevOps Principles
Effective Date: 1 April 2017
Management Instruction CIS-OIT-003 Appendix

Appendix A. Generally Accepted Agency Practices

In pursuit of the Required Outcomes called out in CIS OIT Management Instruction CIS-OIT- 003, the following generally accepted practices may be used to achieve successful software development. The Key Questions for each Required Outcome help identify and measure areas of improvement. Table 1 depicts the outcomes supported by each of the practices.

Teams planning to practice Team Managed Deployment (TMD) are expected to have a higher level of Agile discipline than the minimal guidelines.

The team-chosen enabling practices commonly include the following:

Delivery Cadence

The development teams deliver incremental improvements to the agency on a regular and frequent basis.
These deliveries of working functionality allow the work completed so far to be experienced, providing an unambiguous indicator of progress and a potential discovery of previously unknown needs.
- Deliver to production no less frequently than quarterly
- For TMD, deliver to production no less frequently than the development cadence, and potentially multiple times per day Delivery Environment
  Development delivery must be able to provide value to the agency, either to allow stakeholders to experience the current system capabilities and limitations, or to end users for actual use.
- At minimum, to an internal environment where stakeholder can examine and evaluate the system

- Customarily to an environment that mimics production
- For TMD, to production use

Iterative, Incremental Development

Development should proceed in small slices of functionality. As development proceeds, existing functionality should be revisited to add additional or modify existing functionality (iterative). New or modified functionality should extend existing working functionality, leaving the whole in a working state (incremental).

- Development cadence of no longer than 4 weeks
- For TMD, development cadence no longer than 2 weeks
- Short enough for effectively steering the project
- Small increments of functionality are validated as they are developed
- Projects shall use time boxes or limited work in progress (WIP) policies to enforce short cadences for planning, completing, demonstrating, and deploying working tested features
- For TMD, validation of accumulated functionality is continually validated, mostly with automated checks, to enable development flow without regressions

Embedded Product Ownership

The direction of development, what functionality should be developed and in what order, should be embedded with the development team, authorized and available to make decisions as needed without delay.

- The Agency needs are represented by a single clear voice to development, dedicated to the development effort
- Product Owner has full authority to make timely decisions regarding development, prioritization, and acceptance of development
- Product Owner has full authority to make decisions about when functionality is deployed either by turning on a feature toggle or by direct code push to production
- Close collaboration between dedicated representative and actual stakeholders and users
- Teams are encouraged to include Product Owner approval as part of the continuous delivery pipeline
- For TMD, frequent feedback of the developing system from the actual stakeholders and users, informing future development, priorities, and fitness for purpose

Representation of Requirements

The documentation of requirements for development should be tuned to the needs of the development process and regarded as ephemeral. Any need to document beyond the development process should be regarded as separate and designed to meet that need.

- Explicit conditions of satisfaction that may be validated
- Acceptance criteria describing the intent
- Acceptance scenarios illustrating essential cases
- Use of low over-head, low fidelity assets such as user stories, augmented as needed with elaborations such as paper prototypes, or sample reports to convey the essential behavior
- Independent pieces capable of being sequenced in almost any order
- Small enough to easily fit within the delivery cadence

Automated Testing

In keeping with "test early, test often" principles, test criteria defined early in the life of a user story drives creation of automated test code that is stored in the version control system along with all other code. Automated tests should include appropriate testing such as unit testing, functionality, and system-to-system interfaces. While complete automated testing is desired, security and Section 508 accessibility testing will be automated when tools are available to support. Risk-based approaches should be used to determine which automated tests are included in regression suites.

- The explicit conditions of satisfaction determined in the requirements are automated as acceptance tests
- Functionality is typically tested over the smallest scope possible, and includes edge conditions

The Agile Testing Pyramid may be used to visualize this

- For TMD, high level of reliable automated testing
- For TMD, performance measures are tracked over time by the development teams

Fail-Safe

Concern should be paid to execution that may not proceed as desired and what consequences this will have. Negative consequences should be minimized and recovery procedures should be considered.

- •System design shall anticipate environmental and implementation failures and mitigate the consequences
  This may be monitored by the consequences and time-to-fix for production incidents
- For TMD, tests are treated as valuable as code, and gaps or failures are treated as first- class issues
- For TMD, perform as many infrastructure tasks as possible programmatically
- For TMD, it should be feasible to revert to the previous version, including database schema or data changes and environment

In close coordination with operations engineers, development teams implement and test methods to monitor, minimize, and correct unanticipated issues associated with deployments. Preferably, these methods are automated. These methods may include blue/green deployments, feature toggles, rollback scripts, and "fail forward" approaches that enable rapid replacement of faulty elements. Recovery methods should be executed quickly to minimize impact to data, system performance, and other critical aspects of production applications.

Extrinsic Quality

Care should be taken to keep the external quality of the system, as seen by the users, sufficiently high at all times to give correct operation and ease of use.

- Every feature is specified with one or more essential tests representing the intended functionality
- External expertise is engaged for extended verifications (e.g., security, accessibility) on a regular basis
- Testing activities happen within development cadence
- Testing capabilities are embedded within the teams

Intrinsic Quality

Care should be taken to keep the internal quality of the system, as seen by the developers, sufficiently high at all times to promote ease of development, understanding, and modification.

- System implementation shall not impede the addition or modification of functionality
- This may be measured in arrears by counting the number of modules that must be modified for a change
- As units of code are created, they are simultaneously tested for proper operation, resilience to unexpected inputs, and boundary conditions
- Unit tests document the code behavior intended by the programmer and verify that the code exhibits this behavior

Emergent Design

- The design of the system should be envisioned and realized over time.
- The more we work on the system, the better we understand the needs of the mission and the needs of the implementation context.
- At any given time, the system design must support current functionality without being overdesigned to support future functionality.
- Anticipated future needs of the system should be designed as needed.
- Care should be taken to keep such needs in mind so that they may be feasibly implemented when the time comes.
- Such an approach not only maximizes the realized benefit of the design, but leaves the agency best prepared for future changes in mission needs.
- Avoid building unused "hooks" anticipating future needs
- Keep the design simple so that future needs are easy to accommodate as they arise

Refactoring

As the needs of the design shift, it's often necessary to modify existing code without changing its functionality.

This process is called Refactoring, a term attributed to William Opdyke and Ralph Johnson after their September 1990 article on the topic. The best known reference to this technique is Martin Fowler's book, *Refactoring. Improving the Design of Existing Code.*

By reshaping code without changing its functionality, we can correct deficiencies we discover in our design or make the design amenable to new demands we place on it.

- Separate changes in code structure from changes in code functionality
- Use well-known refactoring techniques that are known to preserve functionality

- Make restructuring changes as a series of small changes, keeping the code functional at each step

Intentional Architecture

Make design decisions intentionally, rather than through expedience. Anticipate technical risks and design the architecture to meet them as they are addressed.

- Keep an eye on the long-term goals and technical issues as the design emerges
- Communicate the issues and current thinking on architectural approaches to all members of the development team
- Listen to any questions or objections concerning the suitability of the design

Managing Technical Debt

Ward Cunningham invented the term Technical Debt to describe the difference between how we currently understand the problem domain and how it is represented in our code. This difference naturally creates difficulties as we expand our coverage of the problem domain.

For example, we might model a domain construct as a hierarchical tree, but later find that some nodes are referred by more than one node. Our tree implementation cannot model that. Refactoring the code to a directed acyclic graph implementation will model our current understanding of the problem domain more directly.

Since then, others have come to use the phrase Technical Debt any perceived deficiency in the code design.

Whether using a strict or loose definition, it's important to manage these deficiencies so that the code does not become difficult to maintain and extend.

- Keep duplication of functionality at a minimum
- Write code that expresses the concepts on the mind of the programmer, such that they are obvious to the next person to touch this code
- In object-oriented code, follow Robert C. "Uncle Bob" Martin's SOLID design principles
- In all code, maximize cohesiveness of any module or grouping, and minimize its coupling to other modules or groupings

Version Control

Teams frequently commit working code to a USCIS-owned repository using an automated mechanism. In this context, code implies all system source code, configuration files, automated test scripts, build scripts, deployment scripts, or other computer files needed to build the system or the supporting Continuous Delivery pipeline.

- All code is version-controlled
- Developers and teams should integrate their code frequently
- Code is merged into common branch more frequently than development cadence
- Code from the common branch is frequently merged into each developer's working copy, preferably multiple times a day
- Minimal time between introducing a change and other teams accounting for that change – For TMD, multiple times a day
- Documented procedures for build, test and deploy are version-controlled with the code
- It shall be feasible to retrieve and build any previous version, preferably by name, date or tag
- It shall be feasible to see the history of changes and to compare any two versions Scripted Builds
- Build processes should be well-defined so that they are repeatable as a matter of course.
- Build processes are scripted to allow anyone to build any portion of the system in a repeatable manner
- Build scripts should be version-controlled with the code
- Build scripts should contain segregated build steps for compiling, unit testing, producing deployable artifacts, and other desirable units of work

Automated Builds

To the extent feasible, build processes should not rely on manual intervention for execution. Human intervention should be reserved for decision making.

- Builds are performed via automated, script-driven retrieval of source code from a repository monitored by a dedicated build server
- Builds should run on code check in, on a set frequency, on demand, or any combination of these
- Builds should run a sequence of build scripts to compile, unit test, and produce deployable artifacts. Builds may automatically deploy artifacts and test them in situ
- Builds should complete within a short duration

The build server should produce appropriate build notifications and always present build status

Scripted Deployment
Deployment procedures should be well-defined so that they are repeatable as a matter of course.
- The same documented procedures are used to deploy to any environment, including Production
- For TMD, these procedures should be scripted and version-controlled

Deployment with minimal downtime for users
- Small releases
- Decoupled services
- Zero downtime (e.g., blue-green) deployments
- Database migration scripts
- Forward and backward compatibility of components
- Backout capability

Automated Deployment
To the extent possible, deployment scripts should not rely on manual intervention for execution.
- Teams maintain an automated process (or set of processes) that executes a list of deployment steps via script or via a deployment tool
- Automated deployments should be rapid, reliable, testable, and repeatable
- Steps include running acceptance tests, pushing code to downstream environments, and automated smoke testing
- Communication artifacts, such as tickets and release notes, should also be
automatically generated. Deployment configuration scripts should be stored as code and placed under configuration management

Approved Pipeline
The components and procedures to build, test and deploy software should be reliable and trusted.
- Teams implement a Continuous Delivery pipeline approved by USCIS.
- – Pipeline components may already be in use at USCIS or, per agreement, may be emerging tools in the market that are new to USCIS
- For TMD, procedures for build, test and deploy are automated

System Monitoring
Systems should be monitored in production to detect problems in a timely fashion for quick action, and to provide the business with information about normal use.
- Teams shall have procedures and tools in place to monitor the performanc e and health of the system in production
- Key elements should be displayed in a dashboard viewable at any time
- Automated systems may monitor that operations are within define thresholds
- – Appropriate personnel should be alerted when thresholds are breached
- – Incident management and escalation procedures should be defined

Release Planning
Planning for future releases should provide guidance to external stakeholders while providing flexibility for the appropriate definition and delivery of system details.
- Adaptive Rolling Wave Planning to maintain a clear vision of immediate capability delivery in the context of a longer range view

Visibility of progress
The progress being made toward program goals should be easily visible and reflect the current reality.
- Visibility into team's progress toward program goals (e.g., burn-up)
- Practices in place for communication and collaboration across teams (e.g., Scrum of Scrums, Portfolio Alignment Wall)

Peer Reviews

Avoid single points of failure by collaborating with others, filling in knowledge gaps, catching oversights, and considering a diverse set of options.

- Peers should review each other's code, tests, and other development artifacts
- Reviews should attempt to identify system risks not caught by tests and automated analysis
- Reviews should share information and development styles across the development team

Integrated Experimentation & Learning

In recognition that the beginning of a program is the point in time at which the least is known about it, experimentation and learning should be conducted to maximize improvement as development proceeds.

- team retrospectives at development cadence with tangible results
- Periodic program retrospectives over larger intervals and participants
- Capacity is allocated for experiments and improvements as a normal part of development

Culture of learning

In recognition that the majority of the time and effort in a program is spent learning what and how to do things, institutionalize learning as a major part of the program execution.

- Outside the development process, institute periodic sharing of technical and process learning
  - Communities of Practice, Guilds, Brown Bags

Deployment History and Consistency

Place the highest value on meeting needs through the life of the program, demonstrating trustworthiness.

- Teams should demonstrate a record of successful deployments
  - Success measures include avoidance of emergency conditions and post-release issues
  - Should a problem occur as an aberration, teams should demonstrate an ability to eliminate the root cause, ensuring a one-time issue does not become a pattern of dysfunction

Appendix B:
MI-CIS-OIT-004

Management Instruction for Agile Independent Verification and Validation

Effective Date: 26 June 2017 Management Instruction: CIS-OIT-004

I. Purpose

This Management Instruction (MI) establishes the U.S. Citizenship and Immigration Services (USCIS) policy for the use of risk-based Independent Verification and Validation (IV&V) to inform management and make oversight decisions ensuring that Information Technology (IT) programs adhere to USCIS Management Instruction CIS-OIT-003 and its Appendices.

The primary functions of USCIS IV&V are:
- Provide transparency and accountability to the public;
- Provide timely feedback to program executors to continuously improve processes, practices, and outcomes;
- Ensure that projects deliver solutions that meet business objectives, support mission needs, and deliver value;
- Inform management and oversight bodies with an independent assessment of program execution based on data and analysis;
- Ensure compliance with regulatory requirements, USCIS Management Instructions, and Department of Homeland Security (DHS) Management Directives

To fulfill these functions, USCIS IT programs will use a risk-based IV&V approach to verify and validate the outcomes defined in Management Instruction CIS-OIT-003 and its Appendices. The IV&V process will ensure that the appropriate controls and analyses are applied to each program based on its assessed risk. The approach for each program will be agreed upon through a collaboration of program executors, USCIS management, IV&V teams, and external stakeholders, and will be documented in a new document called the Independent Assessment Plan (IAP).

II. Scope

This Management Instruction focuses on the IV&V program at USCIS but applies to all employee and contractor teams involved in the planning, development, and deployment of software and systems throughout USCIS.

Office of Information Technology

III. Authorities

The following laws, regulations, orders, policies, directives, and guidance authorize and govern this Management Instruction:

1. DHS Management Directive (MD) 102-01"Acquisition Management Directive," and associated Instructions and Guidebooks
2. Section 5202 of the Clinger-Cohen Act of 1996
3. Office of Management and Budget (OMB) Circulars A-130 and A-11
4. 25 Point Implementation Plan to Reform Federal Information Technology Management (U.S. Chief Information Officer, December 9, 2010)
5. Contracting Guidance to Support Modular Development (OMB, June 14, 2012)
6. Memorandum on Agile Development Framework for DHS, by DHS CIO Richard A. Spires, issued June 1, 2012
7. Digital Services Playbook (https://playbook.cio.gov)

IV. Policy, Procedures, and Requirements

Except in cases where a waiver is granted by the Chief Information Officer (CIO), all systems development and maintenance projects at USCIS will require IV&V. Such projects include, for example, custom software development, Commercial Off-The-Shelf (COTS) integration and configuration, business intelligence, and reporting capabilities.

USCIS Office of Information Technology (OIT) management will ensure that appropriate training, coaching, and tools are available to facilitate the success of all projects. Teams are encouraged to work with OIT support groups to implement this Management Instruction in a manner appropriate for their particular context.

A. IV&V Approach
The IV&V approach to each release cycle of each project is based on a holistic assessment of the project, the team's development history, the release plan, and the deployment plan. This assessment is based on the unique characteristics and measures of each assessed element. Some examples include:
- DHS program level or CIO designation for the project
- Visibility to the public
- Impact on mission critical systems
- Number of internal and external users affected
- Federal Information Processing Standard (FIPS) rating and security or privacy impacts
- Reliance on interfaces to external systems
- Development process
- Outcomes to date (e.g., technical debt, escaped defects, user satisfaction)

At the beginning of each project, the IV&V stakeholders will evaluate the project's risk and create an Independent Assessment Plan (IAP). The IAP will be re-evaluated from time to time during the course of the project to see if it needs to be changed. The IAP will indicate what level of assessment will be conducted, what resources will be allocated, and what templates will be used for assessment. Appendix C to this document shows an example of an IAP template (the template may vary over time). The IAP will serve as a guide for IV&V as the program proceeds.

USCIS has also developed an assessment tool called the Product Quality Assessment (PQA) that will be continuously refined as USCIS OIT gains experience determining the success factors for projects. An example is shown in Appendix B of this document. This instrument will be the default template for IV&V assessments of major programs. The PQA compares the program's practices and status to the instructions given in Management Instruction CIS-OIT-003 and in its Appendix A. The IV&V process therefore functions as a control to ensure that programs implement the direction specified in Management Instruction CIS-OIT-003 and its Appendices.

There will be a direct correlation between risk and the level of IV&V engagement. High risk programs (all level one and two programs and certain level three programs) will have embedded IV&V analysts and testers working with the development team, while low risk programs may only be audited. . High risk programs will also be assessed more frequently than low risk programs. IV&V will also evaluate and provide feedback on all Systems Engineering Lifecycle (SELC), Acquisition Lifecycle Framework (ALF), and other oversight documents and artifacts.

Key documents, artifacts, and relevant risk assessments will be revisited in each Release Planning Review (RPR) and will be updated as necessary, depending on the level of IV&V engagement, throughout the release cycle.

During project execution, IV&V teams will monitor team progress toward the outcomes set forth in USCIS Management Instruction CIS-OIT-003 and its Appendices. Depending on the needs of the project, IV&V teams may also include other activities such as:
- Sample testing for Section 508 conformance
- Code quality scanning and manual code review
- Unit test review
- Functional testing and test review
- Integration testing
- Performance testing
- End User testing

These activities will inform IV&V teams' analysis as documented in the PQA. IV&V will execute these activities in a manner that supports agile delivery practices and methods.

B. Team Managed Deployment
In order to support best practices for DevOps and Continuous Delivery techniques, USCIS has developed a methodology called, Team Managed Deployments (TMD). In order to engage in this methodology, a program must be onboarded to TMD by the IV&V stakeholders. In assessing eligibility for TMD, IV&V stakeholders will evaluate a program's readiness relative to CIS-OIT-003 Outcomes #7, #8, #9, and #10. The results of the evaluation and a determination for TMD certification will be conducted as part of the program's next RPR, in accordance with Management Instruction CIS-OIT-003. Example measurements are provided in Appendix A.

C. Value Delivery

A primary function of IV&V at USCIS is to ensure projects deliver solutions that meet business objectives, support mission needs, and deliver value. This work begins in release planning, when the IV&V team works with Product Owners to ensure that teams plan to deliver capabilities that clearly meet mission needs and priorities, as outlined in the Capabilities and Constraints (CAC) document.

At RPR, IV&V ensures alignment with business needs by validating that the appropriate stakeholders (product owners, line of business executives, etc.) are present in person or by delegation and fully approve release plans. During the development cycle, IV&V monitors projects to ensure that business representatives are involved in work planning sessions, and in monitoring and participating in test efforts.

For Level 1 and other designated projects, IV&V also supports Operational Test & Evaluation (OT&E). OT&E, or Operational Testing, is a testing process that takes place on production systems with production data with real end users. Its purpose is to determine whether Key Performance Parameters (KPPs) articulated in the Measures of Effectiveness (MOEs) and Measures of Suitability (MOSs) set forth in the Operational Requirements Document (ORD) by the business sponsor at program authorization have been met, or not. Many experts consider this the ultimate test of business value, as it was what was promised when the program was authorized.

D. Questions, Comments, and Suggestions

Please address any questions, comments, or suggestions to: USCIS-QA-TEAM@uscis.dhs.gov VI. Approval

Signed: _____ Date: _____

Example Metrics

Below are examples of measurements supporting evaluation of objective outcomes. Key measurements must be agreed among program management, IV&V, and USCIS OCIO for regular reporting. The agreement on measurements must be recorded in the POP, and revisited in each RPR. This list is neither mandatory nor exhaustive, but serves as an indicator of the types of measurements that should be considered in crafting the POP for a specific program.

MI CIS-OIT-003 Outcome	Examples of IV&V Decision Support Measurements (Trending Preferred)
Outcome #1: Programs and projects frequently deliver valuable product	• Quantitative measurements of program goals (business KPIs) • Number of deployments • User satisfaction • Strategic stakeholder satisfaction • Usage statistics
Outcome #2: Value is continuously discovered and aligned to mission	• Lead times for new functionality • Evidence of feedback being incorporated
Outcome #3: Work flows in small batches and is validated	• Work item flow measurements (e.g. cycle time) • Batch size • Evidence of test coordination • Evidence product demonstration feedback is incorporated in requirements
Outcome #4: Quality is built in	• Incident count (escaped defects) • Code quality measurements • Test coverage • Evidence of appropriate tool configuration and use
Outcome #5: The organization continuously learns and improves	• Amount of effort spent on improvement • Outcomes of retrospective experiments • Implementation of retrospective action items • Evidence of appropriate measurement activities • Evidence of feedback being incorporated • Evidence of practice transfer across organization
Outcome #6: Teams collaborate across groups and roles to improve flow and remove delays	• Continuous integration availability • Lean measurements • "Health check" assessment of team practices

continued on page 228

continued from page 227

MI CIS-OIT-003 Outcome	Examples of IV&V Decision Support Measurements (Trending Preferred)
Outcome #7: Security, accessibility and other compliance constraints are embedded and verifiable	• Cost of compliance issues to customers, users, and agency • Number of open issues • Security risk level • Section 508 risk level • Privacy risk level • Performance risk level
Outcome #8: Consistent and repeatable processes are used across build, deploy, and test	• Rate of broken builds, particularly in later stage gates • Number/percentage of escaped defects
Outcome #9: The entire system is deployable at any time to any environment	• Percentage of deployments needing rollback • Pipeline and repository unavailability incidents
Outcome #10: The system has high reliability, availability, and serviceability	• Incident count • Incident aging and inventory • Escaped defect count • Uptime • Production performance • Mean time to repair • Mean time between failures • Production error count

BIBLIOGRAPHY

Adler, Paul. "The 'Learning Bureaucracy': New United Motor Manufacturing, Inc." In *Research in Organizational Behavior*. Vol. 15, edited by Barry M. Staw and Larry L. Cummings, 111–94. Greenwich, CT: JAI Press, 1992. Source consulted was Draft 3.1, available at http://faculty.marshall.usc.edu/Paul-Adler/research/NUMMI(ROB)-1.pdf.

Adler, Paul. "Time and Motion Regained." *Harvard Business Review* (January/February 1993): https://hbr.org/1993/01/time-and-motion-regained.

Adler, Paul. "Building Better Bureaucracies." The Academy of Management Executive 12, no. 4 (1999): 36.

Adler, Paul, and Bryan Borys. "Two Types of Bureaucracy: Enabling and Coercive." *Administrative Science Quarterly* 41, no. 1 (March 1996): 61–89.

Adzic, Gojko. *Impact Mapping: Making a Big Impact with Software Products and Projects*. Surrey, UK: Provoking Thoughts, 2012.

Amy, D. J. "The Case for Bureaucracy: An Unapologetic Defense of a Vital Institution." GovernmentIsGood.com. Accessed May 1, 2020. http://www.governmentisgood.com/articles.php?aid=20.

Arendt, Hannah. "A Special Supplement: Reflections on Violence." *NY Review of Books*, February 27, 1969. http://www2.kobe-u.ac.jp/~alexroni/IPD%202019%20readings/IPD1%202019%20No.8/A%20Special%20Supplement_%20Reflections%20on%20Violence%20by%20Hannah%20Arendt%20_%20The%20New%20Yor.pdf.

Arendt, Hannah. *Eichmann in Jerusalem: A Report on the Banality of Evil*. New York: Penguin Books, 2006.

Avery, Christopher. "Responsible Change." *Cutter Consortium Agile Project Management Executive Report* 6, no. 10 (2005): 1–28.

Batkins, Sam. "Testimony." AmericanActionForum.org. March 29, 2017. https://www.americanactionforum.org/testimony/evaluating-paperwork-reduction-act-burdens-reduced/.

Balzac, Honoré de. *The Bureaucrats*. Translated by Charles Foulkes. Evanston, IL: Northwestern University Press, 1993.

Beetham, David. *Bureaucracy*. Minneapolis: University of Minnesota Press, 1987.

Beniger, James R. *The Control Revolution*. Cambridge, MA: Harvard University Press, 1986.

Blair, Elizabeth. "A History of 'Pettifogging' for the Pettifoggers Among You." NPR. January 22, 2020. https://www.npr.org/2020/01/22/798486578/a-history-of-pettifogging-for-the-pettifoggers-among-you.

Blau, P. M. *The Dynamics of Bureaucracy: A Study of Interpersonal Relations in Two Government Agencies*. Chicago: University of Chicago Press, 1963.

Blau, P. M., and M. W. Meyer. *Bureaucracy in Modern Society*. 2nd ed. New York: Random House, 1971.

Bogsnes, Bjarte. *Implementing Beyond Budgeting: Unlocking the Performance Potential*. Hoboken: John Wiley and Sons, 2009.

Bozzuto, Brian. "Coercive vs. Enabling Bureaucracy." *SolutionsIQ*. August 21, 2011. https://www.solutionsiq.com/resource/blog-post/enabling-bureaucracy/.

Brady, John. "Analytics Without Limits: FINRA's Scalable and Secure Big Data Architecture—Part 1." *AWS Public Sector Blog*. October 3, 2017. https://aws.amazon.com/blogs/public sector/analytics-without-limits-finras-scalable-and-secure-big-data-architecture-part-1/.

Buchanan, David A., and Louise Fitzgerald. "New Lock, New Stock, New Barrel, Same Gun: The Accessorized Bureaucracy of Health Care." In Clegg, Harris, and Höpfl, *Managing Modernity*, 56–80.

Burke, Jason, and Ian Black. "Al-Qaida: Tales from Bin Laden's Volunteers." *The Guardian*. September 10, 2009. https://www.theguardian.com/world/2009/sep/10/al-qaida -terrorism-bin-laden.

"Bureaucracy: The Piazza Tales." UNT University Libraries Exhibits website. Accessed January 1, 2020. https://exhibits.library.unt.edu/bureaucracy-love-story/items/piazza-tales-1.

Burns, Tom, and G. M. Stalker. *The Management of Innovation*. London: Tavistock Publications: 1961.

Cantoni, Craig J. *Corporate Dandelions: How the Weed of Bureaucracy Is Choking American Companies—and What You Can Do to Uproot It*. New York: American Management Association, 1993.

Chrystal, K. Alec, and Paul D. Mizen. "Goodhart's Law: Its Origins, Meaning, and Implications for Monetary Policy." November 12, 2001. https://pdfs.semanticscholar.org/0062/a8e2 981230185c88819776e600419ed1426d.pdf.

Clegg, Stewart, Martin Harris, and Harro Höpfl, eds. *Managing Modernity: Beyond Bureaucracy?* Oxford: Oxford University Press, 2011.

Clegg, Stewart. "Under Reconstruction: Modern Bureaucracies." In Clegg, Harris, and Höpfl, *Managing Modernity*, 202–229.

Clinger-Cohen Act of 1996. Congress U. N. Public Law: 104–106.

Cohn, Mike. *Succeeding with Agile: Software Development Using Scrum*. Upper-Saddle River, NJ: Addison-Wesley, 2010.

Conway, Melvin E. "Conway's Law." MelConway.com. Accessed May 1, 2020. http://www .melconway.com/Home/Conways_Law.html.

Crooks, Peter, and Timothy H. Parsons. *Empires and Bureaucracy in World History: From Late Antiquity to the Twentieth Century*. Cambridge: Cambridge University Press, 2016.

Cyert, Richard M., and James G. March. *A Behavioral Theory of the Firm*. Englewood Cliffs, NJ: Prentice-Hall, 1963.

Department of Homeland Security, Management Directive 102.

Department of Homeland Security. "Acquisition Directive 102-01," November 7, 2008.

Department of Homeland Security. "Acquisition Instruction/Guidebook 102-01-001," November 7, 2008.

Department of Homeland Security. "Management Instruction: CIS-OIT-003," April 1, 2017.

Department of Homeland Security. "Management Instruction: CIS-OIT-004," June 26, 2017.

Dickens, Charles. *David Copperfield*. Hampshire, UK: Macmillan Collectors Library, 2016.

Dickson, Del. *The People's Government: An Introduction to Democracy*. New York: Cambridge University Press, 2015.

"'Did You Lose the Keys Here?' 'No, But the Light Is Much Better Here.'" Quote.Investigator. com. Accessed March 7, 2017. https://quoteinvestigator.com/2013/04/11/better-light/.

Doerr, John. *Measure What Matters: How Google, Bono, and the Gates Foundation Rock the World with OKRs*. New York: Portfolio/Penguin, 2018.

Duval, Jacqueline Raoul. "Flaubert & Kafka Part One: Life, Literature, and Love." *Versopolis/ Review*. April 14, 2017. https://www.versopolis.com/arts/to-read/368/flaubert-kafka -part-1.

"FISMA NIST 800-53 Rev. 4 Controls—by the Numbers," BSC website. Accessed May 1, 2020. https://www.passfisma.com/fisma-nist-800-53-rev-4-controls-numbers/#.

Emery, D. H. "Resistance as a Resource." *Cutter IT Journal* 14, no. 10 (2001): 35–43.

Enders, Giulia. *Gut: The Inside Story of Our Body's Most Underrated Organ*. Vancouver, Canada: Greystone Books, 2015.

Galore, Edward. "The Bureaucracy of Terror: The Middle Managers of Murder." Galorebot .com (2004): http://www.galorebot.com/bureaucracy/essay.htm. Available in the Internet Archive WayBack Machine, archived 10/19/2019. https://web.archive.org /web/20191018195533/http://www.galorebot.com/bureaucracy/essay.htm.

Gaunt, Jeremy. "Corporations Are Becoming Expert at Doublespeak to Mask Bad News." *LA Times*. December 2, 1990. https://www.latimes.com/archives/la-xpm-1990-12-02-fi -7858-story.html.

Gawande, Atul. *The Checklist Manifesto: How to Get Things Right*. New York: Picador, 2010.

du Gay, Paul. "'Without Regard to Persons': Problems of Involvement and Attachment in 'Post-Bureaucratic' Public Management." In Clegg, Harris, and Höpfl, *Managing Modernity*, 11–29.

Gouldner, Alvin W. *Patterns of Industrial Bureaucracy*. New York: The Free Press, 1954.

"Government Paperwork Elimination Act." US Department of Interior website. Accessed May 1, 2020. https://www.doi.gov/ocio/policy-mgmt-support/govt-paperwork-elimination -act.

Graeber, David. *The Utopia of Rules: On Technology, Stupidity, and the Secret Joys of Bureaucracy*. Brooklyn, NY: Melville House, 2015.

Graeber, David. "In Regulation Nation." *Harper's Magazine* (March 2015): 13.

Green, Mark, and John F. Berry. *The Challenge of Hidden Profits: Reducing Corporate Bureaucracy and Waste*. New York: William Morrow, 1985.

Harline, Craig E. *The Rhyme and Reason of Politics in Early Europe: Collected Essays of Herbert H. Rowen*. Dordrecht, Netherlands: Springer, 1992.

Harris, Martin, Stewart Clegg, and Harro Höpfl. "Introduction: Managing Modernity: Beyond Bureaucracy?" In Clegg, Harris, and Höpfl, *Managing Modernity*, 1–10.

Harris, Michael, and Bill Tayler. "Don't Let Metrics Undermine Your Business." *Harvard Business Review* 97, no. 5 (September/October 2019): 63–69.

Hašek, Jaroslav. *The Fateful Adventures of the Good Soldier Švejk During the World War (Book One)*. Translated by Zdenek K. Sadlon. Zenny.com. 2018.

"History." Department of Homeland Security webpage. Accessed May 1, 2020. https://www .dhs.gov/creation-department-homeland-security.

Hlavacek, James D., and Victor A. Thompson. "Bureaucracy and New Product Innovation." *The Academy of Management Journal* 16, no. 3 (September 1973): 361–372.

Hubbard, Douglas W. *How to Measure Anything: Finding the Value of "Intangibles" in Business.* New York: Wiley & Sons, 2014.

Hunter, Ian, *Rethinking the School: Subjectivity, Bureaucracy, Criticism (Questions in Cultural Studies).* Sydney: Allen & Unwin, 1994.

Johnston, Louis D. "History Lessons: Understanding the Decline of Manufacturing." *MinnPost.* February 22, 2012. https://www.minnpost.com/macro-micro-minnesota/2012/02 /history-lessons-understanding-decline-manufacturing/.

Kafka, Franz. *The Trial.* New York: Schocken Books, 1998.

Kafka, Franz. *The Castle.* Oxford: Oxford University Press, 2009.

Kagan, Shelly. *Death.* New Haven: Yale University Press, 2012.

Kallinikos, Jannis. "Bureaucracy under Siege: On Information, Collaboration, and Networks." In Clegg, Harris, and Höpfl, *Managing Modernity*, 130–153.

Katz, D., and R. L. Kahn. *The Social Psychology of Organizations.* New York: Wiley, 1966.

Kelman, Steve. "Bureaucracies as Learning Organizations." Federal Computer Week (FCW). April 2, 2019. https://fcw.com/blogs/lectern/2019/04/kelman-learning-organizations .aspx.

Kersten, Denise. "How to Bend the Rules of Corporate Bureaucracy." *USA Today* (November 8, 2002). http://usatoday30.usatoday.com/money/jobcenter/workplace/rules/2002-11 -08-corporate-bureaucracy_x.htm.

Kherdian, David. *Monkey: A Journey to the West.* Boston: Shambala, 1992.

Lactantius. *Of the Manner in Which the Persecutors Died.* Accessed May 1, 2020. http://people. ucalgary.ca/~vandersp/Courses/texts/lactant/lactperf.html.

Landau, M. *Political Science and Political Theory.* New York: MacMillan, 1972.

Lewis, Lowell. "Toward a Unified Theory of Cultural Performance." In *Victor Turner and Contemporary Cultural Performance*, Graham St. John, ed. London: Berghahn, 2008, 41–58.

Lucas, Matt, and David Walliams. *Little Britain.* London: Pinewood Studios, 2003–2006.

Luebke, Neil R. "Presidential Address: For and Against Bureaucracy." *Philosophical Topics* 13, no. 2 (1985): 143–154. www.jstor.org/stable/43153936.

McChrystal, Gen. Stanley, *Team of Teams: New Rules of Engagement for a Complex World.* New York: Penguin Random House, 2015.

Melville, Herman. "Bartleby the Scrivener." In *The Piazza Tales.* Evanston, IL: Northwestern University Press, 1996.

Melville, Herman. *Moby-Dick (Norton Critical Edition).* 3rd ed. New York: W. W. Norton, 2018.

Merton, Robert K. *Social Theory and Social Structure.* Glencoe, IL: Free Press, 1957.

Mikkelson, David. "Did Dr. Seuss Write 'Green Eggs and Ham' on a Bet?" Snopes.com. February 25, 1999. https://www.snopes.com/fact-check/green-eggs-and-ham/.

Mill, John Stuart. *Considerations on Representative Government.* 2nd ed. London: Parker, Son, and Bourn, 1865.

Mill, John Stuart. *On Liberty.* London: Forgotten Books, 1960.

von Mises, Ludwig. *Bureaucracy.* Dead Authors Society, 2018.

Muller, Jerry Z. *The Tyranny of Metrics.* Princeton: Princeton University Press, 2018.

Neiman, Susan. *Evil in Modern Thought: An Alternative History of Philosophy.* Princeton: Princeton University Press, 2002.

NPR Staff. "Who Oversees Homeland Security? Um, Who Doesn't?" *All Things Considered.* July 20, 2010. https://www.npr.org/templates/story/story.php?storyId=128642876.

Nussbaum, Frederick J. *A History of the Economic Institutions of Modern Europe.* New York: F. S. Crofts and Co., 1933.

William of Ockham. *Sentences of Peter Lombard* (Quaestiones et decisiones in quattuor libros Sententiarum Petri Lombardi; ed. Lugd., 1495, i, dist. 27, qu. 2, K).

Office Inspector General. *USCIS Automation of Immigration Benefits Processing Remains Ineffective.* Washington, DC: Department of Homeland Security. March 9, 2016. https://www.oig.dhs.gov/assets/Mgmt/2016/OIG-16-48-Mar16.pdf.

Orwell, George. "Politics and the English Language." In *The Collected Essays, Journalism, and Letters of George Orwell*, edited by Sonia Orwell and Ian Angus, 127–140. Vol. 4, ed. 1. New York: Harcourt, Brace, Jovanovich, 1968. https://faculty.washington.edu/rsoder/EDLPS579/HonorsOrwellPoliticsEnglishLanguage.pdf.

Parks, Tim. "Literature and Bureaucracy." *New York Review of Books—NYR Daily.* December 2, 2013. https://www.nybooks.com/daily/2013/12/02/literature-and-bureaucracy/.

Patrick-Goudreau, Colleen. "A Gaggle of Geese, A Pride of Lions, A School of Fish, and More Collective Animal Nouns." *Food for Thought* podcast. August 17, 2016. https://www.colleenpatrickgoudreau.com/a-gaggle-of-geese-a-pride-of-lions-a-school-of-fish-and-more-collective-animal-nouns-2/.

Pearce, Laurie. "The Scribes and Scholars of Ancient Mesopotamia." In *Civilizations of the Ancient Near East.* Edited by Jack Sasson. 4: 2265–2278. New York: Macmillan, 1995.

Poppendieck, Mary, and Tom Poppendieck. *Implementing Lean Software Development: From Concept to Cash.* Upper Saddle River, NJ: Addison-Wesley, 2007.

Pugh, D. S. "Modern Organization Theory: A Psychological and Sociological Study." *Psychological Bulletin* 66, no. 4 (1966): 235–251.

Pynchon, Thomas. *The Crying of Lot 49.* New York: Harper & Row, 1966.

Reed, Michael. "The Post-Bureaucratic Organization and the Control Revolution." In Clegg, Harris, and Höpfl, *Managing Modernity*, 230–256.

Ries, Eric. *The Lean Startup: How Today's Entrepreneurs Use Continuous Innovation to Create Radically Successful Businesses.* New York: Crown Business, 2011.

Rhodes, Michael L, Office of the Deputy Chief Management Officer. "Revised Department of Defense Order of Precedence," Memorandum. July 15, 2016. https://execsec.defense.gov/Portals/34/Documents/Revised%20DoD%20Order%20of%20Precedence-15July2016.pdf.

Rockwell, Mark. "CBP Closes In on Completing 17-Year Multibillion IT Project." *Federal Computer Week* (FCW). March 5, 2018. https://fcw.com/articles/2018/03/05/cbp-ace-cargo-system.aspx.

Sade, Marquis de. *120 Days of Sodom.* New York: Penguin Classics, 2016.

Schein, Edgar H. *The Corporate Culture Survival Guide.* San Francisco: Jossey-Bass, 2009.

Schwaber, Ken, and Jeff Sutherland. *The Scrum Guide: The Definitive Guide to Scrum: The Rules of the Game*, 2017. https://www.scrumguides.org/docs/scrumguide/v2017/2017-Scrum-Guide-US.pdf#zoom=100.

Schwartz, Mark. *The Art of Business Value.* Portland, OR: IT Revolution Press, 2016.

Schwartz, Mark. *A Seat at the Table: IT Leadership in the Age of Agility.* Portland, OR: IT Revolution Press, 2017.

Schwartz, Mark. *War and Peace and IT: Business Leadership, Technology, and Success in the Digital Age*. Portland, OR: IT Revolution Press, 2019.

Scott, James C. *Seeing Like a State: How Certain Schemes to Improve the Human Condition Have Failed*. New Haven, CT: Yale University Press, 1998.

Shapiro, Jacob N. *The Terrorist's Dilemma: Managing Violent Covert Organizations*. New Jersey: Princeton University Press, 2013.

Shook, John. "How to Change a Culture: Lessons from NUMMI," *MIT Sloan Management Review* 51, no. 2 (Winter 2010): 63–68. https://www.lean.org/Search/Documents/35.pdf.

Smart, Jon. "LKCE18 Jonathan Smart—Better Value Sooner Safer Happier." Slideshare.net. Posted by Lean Kanban Central Europe. November 8, 2019. https://www.slideshare .net/lkce/lkce18-jonathan-smart-better-value-sooner-safer-happier.

Smith, Perry M., and Daniel M. Gerstein. *Assignment: Pentagon: How to Succeed in a Bureaucracy*. Washington, DC: Potomac Books, Inc., 2007.

"Spherical Cow: A Simple Model." Physics.CSBSJU.edu website. http://www.physics.csbsju .edu/stats/WAPP2_cow.html

Starr, Kevin. *Golden Dreams: California in an Age of Abundance, 1950-1963*. Vol. 6, (*Americans and the California Dream*). Oxford: Oxford University Press, 2009.

Stravinsky, Igor. *Poetics of Music in the Form of Six Lessons*. Cambridge, MA: Harvard University Press, 1970.

Swedberg, R., and O. Agevall. *The Max Weber Dictionary: Key Words and Central Concepts*. 2nd ed. Stanford, CA: Stanford University Press, 2005.

Takeuchi, Hirotaka, and Ikujiro Nonaka. "The New New Product Development Game." *Harvard Business Review* (January-February 1986): 137–146.

Taub, Amanda. "The US Just Declassified Al-Qaeda's Job Application Form. It's bizarrely Corporate." *Vox*. May 20, 2015. https://www.vox.com/2015/5/20/8630669/bin-laden -al-qaeda-application.

"Testimony of John Roth, former Inspector General, Department of Homeland Security, before the Committee on Homeland Security, United States House of Representatives, May 1, 2019." Homeland.house.gov. Accessed May 1, 2020. https://homeland.house .gov/imo/media/doc/Testimony-Roth.pdf.

"The Signifying Monkey: Two Versions of a Toast." UBU Web Ethnopoetics. Accessed May 1, 2020. http://www.ubu.com/ethno/soundings/monkey.html.

"The World's Most Valuable Brands." *Forbes.com*. Accessed May 1, 2020. https://www.forbes .com/powerful-brands/list/#tab:rank

United States Office of Personnel Management. "Paperwork Reduction Act (PRA) Guide." Version 2.0. 4/27/2011. https://www.opm.gov/about-us/open-government/digital -government-strategy/fitara/paperwork-reduction-act-guide.pdf.

Wallace, David Foster. *The Pale King*. New York: Little, Brown and Company, 2011.

Weber, Max. *The Theory of Social and Economic Organization*. Edited by Talcott Parsons. Translated by A. M. Henderson and Talcott Parsons. New York: Free Press, 1947.

Weber, Max. *Economy and Society: An Outline of Interpretive Sociology*. Edited by Guenther Roth and Claus Witch. Berkeley, CA: University of California Press, 1978.

Weber, Max. *Selections in Translation*. Edited by W. G. Runciman. Translated by Eric Matthews. Cambridge: Cambridge University Press, 1978.

Weber, Max. *The Protestant Ethic and the "Spirit" of Capitalism and Other Writings*. New York: Penguin Books, 2002.

Wiesche, Manuel, Michael Schermann, and Helmut Krcmar. "When IT Risk Management Produces More Harm Than Good: The Phenomenon of 'Mock Bureaucracy.'" Paper presented at 46th Hawaii International Conference on System Sciences, Wailea, HI, January 7–10, 2013.

Whyte, William H. *The Organization Man*. Philadelphia: University of Pennsylvania Press, 1956.

Willmot, Hugh. "Back to the Future: What Does Studying Bureaucracy Tell Us?" In Clegg, Harris, and Höpfl, *Managing Modernity*, 257–294.

Wilson, J. Q. *Bureaucracy: What Government Agencies Do and Why They Do It*. New York: Basic Books, 1989.

Wilson, Sloan. *The Man in the Gray Flannel Suit*. Cambridge, MA: Da Capo Press, 1955.

Wikipedia. "Spherical Cow." Wikipedia.org. Last modified April 17, 2020. https://en.wiki pedia.org/wiki/Spherical_cow.

Wren, Daniel A., and Arthur G. Bedeian. *The Evolution of Management Thought*. Chichester, England: Wiley, 2009.

NOTES

Editor's Preface
1. Melville, *Moby Dick*, 332.

Introduction
1. Graeber, *The Utopia of Rules*, 192. He references Lewis, "Toward a Unified Theory of Cultural Performance," 47.
2. Kherdian, *Monkey*, 58.
3. See, for example, Pseudo-Dionysius *On the Celestial Hierarchy* (De Coelesti Hierarchia), as well as Thomas Aquinas, The Mishnah Torah, St. Ambrose, and others.
4. Harris, et al, "Introduction: Managing Modernity: Beyond Bureaucracy," in Clegg, Harris, and Höpfl, *Managing Modernity*, 1.
5. Clegg, "Under Reconstruction," in Clegg, Harris, and Höpfl, *Managing Modernity*, 202, citing Landau, *Political Science*, 167, and Blau and Meyer, *Bureaucracy in Modern Society*, 10.
6. Clegg, Harris, and Höpfl, *Managing Modernity*, 203.
7. Mill, *Considerations on Representative Government*, 114. Mill didn't like bureaucracy much, though.
8. Wren and Bedeian, *Evolution of Management Thought*, 233.
9. Shapiro, *Terrorist's Dilemma*, 16.
10. Taub, "US Just Declassified al-Qaeda's Job Application Form."
11. Shapiro, *Terrorist's Dilemma*, 18.
12. Reed, "Post-Bureaucratic Organization" in Clegg, Harris, and Höpfl, *Managing Modernity*, 230, citing Burke and Black, "Al-Qaida."
13. Weber, *Economy & Society*, 971.
14. Wren and Bedeian, *Evolution of Management Thought*, 15.
15. Wren and Bedeian, *Evolution of Management Thought*, 16.
16. Wren and Bedeian, *Evolution of Management Thought*, 14.
17. Weber, *Economy & Society*, 970.
18. von Mises, *Bureaucracy*, Kindle loc. 285.
19. Wren and Bedeian, *Evolution of Management Thought*, 19.
20. Dickson, *People's Government*, 176.
21. von Mises, *Bureaucracy*, Kindle loc.1502.
22. Wren and Bedeian, *Evolution of Management Thought*, 17. Compare to Weber's definition of bureaucracy in Chapter 1.

23. Lactantius, "Of the Manner," 7.

24. Lucy Ives in *Lapham's*. She attributes the term to Vicent de Gournay.

25. Merton, *Social Theory and Social Structure*, 251.

26. Lucy Ives, *Lapham's*.

27. von Mises, *Bureaucracy*, Kindle loc. 112.

28. Graeber, *The Utopia of Rules*, 192.

29. Graeber, *The Utopia of Rules*, 192.

Part I

Overture

1. "History," Department of Homeland Security website.

2. NPR Staff, "Who Oversees Homeland Security?"

Chapter 1

1. Quoted in *Moby Dick*, opening sentence of Hobbes's Leviathan.

2. There are nuances here; see "'L'état C'Est à Moi': Louis XIV and the State," in Harline, *Rhyme and Reason of Politics*, 185–198, for a more thorough discussion.

3. Wren and Bedeian, *Evolution of Management Thought*, 194.

4. Clegg, Harris, and Höpfl. *Managing Modernity*, 203.

5. Merton, *Social Theory and Social Structure*, 249.

6. Weber, *Economy & Society*, Kindle loc. 6266.

7. Weber, *Economy & Society*, Kindle loc. 6215–6228.

8. Weber, *Selections in Translation*, Kindle loc. 7991.

9. Merton, *Social Theory and Social Structure*, 250.

10. Weber, *Economy & Society*, 974.

11. Buchanan & Fitzgerald, "New Lock, New Stock," in Clegg, Harris, and Höpfl, *Managing Modernity*, 58, citing Burns & Stalker, Management of Innovation.

12. Clegg, "Under Reconstruction," Clegg, Harris, and Höpfl, *Managing Modernity*, 204, citing Pugh, "Modern Organization Theory."

13. Weber, *Economy & Society*, 974.

14. Wilson, *Bureaucracy*, 375.

15. Wilson, *Bureaucracy*, 114.

16. "The World's Most Valuable Brands," *Forbes.com*.

17. Graeber, *The Utopia of Rules*, 11.

18. Graeber, "In Regulation Nation," 13.

19. Weber, *Economy & Society*, 974.

20. Weber, *Economy & Society*, 975.

21. Graeber, *The Utopia of Rules*, 15.

22. Conway, "Conway's Law."

23. Gaunt, "Corporations Are Becoming Expert."

24. Orwell, "Politics and the English Language," 133, in Orwell and Angos, *Collected Essays, Journalism, and Letters*.

25. Galore, "The Bureaucracy of Terror."

26. Weber, *Economy & Society*, 983.
27. Balzac, *The Bureaucrats*.
28. Dickens, *David Copperfield*, Chapter 43.
29. Weber, *Economy & Society*, 973.
30. Arendt, "A Special Supplement."
31. Weber, *Economy & Society*, 987.
32. Weber, *Economy & Society*, 993.
33. Adler, "Building Better Bureaucracies," 36.
34. Adler, "Building Better Bureaucracies," 36.
35. Wilson, *Bureaucracy*, 128.
36. Wilson, *Bureaucracy*, 324.
37. Graeber, *The Utopia of Rules*, 9.

Chapter 2

1. Clinger Cohen Act of 1996.
2. Patrick-Goudreau, "A Gaggle of Geese."
3. Avery, "Responsible Change," 22–23.
4. Department of Homeland Security, Acquisition Directive 102-01, November 7, 2008, B42-45.
5. Department of Homeland Security, Acquisition Directive 102-01, November 7, 2008, B60.
6. Schwaber and Sutherland, *The Scrum Guide*.
7. The team of brilliantly creative bureaucracy savants included Josh Seckel, Suzi Rizzo, Ken Moser, Darren Hoevel, Bob Payne, Raj Indugula, John Hughes, Rob Brown, Roland Cuellar, Melinda Solomon, and George Dinwiddie.
8. Rhodes, Office of the Deputy Chief Management Officer, "Revised Department of Defense Order of Precedence." *Under Code 5, for example.
9. Office Inspector General, *USCIS Automation of Immigration Benefits*, 22. This report is filled with inaccuracies and misleading information, so please read it with some skepticism.
10. "Government Paperwork Elimination Act."

Chapter 3

1. Weber, *Economy & Society*, 88.
2. Beetham, *Bureaucracy*, 14, referencing Weber, *Theory of Social and Economic Organization*, 214.
3. Gouldner, *Patterns of Industrial Bureaucracy*, 179, citing Nussbaum, *History of the Economic Institutions*, 379.
4. Adler, "Two Types of Bureaucracy," 67, citing Cyert and Marsh, *A Behavioral Theory of the Firm*, and Beniger, *The Control Revolution*.
5. Weber, *Economy & Society*, 973.
6. Scott, *Seeing Like a State*, 76.
7. Scott, *Seeing Like a State*, 2.
8. Scott, *Seeing Like a State*, 6.

9. Schwaber and Sutherland, *The Scrum Guide*, 6.

10. Schwaber and Sutherland, *The Scrum Guide*, 19.

Chapter 4

1. Shook, "How to Change a Culture," 83–84.

2. Wilson, *Bureaucracy*, 375.

3. Wilson, *Bureaucracy*, xviii.

4. Clegg, "Under Reconstruction," in Clegg, Harris, and Höpfl, *Managing Modernity*, 207.

5. Elizabeth Blair, "A History of 'Pettifogging.'"

6. von Mises, *Bureaucracy*, Kindle loc. 950.

7. Merton, *Social Theory and Social Structure*, 253.

8. Merton, *Social Theory and Social Structure*, 254.

9. Hlavacek, "Bureaucracy and New Product Innovation," 363–364.

10. Wilson, *Bureaucracy*, 221.

11. Merton, *Social Theory and Social Structure*, 252.

12. Merton, *Social Theory and Social Structure*, 252.

13. Merton, *Social Theory and Social Structure*, 251–252.

14. Muller, *Tyranny of Metrics*, 41.

15. Merton, *Social Theory and Social Structure*, 252.

16. Merton, cited in Gouldner, *Patterns of Industrial Bureaucracy*, 19.

17. Scott, *Seeing Like a State*, 76–77.

18. Merton, *Social Theory and Social Structure*, 256.

19. Graeber, *The Utopia of Rules*, 7.

20. Graeber, *The Utopia of Rules*, 7.

21. Lucas and Walliams, *Little Britain*.

22. Brady, "Analytics Without Limits."

23. von Mises, *Bureaucracy*, Kindle loc. 1029.

Chapter 5

1. du Gay, "Without Regard," in Clegg, Harris, and Höpfl, Managing Modernity, 18, citing Hunter, *Rethinking the School*, 157.

2. du Gay, "Without Regard," in Clegg, Harris, and Höpfl, *Managing Modernity*, 19.

3. Clegg, "Under Reconstruction," in Clegg, Harris, and Höpfl, *Managing Modernity*, 203.

4. du Gay, "Without Regard," in Clegg, Harris, and Höpfl, *Managing Modernity*, 18.

5. Willmot, "Back to the Future," in Clegg, Harris, and Höpfl, *Managing Modernity*, 259, citing Amy, "The Case for Bureaucracy."

6. Merton, *Social Theory and Social Structure*, 249.

7. Willmot, "Back to the Future," in Clegg, Harris, and Höpfl, *Managing Modernity*, 260.

8. Clegg, "Under Reconstruction," in Clegg, Harris, and Höpfl, *Managing Modernity*, 206.

9. Clegg, "Under Reconstruction," in Clegg, Harris, and Höpfl, *Managing Modernity*, 206.

10. Adler, "Better Bureaucracies," 38.

11. Adler, "Two Types of Bureaucracy," 65.

12. Adler, "Two Types of Bureaucracy," 64.

13. Wische, "IT Risk Management," 2, citing Gouldner, *Patterns of Industrial Bureaucracy*, 10.

14. Adler, "Better Bureaucracies," 38.
15. Willmot, "Back to the Future," in Clegg, Harris, and Höpfl, *Managing Modernity*, 257.
16. Schein, *The Corporate Culture Survival* Guide, 134.
17. Schein, *The Corporate Culture Survival Guide*, 140.
18. Schein, *The Corporate Culture Survival Guide*, 47.
19. von Mises, *Bureaucracy*, Kindle loc. 767.
20. Wilson, *Bureaucracy*, 339.
21. Adler, "Better Bureaucracies," 36.
22. Adler, "Two Types of Bureaucracy," 67, citing Cyert and Marsh, *A Behavioral Theory of the Firm*, and Beniger, *The Control Revolution*.
23. Takeuchi and Nonaka, "New New Product Development Game," 144.
24. du Gay, "Without Regard," in Clegg, Harris, and Höpfl, *Managing Modernity*, 20.
25. Weber, *Economy and Society*, Kindle loc. 6215.
26. Willmott, "Back to the Future," in Clegg, Harris, and Höpfl, *Managing Modernity*, 261.
27. Stravinsky, *Poetics of Music in the Form of Six Lessons*, 65.
28. Mikkelson, David. "Did Dr. Seuss Write." *Forty-nine of the words were just a single syllable long!
29. von Mises, *Bureaucracy*, Kindle loc. 691–696.
30. von Mises, *Bureaucracy*, Kindle loc. 699.
31. Adler, "Two Types of Bureaucracy," 78.
32. Clegg, Harris, and Höpfl, *Managing Modernity*, 25.

Part II

Chapter 6

1. Johnston, "History Lessons."
2. Adler, "Better Bureaucracies," 37.
3. Schwartz, *A Seat at the Table*, 105–107; Schwartz, *War & Peace & IT*, 107–110.
4. Weber, *Economy and Society*, 974.
5. Weber, *Economy and Society*, 223.
6. Weber, *Selections in Translation*, Kindle loc. 7973.
7. Buchanan and Fitzgerald, "New Lock, New Stock," in Clegg, Harris, and Höpfl, *Managing Modernity*, 58.
8. Buchanan and Fitzgerald, "New Lock, New Stock," in Clegg, Harris, and Höpfl, *Managing Modernity*, 74.
9. Buchanan and Fitzgerald, "New Lock, New Stock," in Clegg, Harris, and Höpfl, *Managing Modernity*, 74.
10. Gouldner, *Patterns of Industrial Bureaucracy*, 164.
11. Willmott, "Back to the Future," in Clegg, Harris, and Höpfl, *Managing Modernity*, 285.
12. Reed, "The Post-Bureaucratic Organization," in Clegg, Harris, and Höpfl, *Managing Modernity*, 237.
13. Gouldner, *Patterns of Industrial Bureaucracy*, 164.
14. Willmott, "Back to the Future," in Clegg, Harris, and Höpfl, *Managing Modernity*, 285.

Chapter 7

1. Adler, "Two Types of Bureaucracy," 623.
2. Weber, *Economy and Society*, Kindle loc. 6254, and *The Theory of Social and Economic Organization*, 349.
3. Muller, *Tyranny of Metrics*, 33, citing Frederick W. Taylor, Principles of Scientific Management, cited by David Montgomery, *The Fall of the House of Labor*, (New Haven, 1989), 229. *This quote is just too good—it's obviously making the rounds.
4. Muller, *Tyranny of Metrics*, 32.
5. Weber, *Economy & Society*, 967–968.
6. Adler, "Better Bureaucracies," 41.
7. Bogsnes, *Implementing Beyond Budgeting*, Kindle loc. 181–185.
8. Gouldner, *Patterns of Industrial Bureaucracy*, 163; 170; 174.
9. Gouldner, *Patterns of Industrial Bureaucracy*, 162.
10. Gouldner, *Patterns of Industrial Bureaucracy*, 207.
11. Gouldner, *Patterns of Industrial Bureaucracy*, 208.
12. Gouldner, *Patterns of Industrial Bureaucracy*, 187.
13. Gouldner, *Patterns of Industrial Bureaucracy*, 189.
14. Adler, "Coercive vs Enabling," 75.
15. Adler, "The 'Learning Bureaucracy': New United Motor Manufacturing, Inc.," 75, citing Herzberg, F., *Work and the Nature of Man*, Cleveland: World Publishing, 1966.
16. Adler, "Two Types of Bureaucracy," 62.
17. Adler, "Two Types of Bureaucracy," 63.
18. Adler, "Two Types of Bureaucracy," 69.
19. Adler, "Two Types of Bureaucracy," 65.
20. Adler, "Two Types of Bureaucracy," 66.
21. Gouldner, *Patterns of Industrial Bureaucracy*, 192.
22. Adler, "Two Types of Bureaucracy," 64, citing Ronald E. Michaels, William L. Cron, Alan J. Dubinsky, and Erich A. Joachimsthaler, "Influence of formalization on the organizational commitment and work alienation of salespeople and industrial buyers." *Journal of Marketing Research*, 25: 376–383, 1988.
23. Adler, "Two Types of Bureaucracy," 66.
24. Adler, "Two Types of Bureaucracy," 64, citing Fariborz Damanpour, "Organizational innovation," *Academy of Management Journal*, 34: 555–591, 1991.
25. Adler, "Two Types of Bureaucracy," 67.
26. Buchanan and Fitzgerald, "New Lock, New Stock," in Clegg, Harris, and Höpfl, *Managing Modernity*, 75.
27. Gawande, *The Checklist Manifesto*, 48.
28. Gawande, *The Checklist Manifesto*, 79.
29. Gawande, *The Checklist Manifesto*, 73.
30. "FISMA NIST 800-53 Rev. 4 Controls—by the Numbers."
31. Adler, "Better Bureaucracies," 41.
32. Adler, "Better Bureaucracies," 42–44.

Chapter 8

1. Batkins, "Testimony."
2. "Testimony of John Roth."
3. Rockwell, "CBP Closes In."
4. Scott, *Seeing Like a State*, 327.
5. Scott, *Seeing Like a State*, 327.
6. Starr, *Golden Dreams*," 251–254.
7. Kelman, "Bureaucracies as Learning Organizations."
8. Kelman, "Bureaucracies as Learning Organizations."
9. Shook, "How to Change a Culture," 64.
10. Adler, "Time and Motion Regained."
11. Adler, "Time and Motion Regained," 21.
12. Shook, "How to Change a Culture," 67.
13. Weber, *Economy and Society*, Kindle loc. 6254.
14. Adler, "The 'Learning Bureaucracy': New United Motor Manufacturing, Inc.," 66.

Chapter 9

1. United States Office of Personnel Management, "Paperwork Reduction Act (PRA) Guide."
2. This description of the classics of literature comes from Parks, "Literature and Bureaucracy."
3. MD-102, Appendix B, 22.
4. Department of Homeland Security. "Acquisition Instruction/Guidebook #102-01-001."

Chapter 10

1. Doerr, *Measure What Matters*, 8, 10.
2. Attributed to Peter Drucker. Some have traced the concept as far back as Rheticus in the 16th century. See: http://www.matthewcornell.org/blog/2007/7/30/whats-your-feed-reading-speed.html#1.
3. The term "hyper-bureaucratic" is used, for example, in Willmot, "Back to the Future," in Clegg, Harris, and Höpfl, *Managing Modernity*, 262, to refer to various types of "post-bureaucratic" organizations.
4. Willmot, "Back to the Future," in Clegg, Harris, and Höpfl, *Managing Modernity*, 276.
5. Willmot, "Back to the Future," in Clegg, Harris, and Höpfl, *Managing Modernity*, 276–277.
6. Willmot, "Back to the Future," in Clegg, Harris, and Höpfl, *Managing Modernity*, 276.
7. Graeber, *The Utopia of Rules*, 19–20.
8. Graeber, *The Utopia of Rules*, 21.
9. Muller, *Tyranny of Metrics*, 8.
10. Muller, *Tyranny of Metrics*, 8, 45, 74.
11. Muller, *Tyranny of Metrics*, 170.
12. Muller, *Tyranny of Metrics*, 171.
13. This includes reporting against the budget. Bogsnes, *Implementing Beyond Budgeting*, Kindle loc. 986, citing Hackett Group study. Bogsnes provides no further details on the study.
14. Reed, "Post-Bureaucratic Organization," in Clegg, Harris, and Höpfl, *Managing Modernity*, 242.

15. Muller, *Tyranny of Metrics*, 169. The term surrogation is defined in "Don't Let Metrics . . .".
16. Muller, *Tyranny of Metrics*, 116.
17. Harris and Tayler, "Don't Let Metrics Undermine Your Business," 64–66.
18. Scott, *Seeing Like a State*, 47.
19. Muller, *Tyranny of Metrics*, 20.
20. Muller, *Tyranny of Metrics*, 36.
21. Chrystal and Mizen, "Goodhart's Law," 4.
22. "'Did You Lose the Keys Here?'"
23. Scott, *Seeing Like a State*, 81.
24. Wilson, *Bureaucracy*, 161.
25. Bogsnes, *Implementing Beyond Budgeting*, Kindle loc. 869, citing benefits consulting firm William S. Mercer.
26. Scott, *Seeing Like a State*, 289.
27. Wikipedia, "Spherical Cow"; see also "Spherical Cow."
28. Muller, *Tyranny of Metrics*, 45.
29. Graeber, *The Utopia of Rules*, 75.
30. Muller, *Tyranny of Metrics*, 61.

Part III

Chapter 11

Chapter 12

1. Kafka, *The Trial*.
2. Avery, *Responsible Change*, 3.
3. Weber, *Economy & Society*, 971.
4. Shook, "How to Change a Culture," 66.
5. "The Signifying Monkey."

Chapter 13

Chapter 14

Chapter 15

1. Muller, *Tyranny of Metrics*, 41.
2. Cohn, *Succeeding with Agile*, 115.
3. Cohn, *Succeeding with Agile*, 221. Italics mine.

ACKNOWLEDGMENTS

I can't tell you how honored I am, and how fortunate, to have worked with the passionate and hard-working civil servants, both trolls and chaos monkeys, at DHS. I thank them for putting up with my provocations when they were just trying to do their jobs. Among the government folks who taught me the meaning of bureaucracy and how to work within it (and who appear in some of the stories I tell in the book), I'd include Keith Jones, Tracy Renaud, Rendell Jones, Larry Denayer, Leslie Hope, the folks at PARM and OIRA, Ken Moser, Suzi Rizzo, Sarah Fahden, Chad Tetrault, Mary Kay Rau, Tammy Meckley, Rafaa Abdalla, Mike Hermus, Luke McCormack, Chip Fulgham, Richard Spires . . .

Josh Seckel was responsible for much of our chaos monkey strategy and led the creation of our splendid bureaucratic artifacts, MI-CIS-OIT-003 and 004. A lot of our bureaucracy became more visible when a few of our friends from US Digital Services dropped in to help us, including Eric Hysen and Stephanie Neill.

I learn every day from my teammates at AWS. With them, I've explored the worlds of digital transformation and how it can be stopped dead by poorly implemented corporate bureaucracy, and I've gained some perspective on my earlier government experience. Thanks to Phil Potloff, Miriam McLemore, Jonathan Allen, Thomas Blood, Phil Le-Brun, Xia Zhang, Clarke Rodgers, Joe Chung, Jake Burns, Ishit Vachhrajani, Bryan Landerman, Tom Godden, and Gregor Hohpe.

Thanks to my reviewers: John Millay, who did the crucial work of making sure I wasn't saying anything outrageously stupid about Weber or Merton; Jonathan Allen; Jennifer Anastasoff; and Thomas Blood. And Professor Paul Adler, who let me borrow so many of his ideas.

And, of course, to the inspirational Gene Kim and all the folks at IT Revolution, especially my editors Anna Noak and Leah Brown. I'm hoping to recycle all the extra commas they deleted from this book into the next dozen or so books I write.

And Jenny, who let me use the comfy armchair every morning to edit the manuscript. She still doesn't believe that *Moby Dick* has anything to do with bureaucracy.

ABOUT THE AUTHOR

Mark Schwartz is a profilic author best known for his bureaucratic classic, *MI-CIS-OIT-003*. In 2010 he made it through the security gates of a federal office building in Washington, DC, and threatened to stay there until government IT became agile. After seven years he agreed to depart for the public cloud and the government gave him a pile of souvenir plaques.

Under his influence as CIO, US Citizenship and Immigration Services became a model for DevOps, microservices, cloud architectures, and new security models in the government, shrinking their IT release time from eighteen months to less than a day.

Since then, he's been an enterprise strategist at Amazon Web Services, helping senior executives of Global 2000 companies overcome cultural and organizational barriers to digital transformation, speaking at conferences around the world, and writing. Before his perilous adventure in the government, he was CIO at Intrax and CEO at Auctiva. He's also the author of *The Art of Business Value*, *A Seat at the Table: IT Leadership in the Age of Agility*, and *War and Peace and IT: Business Leadership, Technology, and Success in the Digital Age*. He has a BS degree in computer science, an MA in philosophy from Yale, and an MBA from Wharton.